Redemptive Encounters

Comparative Studies in Religion and Society

Mark Juergensmeyer, Editor

Redemptive Encounters

Three Modern Styles in the Hindu Tradition

Lawrence A. Babb

University of California Press

Berkeley / Los Angeles / Oxford

University of California Press
Berkeley and Los Angeles, California

University of California Press, Ltd.
Oxford, England

Library of Congress Cataloging-in-Publication Data

Babb, Lawrence A.
  Redemptive Encounters
  Bibliography: p.
  1. Hinduism—History—1765–   . 2. Radhasomi Satsang.   3. Brahmakumari.
4. Satya Sai Baba, 1926–   I. Title.
BL1153.5.B33   1986   294.5'56   85-28897
ISBN 0-520-07636-2

Printed in the United States of America
1   2   3   4   5   6   7   8   9

To the memory of my father

Contents

Preface

The research on which this volume is based took place between July 1978 and May 1979 and was conducted mainly in the immediate Delhi–New Delhi area. My overall project was an investigation of forms taken by the Hindu tradition in modern, urban environments. Information on the three religious movements described in this book was collected during my inquiries into a broad range of modern manifestations of that tradition. As will be seen, however, what is stressed in these pages is not modernity, but continuity. In the end what came to interest me most about these particular movements was the way each, in its own highly distinctive manner, seemed to exemplify enduring Hindu motifs. Taken together, the three movements provide a vivid lesson in the way the Hindu tradition has combined underlying coherence with a kind of boundless spiritual inventiveness. Themes and variations are what this book is about, and from this standpoint whatever 'modernity' the movements possess—and each is indeed modern in its own way—is of tangential interest.

I was assisted in my inquiries by too many devotees and adherents for all to be named here. Indeed, some were not known to me by name, having been encountered only briefly and casually at various devotional gatherings; because this was an urban study, brief meetings, typical of urban life, were common. Obviously without the generous assistance of such persons, known well or only casually, I would have understood nothing. I thank them all. It would not be amiss, however, to mention specifically the help I received from Mr. S. D. Maheshwari, a most learned and generous man, who aided me more than anyone else in coming to what understanding I have of the Radhasoami tradition. I am acutely aware that the materials reported in this book are not just 'materials' to believers. Because this book deals with matters of religious conviction from a standpoint outside the beliefs in question, its purposes must necessarily deviate from the

intrinsic purposes of the movements it describes. Knowing that
adherents might choose to present my descriptive accounts differently,
and knowing too that they would certainly come to conclusions
different from mine, I have regarded it as a special obligation to treat
these movements with all the respect that I deeply feel.

I also owe much to the many nondevotee friends and neighbors
whose wise counsel and assistance were essential in securing a comfortable existence for my family in the New Delhi neighborhood
where we lived, and whose acute interpretations of religious matters
were vital in establishing a broader setting for the materials described
in this book. Special thanks are due to Mrs. G. S. Paul, who was a
most helpful language coach and general cultural guide.

It would be hard to exaggerate the importance of the hospitality
and intellectual companionship so generously and unstintingly given
by the Department of Sociology, University of Delhi, during my stay
in India. I owe a great deal to the intellectual stimulation of conversations with these colleagues, especially A. M. Shah, J. P. S.
Uberoi, and Veena Das. Many others have responded critically to
various portions of this manuscript at varying stages of formulation.
Of these my debt is highest to Mark Juergensmeyer and McKim
Marriott. Mark Juergensmeyer has encouraged me in my (by
comparison amateurish) Radhasoami studies and has been a kindly
but forceful critic of this manuscript; what it lacks in coherence is a
result of my inability to meet his high standards. McKim Marriott's
unfailing and selfless responses to materials sent for his perusal, his
ceaseless concern to get matters right, and above all the stimulus of
his ideas have all contributed greatly to the development of this
manuscript and to my continuing education as an interpreter of
culture. I am also much indebted to Jonas Weisel of the University of
California Press for his wise editorial advice and guidance. My wife
Nancy has taken time out from a busy musical life to be my constant
companion in fieldwork, and she has also provided much editorial
assistance in putting together this manuscript. To my expressions of
gratitude to the many who have helped me, however, I add that
responsibility for any error of fact or interpretation is mine alone.

The research was financed by an Indo-American Fellowship, and
for this support I am very grateful. I must also acknowledge the
indispensable assistance of Mr. P. R. Mehendiratta and his staff at
the American Institute of Indian Studies in New Delhi. It was indeed
a relief that so many of the practical details of living and working in
India were in their capable hands.

Some portions of this book represent recastings of text already published in the form of articles. These materials appeared in *Anthropological Quarterly, Asian Folklore Studies, History of Religions, Journal of Anthropological Research*, and *Signs*. I thank the editors of these journals for their kind permission to utilize these materials.

A Note on Transliteration
and Sources

In reproducing Hindi words I have aimed at maximum simplicity
and have compromised on scholarly conventions of transliteration
where it seemed to me that overscrupulousness might confuse rather
than aid the English-speaking reader. Thus, I have used *ch* rather
than *c* to represent the Hindi sound equivalent to the 'ch' in the
English '*chat*'; the aspirated version is here given as *chh*. The sibilants
usually represented as *ś* and *ṣ* are here both given as *sh*, to be
pronounced as in '*sheet*.' Therefore, in this volume Śiva is written as
Shiva. The vocalic *ṛ* I have represented as '*ri*,' as in K*ri*shna. In other
respects I have followed standard transliterating practices. Indic
terms are italicized only on their first appearance in the text.

Many of the words used in this book have both Sanskrit and Hindi
forms, with the Hindi version dropping the final *a* (thus, *prasāda*
becomes *prasād*). When the word in question has become familiar in
its Sanskrit form (such as *yoga*, *yuga* *karma*, *dharma*, etc.) I have used
this version; otherwise I have employed the Hindi form (for example,
darshan instead of *darshana*). All initially italicized words are given
with diacritical marks. Place and personal names are given without
diacritics, which I have done to avoid a clutter of such markings,
especially in those sections where names are repeated frequently. The
names of deities familiar in English (such as Krishna [Krishṇa,
Kṛṣṇa] or Vishnu [Vishṇu, Viṣṇu]) are given without diacritics; less
familiar names or titles of deities (such as Nārāyaṇ) or deitylike
beings (Kāl) are given with diacritics. All these names and terms are
given with full diacritics in the glossary. In the glossary I have
included important and recurrent terms, and other terms for which it
would have been inconvenient to provide definitions in text. Hindi
glosses given in text are not reproduced in the glossary.

The following abbreviations are used for frequently cited works:

S. B. Poetry   Soamiji Maharaj. 1976. *Sār bachan rādhāsvāmī, nazm yānī chhand band.* 14th ed. 2 vols. Soami Bagh (Agra): Radhasoami Satsang.

S. B. Prose   Soamiji Maharaj. 1973. *Sār bachan rādhāsvāmī, nasar yānī bārtik.* 14th ed. Soami Bagh (Agra): Radhasoami Satsang.

S. B. Poetry is internally organized by chapter, hymn, and verse (with some prose material). Citations will be indicated by chapter, hymn, and verse numbers. The same format will be followed in references to Huzur Maharaj's *Prembānī* (Huzur Maharaj 1972).

S. B. Prose consists of two parts, each divided into brief numbered sections. Citations will be given by part and section numbers.

Introduction

My subject is the Hindu religious imagination. By this I mean a distinctive spiritual disposition. a culturally informed capacity to invest the world with religious meaning in certain characteristic ways. As a capacity or propensity, it is not expressed as any particular interpretation of the world, but in the Hindu tradition's ability to generate multiple and various interpretations within a common frame of reference. It is not static but endlessly protean and full of creative possibilities.

In pursuit of this elusive quarry I examine three contemporary religious movements in the Hindu tradition, each representing a distinct interpretation of the world and the human situation. My object is to discover common perspectives in the midst of this diversity, perspectives that unify what are, finally, quite different systems of religious belief and practice. I trace through my three examples the threads of certain shared concepts: ideas about the composition, perceptions, interactions, destinies, and—most of all—identities of selves entangled in a world of ceaseless historical flux. Consensus on these basics (and doubtless others not caught in my net) enables this tradition to 'say' quite different things about the human predicament, but in a common spirit. My story also has a moral, which is that cultural distinctiveness should not be mistaken for human uniqueness. If what we find in common between these three belief-systems is profoundly Hindu, it also suggests links between the inner Hindu world and universals of human experience.

Does Hinduism exist? The answer to this question has always seemed obvious, yet never quite clear. Of course Hinduism exists—but then what exactly is it? This is probably the most enduring puzzle of South Asian studies. The confusion begins with language. Hindus were first called 'Hindu' not by themselves but by foreigners; the word comes from Persian. *Ism*, in its turn, is a perfectly useful suffix, but it belongs to no Indic language. That it has found its way into a marriage with *Hindu* tells us at least as much about the ups and downs of imperialism as it does about the spiritual life of the Indian subcontinent. Yet matters can hardly be dropped here. The existence of a coherent Hindu tradition—'Hinduism'—is intuited by insiders and outsiders alike, and this intuition is far too immediate and powerful to collapse under a little etymological nit-picking. Whatever the origin of the word, Hindus mean something when they call themselves that, and what they mean goes deeper than mere matters of subcontinental politics or cultural chauvinism. To this we must add that when non-Hindus become acquainted with the Hindu tradition, they have the giddy sense not only of being on the outer perimeter of something quite 'other,' but also of being in the presence of a tradition that is—for all of its inner variation—held together by common qualities of otherness.

The basis of such intuitions is the issue; and it is, of course, the immense diversity of the tradition that makes the problem so intractable. What links the austere, world-disenchanting piety of the northern *sant* tradition with the rich magicality of the omnipresent healer-mediums? Or what connects either of these with the fussy ritual formalism of the Shrī Vaishṇava priest? We sense that something does, but just what that something is remains elusive and obscure. The vast web of historical connections between the tradition's many manifestations (near and remote, and sometimes partial or indirect) is obviously an important aspect of the problem, but tracing such connections is not, in itself, a fully satisfying solution. Our real target is a certain unity of outlook for which historical links are certainly a precondition, but of which they are not the present essence.

But where do we find this unity? One thing at least seems clear: if there are common denominators, we will not find them at the level of formal doctrines. We must not be fooled by the 'ism' that history has affixed to the tradition, for there is not now, nor has there ever been, a theology or philosophy that commands anything remotely resembling a consensus in the Hindu world. This tradition shelters highly diverse and endlessly contending schools of thought, and the relationship between such theological systems and popular belief and practice is itself highly complex and often indirect. Certainly no one of them can, on its own, stand as representative of the tradition.

Still, there are other possibilities. Theology aside, certain symbols and ideas seem to bear relatively stable meanings within the widest variety of contexts, cutting across linguistic, geographical, and social boundaries. Various candidates for this unifying role have been suggested: the major Hindu deities, the purity-pollution opposition, basic concepts such as *dharma* and *karma*, and so on. This is a far more promising domain in which to seek the threads that bind the whole together, since at this level of the tradition commonalities can indeed be shown to exist. In fact this is the general approach, roughly speaking, of the present volume.

But here, too, matters are far from simple, and the difficulties take us right to the heart of our problem. Take, for example, the deity Krishna. In the Radhasoami movement (one of the cases discussed in this book), Krishna is said to be an incarnation of Brahm, who in the Radhasoami view is not the Supreme Being, but the lord of an intermediate celestial level—and who is identified, moreover, with a being called Kāl, who is the personification of time and death. In arriving at this conception, the Radhasoami gurus were clearly drawing on a common store of meanings (including Brahm and Kāl, as well as Krishna) shared with others in the Hindu world, but hardly in a way Krishna's devotees would commend. And yet to the deity's devotees the Radhasoami view is at least intelligible, and in this sense Radhasoami teachings and Krishna's devotees have in mind the 'same' deity. Or do they? Obviously Krishna 'means' something both different and the same to his devotees and the Radhasoami tradition. But one need not stop here, for there is the same potential for disagreement about who or what Krishna really is between Krishaite sects. The accord is no doubt greater, but this is essentially a matter of degree.

Similarly, though in a far narrower field of view, when we learn that devotees of the miracle-working Sathya Sai Baba (discussed in part III) believe that his alleged paranormal abilities demonstrate that he is an *avatār* (an earthly descent of God), we are not surprised. Nor do we find it surprising to learn that many Hindus who admire him, but are not devotees, believe that the miracles are genuine, but not evidence of divinity. What is more startling is the fact that many of his severest Hindu critics likewise accept his miracle-performing ability as given and indubitable—though, of course, they certainly do not believe these abilities are divine. Obviously devotees, nondevotees, and critics are all operating in the same world of thought and discourse, but at varying levels of disagreement. Are believers, admirers, and skeptics seeing the same 'miracles'? Yes and no.

What these instances (and many more of the same sort could be given) seem to suggest is that at both macrolevels and microlevels of the Hindu tradition consensus and nonconsensus coexist in a very complex relationship. Certainly one implication is the futility of trying to locate the unity of Hindu religious culture in agreement on any surface particulars; the tradition is vast, and there are fissures of disagreement everywhere. But an even more important implication is that, given the potential depth of disagreement, any search for linking concepts or principles must take variation not simply as a kind of inconvenient fact to be analytically boiled away, but as one of the principal dimensions of its 'findings.' Stated somewhat differently, a valid concept of this tradition's coherence sees continuity manifested in discontinuity, and does not make the tradition seem to be more uniform than it really is. It is not enough merely to point to 'linking concepts'; what has to be shown is *how* such concepts can function in different religious interpretations that might in some respects disagree radically.

There is, of course, no reason why this should be impossible in principle, since disagreement and coherence are not necessarily inconsistent. But in order to show their potential consistency, one must distinguish between different levels of cultural reality. To move momentarily to a different (though related) cultural domain, there are important lessons to be learned from studies of caste. According to some studies, in local settings there can be considerable disagreement about the relative ranking of specific castes, but this disagreement itself can be grounded in a general consensus on the principles utilized in determining and expressing caste rank (see, e.g., Moffatt 1979). Here unity is not necessarily expressed as concord and harmony; it consists, rather, of agreement on certain cultural ground rules that can be invoked (if only implicitly) even in debate and conflict.

There is no prima facie reason why matters should be otherwise with religion. In this sphere, too, it should be possible for dissent and consensus to coexist at different levels within a coherent tradition. While similar religious beliefs or practices probably reflect a more basic agreement on true fundamentals, the reverse does not follow. Quite diverse religious interpretations of the world can also rest on the base of common principles. Below the visible surfaces of particular beliefs and practices, there may be a half-visible or even hidden consensus consisting of shared ideas so basic and accepted as to be beyond the reach of doubt or debate.

In the broadest sense this is how the Hindu tradition ought to be conceived. There is no such thing as a Hindu world-view, or at least not in the narrow meaning of this expression. Rather, the tradition is itself a vast religious world, which has ample room for the most diverse constructions of the cosmos and the human situation. What makes it *one* religious world, rather than many, is the fact that even at its most radically various it can be shown to exemplify common thematic concepts. These common themes—not always explicit, and frequently manifested differently in different contexts—impart to the tradition its characteristic inflections, and in so doing constitute a critical dimension of its living unity.

I have utilized the materials presented in this book as illustrations of this vision of the tradition's ordered diversity. Each of the three movements described here represents an integral system of belief and practices quite distinct from the others. In this respect each movement affords a particularly clear view of specific facets of the wider tradition, which is a point that I'll enlarge upon shortly. In my presentation I have attended carefully to these distinctive emphases. However, I have also tried to sift from the distinguishing features of the three movements common elements bridging the gaps between them. I certainly do not pretend to have produced a true inventory of unifying Hindu themes. Even between my three movements there are commonalities I have not explored, and as far as the wider tradition is concerned, my examples represent something closer to strategic 'soundings' than a survey. Within the limited universe of my three examples, I have tried to discover a few important aspects of what might be called the 'Hindu way' of supplying the world with religious meaning.

Difference is the key to my method. Instead of trying to base my inquiry at the tradition's center—assuming that such exists—I have concentrated on what may seem to be its farthest outposts. Religious movements such as those discussed here are not, by most reckonings, characteristic of the wider tradition, nor are the highly focused soteriological interests of two of the movements central to the tradition at the popular level. Two of the movements, indeed, do not actually regard themselves as 'Hindu.' But they *are* Hindu, and deeply so. I have assumed that the limits of a concept are best tested by cases near or at its boundaries, and it is in the open space between ostensible marginality and underlying continuity that this book operates. Atypicality and divergence are treated not as obstacles, but as allies, because extreme diversity gives us the clearest possible contrast between varying externals and the constant inner core.

The result is not the discovery of a universal Hinduism, since it is not there to be discovered. If these materials suggest one notion above all, it is that one can draw spiritually from the Hindu tradition in fundamentally different ways. In this sense the movements I describe challenge the conventional notion of 'Hinduism'; but in so doing they also confirm the more important and interesting truth that this tradition combines underlying continuity with astounding richness. Depending on context, its essential elements can be emphasized in different permutations and degrees, and turned to quite unexpected purposes. To say that the Hindu tradition is diverse is to understate the case; what is really notable is its apparently endless capacity to surprise.

There is another lesson too. Although the tradition's exterior face might seem quite exotic, its innermost elements turn out not to be as unique as the outside observer might at first suppose. It is as if the deeper we go into the tradition and the more clearly we see its unities, the more insubstantial its outer boundaries become. At its heart we encounter principles of self-discovery that are as social as they are religious, and as generally human as they are specifically South Asian. The Hindu tradition thus not only teaches us about the variousness of religious experience, but may also hint at its common sources.

Three Religious Movements

I encountered and studied the three religious movements described in these pages in the course of field research on modern expressions of the Hindu tradition. The research took place mainly in Delhi, New Delhi, and the vicinity, with occasional excursions further afield. Two of the movements are established sects, and the third is a personal cult centering on a well-known living deity-saint. All three draw their main constituencies from urban India's middle and upper-middle classes.

The Radhasoami movement, the first of my cases, is probably the best described in the scholarly literature (e.g., Barthwal 1978; Gold 1982; Juergensmeyer 1978, 1982, and forthcoming). Because some of the Radhasoami subgroups have been vigorously internationalizing for years, it also has the most established presence abroad. Among the Radhasoami movement's many features of interest is its highly elaborated cosmological system. Quite apart from this system's almost science-fictionesque appeal as an imaginative construct (which I hope my readers will come to appreciate), it is directly relevant to certain key issues in contemporary South Asian cultural studies. Currently there is intense interest in South Asian constructions of personhood, especially in relation to patterns of interpersonal trans-actions, and in fact these are among the most important concerns of this book. To a striking degree these matters are central to Radhasoami world-imagery. If for no other reason than this, the Radhasoami movement has a strong claim on the attention of students of South Asian culture.

Since the Radhasoami world is large and various, any investigation of the Radhasoami movement must decide which subgroup or combination of subgroups to consider. The major split in the move-ment is between the groups associated with Agra, where the movement originated, and the Punjab, where a separate Radhasoami subtradition flourishes today. In my account of the movement I have referred to the Punjab tradition (with which I had relatively little direct contact) as a background of reference, but have concentrated on one of the Agra groups. Headquartered at Soami Bagh on the outskirts of that city, this group was the source of most of the information reported in this book.

In my inquiries into Radhasoami matters there was an important barrier I could not cross. I was an interested outsider, a student of Indian society and culture investigating the contemporary religious scene. As such, I could not become an initiate. This was an impedi-ment, because some of the most important practices in the Radhasoami tradition are disclosed only to initiates. But this was fair enough; there was much to learn in any case. Even as an outsider, I was permitted to attend congregational services (*satsang*), which I did on a regular basis. Many movement adherents, moreover, were extremely generous with their time and knowledge, and gave me what I believe to be a good understanding of this tradition as it is manifested outside the esoteric sphere accessible only to insiders.

The literature of the movement was another valuable source. The Radhasoami tradition, and especially the Agra wing of the tradition, has produced a massive body of sacred and semisacred texts. These texts, consisting largely of the poetic compositions and prose dis-courses of past gurus, are sung and recited during congregational services and are integral to the faith as conceived by most devotees. As will be seen in the next three chapters, this literature—read against the background of my own observations and conversations with devotees—turned out to be a rich ethnographic mine indeed.

Unlike the Radhasoami movement, the Brahma Kumari sect, the second of my cases, is hardly known to Western scholarship. It certainly deserves more notice than it has thus far received. To begin with, the Brahma Kumaris are strongly millenarian. This is unusual in the Hindu world, and indeed is regarded by some scholars as antithetical to the inner spirit of Indic religions. The Brahma Kumaris not only show us that Hindu millenarianism is possible, but demonstrate *how* it is possible. Another notable feature of this movement is that from its start it has had a distinctly feminist coloring. This, too, is exceptional in the Hindu tradition, and invites inquiry on that account. It should also be of interest to anyone concerned with gender issues in cross-cultural perspective.

For a period of many months I regularly attended 'classes' (described in chapter 5) and participated in a variety of other activities in a large Brahma Kumari 'Raja Yoga Center' in New Delhi. This, in turn, led to after-hours contact with individual adherents with whom I discussed Brahma Kumari doctrine and their own perceptions of the movement. As in the case of the Radhasoami tradition, the Brahma Kumaris' abundant literature was another important source of information. During the period of my contact with the movement I read extensively in these materials, bringing questions as they arose to the 'teachers' at the center and other movement members.

The third of my cases is the cult of Sathya Sai Baba, a much-celebrated holy man who is one of modern India's most important religious leaders. With a growing international network of devotees, this movement has become fairly well known in the West. Although most of the available writing on the movement is essentially hagiographic, it has also been reported in a small but good scholarly literature (Swallow 1982; White 1972). Because this cult is so closely associated with the English-educated and very wealthy, it might appear at first glance to be culturally unimportant. But this is far from correct. Sathya Sai Baba's main constituency is in some ways culturally alienated, but this circumstance is itself observationally useful because it establishes a frame of reference in which certain aspects of the Hindu tradition can be seen with special clarity.

One of the most striking features of Sathya Sai Baba's cult is the immense importance his followers attach to his physical miracles (his apparent magical production of substances and objects, his miraculous cures, and so on). Such phenomena receive no emphasis at all in the Radhasoami and Brahma Kumari movements. The question is, why should magical performances be so crucially important in a religious movement so firmly grounded in a sector of modern Indian society that is—to all appearances—the most averse to what is frequently called (in India as well as elsewhere, though with different connotations) 'superstition'? As it turns out, this question is an avenue to more basic issues concerning the general meaning of 'the miraculous' in the Hindu world.

I never met Sathya Sai Baba himself. My concern was only marginally with him in any case, and I seriously doubt whether any outside observer will ever get close enough to him or the inner circles of his cult to learn anything ethnographically useful. For that, perhaps, we must await memoirs. Instead, my inquiries were devotee-oriented and centered on his local (Delhi) following. My object was to discover what his devotees made of him, themselves, and their relations with him. I attended cult-related activities regularly and interviewed many devotees. I also investigated one of the cult's 'miraculous households' (discussed in chapter 8). Though not as central as it was in my investigations of the Radhasoami and Brahma Kumari movements, the cult's literature was another important resource.

In my accounts of these three movements I have treated them not as descriptive ends in themselves but as means to an end. My object has been to present them as contrastive religious styles, each with its own inner coherence and logic, but each also sharing with the others certain constant themes. Complete institutional descriptions have not been attempted, though I have been attentive to wider institutional and historical matters as they bear on the present-day face the movements offer to their followers. As far as their constituencies are concerned, the focus of my research was mainly on local groups of devotees in Delhi and environs. A more intensive study of any one of these movements would necessarily be more concerned with its extralocal (and even international) dimensions, but for present purposes a local context is sufficient. Temporally, my descriptions are located in what is sometimes called the 'ethnographic present.' I use the present tense to describe the realities of 1978–79 when I was in direct contact with the movements. Accounts based on data collected at the time of this writing (mostly 1984) would differ in some particulars but would not, I believe, support substantially different conclusions.

There is no pretense here that I, as an observer, can report my materials from the point of view of an 'insider.' It is one thing to enter, let us say, a village community and assume the role of a participant in its life. Given sufficient powers of empathy and the community's goodwill, such participation can become the basis for something approximating an insider's perspective, and perhaps even an insider's privileges of judgment. But in the case of religious movements the situation is different in principle. To become a full participant in a religious movement requires assent, at some level, to a particular body of beliefs, even if there is no formality of initiation. One can, of course, participate in various activities as an outsider as I did, but to go further would necessitate what can only be called a spiritual commitment, which cannot and must not be feigned. Such commitment would probably be inconsistent with an observer's status anyway, because it is far from clear that the conviction necessary to be a genuine participant in these movements is compatible with reporting in a way that preserves any semblance of detachment. My accounts of these movements are not, nor should they be, accounts that believers would render.

Themes

The main perspectives of this book are established in part I, which deals with the Radhasoami movement. Each of my three movements has its own characteristic preoccupations, and in the Radhasoami case this is a pervasive concern with questions of succession to the spiritual authority of past gurus. Using succession issues as a general frame of reference, I utilize the Radhasoami materials as a means of introducing the principal themes to be pursued in subsequent sections of the book. Of these, the most important is the theme of identity, false and true. In the Radhasoami case, as elsewhere, the problem of identity is closely associated with matters of history, memory, vision, and the self's interactive relations with others in a fluid, ceaselessly changing world.

In the Radhasoami tradition questions of succession and the self's identity directly converge in what I have called the principle of devotional 'recognition.' Radhasoami obsessions with the question of who is, and is not, a legitimate guru turn out to be more than mere matters of sectarian politics; they are in a fundamental sense soteriological. Given Radhasoami assumptions about the way the cosmos works and their implicit notions about the logic of interpersonal transactions, inward recognition of a 'true guru' can be a medium for a special kind of redemptive self-recognition. This involves a social-psychological dimension of religious experience that we shall see exemplified, though differently, in the other movements too.

Millenarianism and feminism are features of the Brahma Kumaris' belief system that distinguish this movement from other manifestations of the Hindu tradition, and these are the principal concerns of part II. We shall see, however, that Brahma Kumari distinctiveness is less extreme than it might seem at first. Brahma Kumari millenarianism represents a particular adjustment, however radical, of the selfsame historical ideas that appear in the Radhasoami tradition, and that are, in fact, nearly omnipresent in the Hindu world. Brahma Kumari feminism can by no means be taken as a given fact; it is expressed in idioms very different from those employed by Western feminists, and part of my task is to show that the Brahma Kumari critique of the contemporary world can be translated into terms familiar to Western feminism. But in the end it remains a very Hindu critique, and the idea of women's (and men's) liberation supported by it is one that could only arise in the Hindu world.

Once we penetrate to the symbolic subsurface of the Brahma Kumaris' millennial expectations and gender concerns, we find ourselves in the presence of themes and principles we have already encountered in the Radhasoami tradition. Here also, identity is finally the key issue, and here too the question of identity implicates matters of history, memory, vision, and interpersonal transactions. In both traditions we find a similar stress on the recognition of spiritually significant others as a basis for a deepened or transformed sense of self.

Sathya Sai Baba and his cult, described in part III, defy any simple characterization; his publicly projected persona is ambiguous and mysterious. Ostensibly his cult focuses mainly on magical performances of a sort that many would regard as religiously superficial. Closer examination of the attitudes fostered by the cult, however, shows that Sathya Sai Baba's magicality is but a special format for the exemplification of certain enduring Hindu ideas of divinity and divine-human relationships. The miracles mobilize transactional principles already seen in the Radhasoami and Brahma Kumari traditions; they also tell a tale to devotees about the meaning of the uncertainty of human life in general. In these materials, too, the theme of recognition is pivotal. Sathya Sai Baba's miracles are crucial to his devotees' recognition of him for what he 'really is,' an incarnation of God. This recognition, in turn, supports an altered sense of self as the beloved of God, and also establishes a special context for devotees' relationships with the world. Through their relations with Sathya Sai Baba, devotees learn to trust a playful, apparently capricious deity; in so doing, they learn to trust existence itself.

The concluding chapter is directly concerned with the issue of deep continuities. Here I examine what I call 'images' shared by the three movements—basic ideas of what the world is like that can be embodied in religious constructions of the human situation that are very different on the surface. These include concepts of cyclical history and the amnesia of temporal beings, unstable personhood in a fluid world, and the special powers of seeing and learning to see anew. The chapter ends with some reflections on the recovery of 'true' identity by means of special transactions with those who are 'recognized' as extraordinary beings. This principle, one that seems to operate somewhere just below the threshold of considered awareness, provides a bridge from the heart of Hindu religious culture to certain general features of human social life. The type of spiritual awakening sometimes characterized as 'self-realization' has a social-psychological basis in the apparently universal process by which self-awareness arises through social interaction.

I. Spiritual Recognition and the Radhasoami Faith

1. Successions

Relics

One has to begin with the *samādh.* A samādh is a resting place for the physical remains of a great religious personage. The great samādh at Soami Bagh (the Garden of the Master), a sectarian community located on the outskirts of the city of Agra, houses the ashes of the community's founder and a portion of those of his wife. Begun in 1904 on the foundations of an earlier and less elaborate structure, abandoned for lack of funds in 1911 and resumed in 1923, its construction continues in infinitesimal increments today. Its projected dimensions are truly impressive: 220 feet square at the base, with a dome over the central hall 171 feet high and surmounted by a 32-foot spire. Though only partly completed, it is in use today. When it will be finished nobody knows.

What matters most about the samādh, however, is not its vast projected size or its lavish appointments but the sacred items within. In a box below the central altar are the ashes of the founder, and at the altar are wooden sandals used by him in life. With great reverence visitors touch their foreheads to these sandals. This is the central and crucial act. Of course, the setting matters too, but the huge sums of money the community has spent on the structure are merely elaborations on that basic gesture of reverent obeisance.

Though central, the great samādh is not the only focus of homage at Soami Bagh. Just to the front of the great samādh is a well. It was once the founder's practice to use the water from this well to wash his feet and mouth. As a result, the well's water is regarded as being charged with religious virtue and is drunk with reverence by devotees. Other physical relics of the founder and his successors are also preserved here at Soami Bagh and at other locations in Agra and beyond: ashes (in other samādhs), sandals, walking sticks, items of clothing, swings, beds, seats, palanquins, and so on. These objects are not just keepsakes, but sacred items, carefully protected and treasured. They are touched and handled in highly formalized ways, because devotees regard them as sources of redeeming power. Contact with them is the same as contact with the Supreme Being, and will aid in achieving salvation from the sorrow and endlessly recurring deaths that are the lot of the beings who inhabit this world.

While not exactly relics, the photographs of the founder and his successors function in the same way. These pictures are ubiquitous. They hang on the walls and stand on the altars of the samādhs, and are fixtures of every devotee's home. They also preside over all ceremonial observances. They are not mere ornamentation; when devotees gaze at these pictures, they believe they are brought into contact with a benevolent power that will pull them upward and out of this world to a higher region where they will enjoy eternal repose at the feet of the Supreme Being.

It was not always thus at Soami Bagh. Though relics and pictures of the great personages of the past have always played a role in the religious life of this community, until 1949 devotional attitudes were mainly focused on a living man. His name was Babuji Maharaj and he was regarded by his followers as a *sant satguru*. A *sant* is a holy man, and *satguru* means 'true master.' More precisely, a sant satguru is a holy man who presides over a *satsang*, a congregation of devotees. He is understood to be the Supreme Being in human form, and is treated as such. During Babuji Maharaj's tenure as sant satguru his person was accorded the same veneration that the relics of past gurus evoked then and continue to command today. Devotees gazed at his face, touched his feet, drank his foot washings, and ate the leavings from his plate. But now the pictures and relics are, to outward appearances, all that is left. Babuji Maharaj died without a successor, and his ashes and relics joined the rest. So matters have stood since 1949.

Soami Bagh

Soami Bagh is the spiritual and physical center of one of the many existing branches of the Radhasoami faith (*rādhāsvāmī mat*).[1] This religious movement is today a loose congeries of sects centered mainly in Agra, Delhi, and at Beas in the state of Punjab. It was founded

---

[1] The Romanization of the Hindi word *rādhāsvāmī* as 'Radhasoami' is technically incorrect, but is preferred by the Agra wing of the movement. In referring to the movement's name I have respected this preference. The tradition renders *mat* as 'faith' in English, another usage I have followed with regard to the movement's name.

(according to some versions) in the mid-nineteenth century by a great saint known to members of the faith as Soamiji Maharaj. His remains are the ones venerated in the great samādh. The heritage within which he conceived and announced his message is called *sant mat*, the creed of the sants, a tradition associated with such figures as Kabir and Nanak.[2] Since its founding the Radhasoami movement has prospered, spread, and split many times over. The existing branches vary greatly in size and vigor; most are small and localized, but a few have acquired international followings.

The movement is split into two main branches. One is associated with Agra, where the movement began; the other with Punjab, where an offshoot took root at Beas around the turn of the century. In Agra itself there are two principal subbranches. One is the Soami Bagh group, the other a group at Dayal Bagh (the Garden of the Merciful) directly across the street. These two communities are bitterly hostile toward each other. In Agra there is also another smaller congregation, linked with Soami Bagh, which is centered at the samādh of Soamiji Maharaj's immediate successor (according to the Agra interpretation) at Pipal Mandi. The Punjab branch, which has been strongly influenced by Sikhism, has produced its own offshoots, at least two of which are now situated in Delhi. There are many other lesser-known Radhasoami groups scattered around northern India.

About one thousand people live at Soami Bagh, many of them elderly retirees. Sequestered from the main road behind an ornate main gate, the colony offers an opportunity for a secluded and quiet life devoted to spiritual pursuits. Congregational observances (called *satsang*) occur four times daily: once in the great samādh, twice at the foot of Babuji Maharaj's bed in the room in which he spent the last years of his life, and once in a building known as the *bhajan ghar* (the House of Listening to Internal Sounds). Many residents do not attend these observances regularly. The presiding authorities at Soami Bagh are the members of a body known as the Central Administrative Council.

Most Soami Bagh devotees do not live in the colony itself, but elsewhere in (mainly) urban northern India. Knowledgeable informants told me that there are about 100,000 devotees in total (a figure I cannot independently verify), and I was also told that in

[2] For excellent accounts of the place of the Radhasoami movement within the wider tradition of sant mat, and its subsequent spread and ramifications, the reader is urged to consult Barthwal 1978; Gold 1982; and Juergensmeyer 1978, 1982, and forthcoming.

Delhi, where much of my contact with the group occurred, there are about 200 affiliated families. The group as a whole is multicaste, and although it is centered in a Hindi-speaking area, it includes devotees from such diverse regional backgrounds as Gujarat, Sind, Punjab, and Bengal. By far the majority of devotees I met in Delhi and Soami Bagh belonged to the English-educated middle and upper-middle classes. Most were either in or retired from some form of government service. 'Outstation *satsangīs*'—that is, devotees who do not live in Agra—ideally maintain strong ties with Soami Bagh and the other sacred centers of the movement. Annual feast-days (*bhaṇḍārā*s) held at the samādhs of past gurus are occasions for general gatherings. I was told that as many as 8000 devotees attended one such occasion during the year of my inquiries.

One would be quite mistaken to think of the Soami Bagh group—the satsang, as members call it—as a community in any normal sense. Within this group there are many divisions, and in any case its territorial dispersion mitigates against the formation of anything resembling corporate ties. The group is probably best conceived as a loose 'congregation' that acquires some measure of identity in relation to Soami Bagh, the place, and the sacred relics kept at Soami Bagh and elsewhere. But this identity is complex and ambiguous. For example, although Babuji Maharaj had no official successor, some members of the congregation have accepted certain living individuals as sant satguru, thus establishing subcongregations within the wider congregation. Moreover, persons outside the Soami Bagh congregation treat some of the relics kept there as sacred. Only Soami Bagh devotees venerate the remains and relics of Babuji Maharaj, but even though the Punjab groups disparage the veneration of the remains of past gurus, I have seen Beas devotees touching the sandals at Soamiji Maharaj's samādh. Also, as we shall see, access to this samādh is one of the main issues dividing the Dayal Bagh and Soami Bagh groups; here coveneration has been more divisive than unifying. Initiation into the movement under the authority of the Central Administrative Council is a potentially unambiguous criterion of allegiance to the Soami Bagh group, but I have met uninitiated individuals who felt such allegiance, and in the past initiates have been involved in factions that have seceded from this group.

One way to visualize the congregation is as three intergrading concentric circles. There is a core of individuals, not necessarily residing at Soami Bagh, who are deeply immersed in the affairs of the satsang. This is the center, though it is far from solid because of disagreements on matters of succession to the guruship. Persons belonging to this category are likely to participate regularly in congregational observances in their own communities and at Agra. As a result, they are highly visible both within the congregation and to an outsider. There is a larger category consisting of persons who are less committed, or at least less involved in the affairs of the satsang. In this group are individuals, often born into affiliated families, who think of themselves as devotees, but who may not have undergone the formality of initiation, and who may not engage in any serious way in the spiritual 'practice' (*abhyās*) taught by the movement. Then there is an outer penumbra of individuals at the very fringe of the congregation or slipping beyond its frontier. This is often the situation of women who marry into nonsatsangī families.

Is the Soami Bagh congregation different from other Radhasoami groups in its beliefs? The answer is yes and no. Many and perhaps most of the teachings promoted under the Soami Bagh umbrella are shared by the other branches of the movement, though there are some crucial exceptions. However, what fundamentally distinguishes this congregation from others is not primarily a matter of doctrine, but of where its devotional energies are focussed. Its members revere the memory of, engage in inner communion with, and venerate the relics of Babuji Maharaj, the last guru of the Soami Bagh line. Other groups do not. This is not primarily a matter of theology, since all Radhasoami groups agree that attachment to some sant satguru is an indispensable precondition for salvation. Rather, disagreement mainly centers on the question of who is, or was, a genuine sant satguru, and on how such matters are decided. This is the level at which beliefs really differ between the various branches of the Radhasoami movement, and here ritual gesture and matters of belief converge. Venerating Babuji Maharaj and his relics means affirming in sentiment and action a certain version of the past. To accept the sanctity of Babuji Maharaj and his relics is to believe that he is in a line of succession to the founder's guruship. That is, to adopt ritual attitudes toward him and his relics is, in a sense, to enact a particular theory of the Radhasoami movement's history.

For this reason it is impossible to understand the Radhasoami faith—as it exists at Soami Bagh or elsewhere—without examining its history and the interpretations that various branches of the movement place on its history. This history is largely defined by a series of succession-episodes, each of which was a point of major schism.

The Founder

According to the Agra wing of the movement, the Radhasoami faith was founded by Shiv Dayal Singh, later known as Soamiji Maharaj.[3] He was born in August 1818 in Panni Gali in Agra. His father was a Punjabi Khatrī moneylender and a follower of Guru Nanak, whose doctrines and verse were very much a part of the religious atmosphere of the household. He was educated in Hindi, Gurmukhi, and Persian, and attained some proficiency in Sanskrit and Arabic. As a young man he apparently found it difficult to settle down to the life of work and householdership expected of men of his background. Following an early marriage, he twice took employment outside Agra, but in neither instance did he stay with his employer long. After his father's death he dissolved the family's moneylending business, and never sought employment again. Income from his younger brother's position in the Post Master General's office apparently sufficed for the family's subsistence. His marriage was without issue.

He is said to have displayed religious proclivities from an early age. However, between the Punjab and Agra wings of the movement there are profound disagreements about the nature of his emergent religious persona, reflecting very different visions of the nature and historical meaning of Soamiji Maharaj's mission.

All agree that his family was under the influence of Tulsi Saheb, an important sant from Hathras (some thirty miles east of Agra), but the Punjab wing of the movement also holds that Tulsi Saheb was Soamiji Maharaj's actual spiritual master (Puri 1972, 6–7). Thus, according to this view, Soamiji Maharaj was not the founder of a new 'faith,' but merely one particularly saintly teacher of sant mat, and heir to a long line of sants. One proponent of the Punjab view has carried this argument even further by suggesting that Tulsi Saheb was a disciple of one of Guru Gobind Singh's disciples, thus putting the Radhasoami tradition in a direct line of descent from the Sikh gurus (Kirpal Singh 1971, 9–19).

According to the contrasting Agra view—and the perspective of this account—Soamiji Maharaj was spiritually autonomous (a *svatah sant*) and neither had nor needed a master (see esp. Maheshwari 1954, 13–14). Proponents of this interpretation hold that Tulsi Saheb was

---

[3] For the Agra interpretation of the movement's history, see esp. Maheshwari 1954 and Mathur 1974. These works are the main general sources for what follows. Other works have been consulted as indicated by citations in text.

the guru of Soamiji Maharaj's parents and a frequent visitor in the household, but not the guru of Soamiji Maharaj himself. Rather, it was Tulsi Saheb who, because of his high spiritual development, first detected the presence of the Supreme Being in Soamiji Maharaj, and announced this fact to his parents. This interpretation is of a piece with the Agra (and, thus, Soami Bagh) contention that Soamiji Maharaj's advent represented an entirely new religious dispensation in the world. His teachings were not simply a new formulation of sant mat, but embodied a salvationary promise that completely superseded all previous religions.

When and how Soamiji Maharaj's following of disciples began to form is difficult to say from existing evidence. We are told that for many years he periodically secluded himself in a room for two- and three-day marathons of meditation, during which he would neither eat nor relieve himself, and such practices must have contributed to his growing reputation as a holy man. At first he was probably a neighborhood saint of purely local fame, but in time the house at Panni Gali became a gathering place for devotees and *sādhus* (mendicants) who listened to his discourses and were initiated by him into special techniques of meditation. On *basant panchmī* day ('Spring Fifth,' a Hindu holiday) in 1861, apparently at the instigation of his closest disciples, he opened his satsang to the public.

He lived for seventeen more years, teaching a faith that blended tantric imagery with elements of the Hindu devotional tradition, and that also incorporated some of the idioms of Islamic mysticism. His fame spread, the satsang grew, and by the time of his death in 1878 he had initiated some eight to ten thousand devotees (Chachaji Saheb 1978, 40). Most were ordinary householders, but there were many sādhus among his followers as well.

The First Succession

The Agra wing of the Radhasoami movement contends that Soamiji Maharaj's sole successor was Rai Saligram, known to the tradition as Huzur Maharaj. This remarkable man was born in 1829 to a Kāyastha family at Pipal Mandi in Agra. He was in many ways very different from Soamiji Maharaj. Unlike Soamiji Maharaj, he was quintessentially a man of government service, and an early representative of India's rather bicultural modern middle class. After completing his education at Agra College, he entered service in the Postal Department, where he remained until his retirement. He was at home with the English language, as Soamiji Maharaj was not, and with Western intellectual styles. He was also fluent in the usages of Anglo-Indian bureaucracy, and an immense success in the world of work. In 1881 he became the first Indian to hold the position of Postmaster General of the North Western Provinces. As a man of the office, he was prototypical of most of the Radhasoami movement's later gurus. Virtually all have been men who spent their working lives in government service, and to a significant degree this has been a characteristic of their followers as well.

Huzur Maharaj first met Soamiji Maharaj in 1858 after learning of his existence from a postal colleague who was Soamiji Maharaj's younger brother, Chachaji Saheb (Lala Pratap Singh Seth).[4] He responded instantly and deeply to Soamiji Maharaj's persona and message. Because of the demands of his career, he was not in continuous contact with Soamiji Maharaj during the years that followed, but he was certainly among the most avid of his devotees, and probably the most favored as well. His devotion had to pass the test of his fellow Kāyasthas' severe disapproval. They objected particularly to his open consumption of Soamiji Maharaj's food leavings (*prasād*), in their view a flagrant compromise of the status of their caste. But he was undeterred, and remained one of the pillars of Soamiji Maharaj's satsang for twenty years.

The question of whether or not Huzur Maharaj was really Soamiji Maharaj's successor is partly what is at issue in the greatest split in the Radhasoami movement, that between its Agra and Punjab branches. According to the Agra interpretation, Huzur Maharaj was Soamiji Maharaj's principal disciple and *gurumukh* (one who faces the guru; that is, his successor). In support of this, proponents of the Agra position maintain that it was not until Huzur Maharaj actually came on the scene that Soamiji Maharaj revealed his highest truth, which was (in the Agra view) that the true name of the Supreme Being is 'rādhāsvāmī.' It was, furthermore, Huzur Maharaj who recognized Soamiji Maharaj's real identity as the Supreme Being incarnate, and began calling him by that name. In the Agra view the disclosure of the name rādhāsvāmī was the decisive revelation that defined a 'Radhasoami faith' as such and distinguished it from all other religions.

---

[4] Chachaji Saheb was also Soamiji Maharaj's biographer. Virtually all that is known about the master's personal life comes from this source (Chachaji Saheb 1978).

The Punjab wing concedes that Huzur Maharaj may have been among the master's most beloved disciples, but holds that there were others of equal status. One was a Sikh soldier by the name of Jaimal Singh. According to the Punjab interpretation, Jaimal Singh received a direct mandate from Soamiji Maharaj to take his teachings to Punjab. This he did, and established the satsang at Beas from which arose the entire Punjab branch of the movement. As already noted, the Punjab branch also contends that Soamiji Maharaj's teachings were not unique but were simply his version of the older tradition of sant mat. In line with this view they also maintain that the name rādhāsvāmī was in no way central to his teachings, and one Punjabi guru has even suggested that this name was Huzur Maharaj's invention (Kirpal Singh 1971, 14–15).

In any case, within months of Soamiji Maharaj's death Huzur Maharaj started the construction of a samādh for his master's remains at Soami Bagh (then mainly used as a sanctuary for sādhus), and began to emerge as Soamiji Maharaj's successor at Agra. Two persons appear to have been crucial to his acceptance as sant satguru. One was Soamiji Maharaj's wife, known as Radhaji, who seems to have played a role in smoothing the way for this succession within Soamiji Maharaj's family (Chachaji Saheb 1978, 146). Another key person was Soamiji Maharaj's younger brother (and biographer), Chachaji Saheb, who had become guru of a congregation of his own at Soami Bagh. In the end he entered Huzur Maharaj's satsang, and in his biography of Soamiji Maharaj (first published in 1902) he gave full sanction to Huzur Maharaj's succession. From the time of his retirement in 1887 until his death in 1898 Huzur Maharaj presided over the satsang from his residence at Pipal Mandi.

Huzur Maharaj was the great consolidator of the Radhasoami faith. For instance, he gave the faith a textual tradition, which was nonexistent at the time of Soamiji Maharaj's death, by editing and in 1884 publishing the master's poetic compositions and prose discourses. These he published as *Sār bachan rādhāsvāmī, chhand band* (hereafter *S. B. Poetry*) and *Sār bachan rādhāsvāmī, bārtik* (hereafter *S. B. Prose*). These two collections are the core of the Radhasoami textual tradition, and are venerated in both the Agra and Punjab wings of the movement.[5]

Huzur Maharaj's own literary output was also huge, and in the

---

[5] Certain changes have been introduced in the Punjab versions. For example, the section of *S. B. Prose* dealing with succession (II, 250) has been considerably altered in the version published by the Beas group (*Sār Bachan* 1974).

Agra wing his writings constitute a second level of sacred texts. His poetry is published in four volumes as *Prembānī rādhāsvāmī*. His prose discourses and other writings are numerous and various, but among them the most important are the collections known as *Prem patra rādhāsvāmī*. Originally published (from 1893 on) as articles in a fortnightly journal of the same name, these discourses were the literary forum in which a systematized Radhasoami theology, only nascently present in Soamiji Maharaj's poetry and discourses, was elaborated for the first time. Much of the highly complex doctrinal system of the Soami Bagh congregation originated in these and other writings of Huzur Maharaj.

The Second Succession

The Soami Bagh congregation holds that Huzur Maharaj's successor was Brahma Shankar Mishra, known to the tradition as Maharaj Saheb. He was born in 1861 in Banaras to the family of a Brāhmaṇ professor of Sanskrit. He obtained an M. A. in English literature in 1884, and after a brief experiment with the study of law, he became a teacher at Bareilly College. In 1885 he was brought into contact with Huzur Maharaj for the first time by Madhav Prasad Sinha, who was an old friend and school chum. Madhav Prasad, who was later to become a sant satguru himself (as Babuji Maharaj), was a member of Soamiji Maharaj's family and a longtime satsangī. Maharaj Saheb quickly became a staunch devotee, and in order to be as close to Huzur Maharaj as possible, then in Allahabad, he and Madhav Prasad took employment together in the Accountant General's office in that city. After Huzur Maharaj's retirement and return to Agra in 1887, the two continued to run the Allahabad satsang, and visited their guru in Agra whenever circumstances permitted.

When Huzur Maharaj died in 1898, a number of satsangīs transferred their allegiance to Maharaj Saheb. His friend Madhav Prasad was probably the key to this transition, since he was the first to accept Maharaj Saheb's guruship openly. As always, however, this succession was not universally accepted. Another of Huzur Maharaj's disciples, Shiva Bharat Lal, established a satsang of his own at Gopiganj near Banaras, and Huzur Maharaj's son, Lalaji Maharaj (Ajudhia Prasad), became the source of a hereditary line of gurus presiding at Pipal Mandi. In any case within a year or two of Huzur Maharaj's death, Maharaj Saheb was attracting large numbers of followers to his satsang at Allahabad. His tenure as sant satguru was not long. In 1907, his health in decline, he moved to Banaras, where he died in October of that year.

Although Maharaj Saheb wrote an important book, *Discourses on Radhasoami Faith* (written in English), the legacies of his guruship are more institutional than intellectual. He began the construction of the great samādh at Soami Bagh in 1904; also under his aegis the issue of the status of sādhus in the movement was finally settled, and the body known as the Central Administrative Council established.

The issue of the sādhus was a crucial matter (see Maheshwari 1954, 59–61). Sādhus had been an important element in the movement's membership under the regimes of Soamiji Maharaj and Huzur Maharaj, and had represented potential rival centers of sacred authority. In those days it was customary for sādhus to initiate devotees and to receive their obeisance. Clearly this was a challenge to what was supposed to be the absolute centrality of the sant satguru. Their presence was awkward in other ways, too. From the start the Radhasoami faith was supposed to be basically a householder's path, and the presence of the sādhus was dissonant with this claim. Moreover, the sādhus probably did not fit well into the bourgeois atmosphere that had become a pervasive feature of the movement's subculture. Maharaj Saheb banned the ochre robe, and attempted to regulate the sādhus' movements and induce them to accept regular employment. He also strongly discouraged the acceptance of any new sādhus into the satsang.

But Maharaj Saheb's most important innovation was the establishment of the Central Administrative Council in 1902 (see esp. ibid., 95–99; Mathur 1974, 109–111). He was motivated by two issues. One was the rise of schismatic factions within the movement, which had become a serious problem by this time. Some organizing framework was needed to keep the faith together. The other issue, and one intimately related to questions of succession, was that of the satsang's property. Sums of money had been given as religious offerings to the first two gurus, and the properties that had been acquired with this money had gone to their principal heirs. Maharaj Saheb intended that the council would consolidate these properties, protect them from the claims of schismatic groups, and manage them on behalf of the sant satguru 'of the time,' whoever he might be.

A postal ballot listing twenty-eight names was sent to senior and influential satsang members. The ten on the list who received the highest number of votes became the council, and Chachaji Saheb (Soamiji Maharaj's younger brother), whose name was not on the ballot, became its first president. Among the other members of the council were, of course, Maharaj Saheb and also his friend and longtime supporter, Madhav Prasad Sinha. Under the rules of the council all future appointments to it would be determined by the council itself.

Once formed, the council quickly moved to rationalize the movement's organization. Initiation was brought under council regulation by vesting the right to initiate and/or sanction initiations in three individuals: Maharaj Saheb, Chachaji Saheb, and one other senior satsangī (Lalaji Maharaj). Branch satsangs were likewise brought under council control. The rule was instituted that a branch could be established only by ten registered satsangīs, and would be subject to the authority of the council, to which it was expected to make remittances and render accounts. In 1904 the council formed the Radhasoami Trust to undertake the actual management of satsang property.

Serious troubles began almost immediately. Baba Jaimal Singh, the founder of the Punjab wing of the movement, had maintained cordial relationships with the parent satsang, though from afar, until the council was formed. Shortly after this new regime took power, he began to find the council's authority irksome. He soon split with the Agra group altogether, and the Punjab wing of the movement remains entirely separate today. Thus, the first result of an attempt to rationalize the movement was a heightening of schismatic tensions.

The End of Succession

In the aftermath of Maharaj Saheb's death in 1907, another crisis arose. Whether or not he named a successor before his death is a debatable point (compare Maheshwari 1954, 67; Mathur 1974, 125), but what is clear is that a period of great confusion followed. A small group of devotees collected around Maharaj Saheb's older sister, an elderly woman known as Buaji Saheba, whom they regarded as his successor. Also forming at the same time was a powerful dissident faction, which finally broke with the council in 1910.

Buaji Saheba was a simple woman in the old style who remained in the seclusion of *parda* all of her life. For this reason she was unable to deliver discourses or accept the normal attentions of devotees. It was especially unfortunate that she could not be seen by most devotees, because visual interaction (*darshan*) between guru and devotee is, as we shall see, fundamental to the soteriologic method of the Radhasoami faith. As a result, the de facto head of her satsang was Maharaj Saheb's old friend, Madhav Prasad Sinha. Such as it was, this satsang functioned under council sanction in Allahabad until Buaji's death in 1913. Because direct contact with Buaji was impossible, save for a select inner group, the satsang never flourished.

In the meantime a very serious defection had occurred. A council member named Kamta Prasad Sinha (later called Sarkar Saheb) had established a satsang of his own in Ghazipur shortly after Maharaj Saheb's demise, and in the absence of a strong center elsewhere he managed to take the allegiance of a large number of satsangīs with him. In 1910 he broke completely with the council and started his own rival organization, the Radhasoami Satsang Sabha. After his death in 1913 he was succeeded by Anand Swarup, who as guru was known as Sahibji Maharaj.

Sahibji Maharaj was one of the most innovative leaders ever produced by the Radhasoami movement. He purchased property directly across the street from Soami Bagh (by then under the control of the council), where he established the Dayal Bagh colony in 1915. Dayal Bagh was intended to be a utopian community, based on a work-as-worship ethic, in which the pursuit of spiritual goals would blend with economic endeavors. How well this ideal was realized is a much debated matter, but in economic and social terms the community was highly successful. Residential buildings, schools, and factories were built, and in later years modernized agricultural operations were started. Today Soami Bagh is nearly surrounded by Dayal Bagh property.

Relations between Dayal Bagh and Soami Bagh are deeply hostile. Often treated as a matter of levity by onlookers, the quarreling between these two groups, each professing the same faith and separated by the width of a street, has been painful indeed for those involved. Bitter conflict arose virtually from the time of their separation. Under Sahibji Maharaj the Dayal Bagh group attempted to challenge the legitimacy of the council at Soami Bagh by demanding the publication of their accounts, and this demand led to a series of litigations that has been continuing since 1923.

The underlying issue was the ownership of the satsang properties at Soami Bagh, especially as this affected Dayal Bagh devotees' rights of access to Soamiji Maharaj's remains in the great samādh. The history of the conflict need not detain us, but it is important to note that one point of considerable theological importance soon arose, namely the question of the relationship between the sant satguru and the worldly institution of property ownership.[6] The essence of the Soami Bagh case seems to have been that the Radhasoami Trust need not answer to any outside group for its management of satsang properties because it is not a trust in the ordinary sense of the term. It is accountable only to the sant satguru, who is the real and sole owner of the property. Since the sant satguru is himself the Supreme Being, he likewise cannot be asked to account in any way for his use or management of satsang property.

The Dayal Bagh case was based on a critical distinction. They contended that when an offering is made to a sant satguru, he accepts it only as a representative of the Supreme Being, with whom he is not actually identified in this context. Therefore, the sant satguru is not the actual owner of the property, and is accountable for his use and management of it to the membership of the satsang. If this is correct, then all 'satsangīs' (i. e., including the Dayal Bagh group in respect to Soami Bagh, since the two groups were one when the property in question was acquired) have a legitimate interest in any property acquired by a sant satguru in the form of religious offerings.

While not wishing to attempt to judge these issues, we may at least observe that if the Dayal Bagh claim is legitimate, its validity seems to be purchased at the expense of what was a central tenet of the Radhasoami faith from the beginning—that is, that the person of a sant satguru and the Supreme Being are, to an awakened awareness, indistinguishable. This is a matter to which we shall return in chapter 3. The long history of the Dayal Bagh–Soami Bagh conflict does illustrate, however, the fundamental difficulty of institutionalizing in legal terms guruship as it was traditionally conceived in the Radhasoami faith. The existence of the council brought matters to a head. As long as there was no mechanism to transfer rights in satsang property from a sant satguru to nonhereditary successors, the question of what belonged to whom fell under the normal laws of inheritance. Alternatively, if the Radhasoami Trust were held to be a normal public trust, then the management of its properties would be

---

[6] My sources for these details are extracts from Babuji Maharaj's, Seth Saheb's, and Sahibji Maharaj's depositions reproduced in Maheshwari (1954, 428–44), and Radhasoami Satsang Sabha (1961, 348–56).

separated from the question of who is, in fact, the sant satguru. But to claim that the sant satguru is the sole owner of satsang properties in virtue of his embodiment of the Supreme Being is to make the question of who embodies the Supreme Being a matter of legal interest. Or, from a different angle, it is to make the decision about who is sant satguru a decision about the disposition of property. Thus arose an intractable legal tangle. All of this is very remote from what is supposed to be at issue in matters of succession to the guruship.

When Buaji Saheba died in 1913, the split between the Soami Bagh council group and what was to become the Dayal Bagh group had already occurred, and Buaji's guruship was never acknowledged by the Dayal Bagh line. The council group accepted her guruship (though when they did so is not clear), and upon her demise acknowledged Madhav Prasad Sinha, Maharaj Saheb's old friend and mainstay of Buaji's satsang, as her successor. This succession, however, was not universally accepted; upon Buaji's death, her eldest son established a group of his own at Banaras called Premashram Satsang.

As guru, Madhav Prasad was known as Babuji Maharaj. He was born in 1861 in Banaras, and was a grandson of Soamiji Maharaj's eldest sister. As a child he was in periodic contact with Soamiji Maharaj and was apparently initiated by him. As already noted, he had spent his working career together with Maharaj Saheb in the Accountant General's office at Allahabad, and after his own succession he conducted his satsang there for many years. He had been a member of the council since its inception and very influential in its affairs; in 1926 he became its president. In 1937 he finally shifted his satsang to Soami Bagh. Because of declining health, in 1943 he took to his bed, where he remained until his death in 1949. Portions of his ashes are enshrined at Radha Bagh (near Soami Bagh), and in the room at Soami Bagh in which he spent the last years of his life.

Babuji Maharaj was basically a caretaker guru. He generated no great doctrinal or institutional innovations, nor was he a poet or writer of books. He was, however, a genuinely learned man and a skilled composer of religious discourses. His discourses have been compiled by S. D. Maheshwari in six volumes and are a rich source of Radhasoami doctrine. An American devotee named Myron Phelps took notes on some of his discourses delivered in 1913–14, and these were later published (in 1947) as *Phelps' Notes*, a book that has acquired semicanonical status in the Soami Bagh tradition. The most notable features of his reign were his able generalship in the continuing wars with Dayal Bagh and his stewardship over the growth and consolidation of the Soami Bagh colony.

Babuji Maharaj did not designate a successor, nor have his followers been able to achieve a consensus on a successor to this day. Thus, for over thirty years the Soami Bagh congregation has been in interregnum. This does not mean that they have been without a guru. They believe that the gurus of the past are, in a sense, still present. Nor does it mean that Babuji Maharaj was actually unsucceeded, for individuals within the Soami Bagh congregation have been recognized as sant satgurus by personal constituencies, and have functioned as such. But nobody has achieved general recognition. For the present, the council administers satsang and sanctions initiations. Meanwhile the advent of a new sant satguru is awaited by the congregation—by some with a continuing sense of expectancy, by others with a mixture of waning hope and growing resignation.

The Lord as Person

There are really two ways of looking at the history I have summarized. One is from the perspective of an outsider, and from this frame of reference the historical map of the Radhasoami movement as a whole appears as an inverted tree with branching lines of descent (Figure 1). One might choose to emphasize any branch—as I have done in stressing the line of succession leading to the present situation at Soami Bagh—but whatever line is emphasized, the general drift of the account would be the same. The movement appears never to have solved the problem of succession to sacred authority. With the passing of every generation there are new disputes and splits, and the branching lines of descent show every sign of continuing to ramify as long as the movement exists.

But from the inside, the history of the movement looks somewhat different. From the Soami Bagh standpoint, for example, the history of the movement appears not as branching lines but as one line. Because there can only be one sant satguru at a time, the other lines of spiritual 'descent' are not really lines of descent at all. The single real line begins with Soamiji Maharaj and continues through Huzur Maharaj, Maharaj Saheb, Buaji Saheba, and Babuji Maharaj. Despite the interregnum, this line continues today, because the redemptive power the line embodies continues to be available in the books,

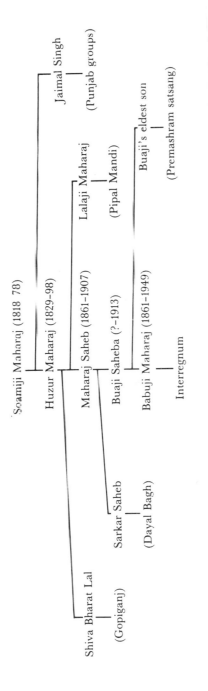

Figure 1. Succession Tree (Simplified): Soami Bagh Perspective

Sources: Gold 1982, 457–59, Maheshwari 1954, and 1971a, 510–11, Mathur 1974.

pictures, and especially the relics of the gurus of the past. It is true that at critical junctures there were those who wandered away from the true line, but they merely wandered into error.

In all of this we can discern an idea of 'error' that may strike readers as peculiar. In the Radhasoami tradition what counts as crucial error seems to be more a matter of historiography than theology, having mainly to do with interpretations of critical succession episodes. Even where there are important doctrinal differences, these seem often to center on matters of succession. Among the Punjab groups, for example, the spiritual 'practice' (abhyās) enjoined on adherents involves a contemplative relationship with five 'names' (discussed more fully in chapter 2), whereas among the Agra groups the emphasis is on one name: rādhāsvāmī. Whatever its salvationary implications, the five-name/one-name question is, however, also a question about who was Soamiji Maharaj's legitimate successor, Huzur Maharaj or Baba Jaimal Singh.

In this tradition error seems finally to be not so much a question of *what* one believes as it is a matter of *in whom* one believes. From the very start everything has centered on the critical question of who is, and who is not, a sant satguru. And in this there is an apparent oddity and a genuine puzzle. As represented by the Radhasoami tradition, the Supreme Being is basically formless and utterly beyond normal powers of human conception, but in fact the religious attitudes fostered by Radhasoami teachings are relentlessly focused on form. In a seeming paradox, devotees of formless divinity love, touch, gaze at, eat the leavings of, and serve the body of a human being, the sant satguru. It is as if the very commitment to the idea of a formless Lord has somehow, by reflex, created its converse. Confronted with an idea of divinity that places the Supreme Being outside the sphere of normal human contact or even comprehension, the tradition has based its salvationary promise on the idea that the Supreme Being, as an act of grace, has become accessible in the most intimate of all possible ways—in the form of a human being whose face can be gazed at, whose feet can be touched, whose leavings can be eaten, and whose relics can be venerated. And because this is the *only* form in which the Lord is accessible, the entire weight of the cosmos rests on the question of who he is.

In the case of the Soami Bagh tradition the result is a religious outlook that might be described as hypertrophically 'interactive.' The entire salvationary promise of this tradition hinges on recognizing a sant satguru for what he is and engaging in interactions with him. To be a 'believer' is to be engaged in such interactions, either with a living sant satguru or, as in the case of the Soami Bagh community today, with an inner image of the sant satguru and the ashes and relics of the gurus of the past.

But in defining the religious situation of devotees in such terms, the Radhasoami faith does not depart from the wider Hindu tradition from which it mainly arose. Not only has the relationship between guru and disciple been central to the Hindu tradition from ancient times, but the relationship between deity and worshipper is an interactive one: worshipper and worshipped engage in transactions with each other, the models for which are essentially social. The Radhasoami tradition merely intensifies this principle in its own way by putting such great weight on guru-disciple interactions. Therefore, to know more about Radhasoami constructions of relations between sant satgurus and their followers is of value in understanding principles that inform a wide range of religious attitudes in the Hindu world, and possibly elsewhere.

My purpose in the next two chapters is to explore in more detail the meanings embodied in guru-devotee relationships in the Radhasoami tradition, particularly as exemplified in the Soami Bagh congregation. What does it really mean to believe that redemptive power can be present in the body of a man? What does it mean to believe that this power can be appropriated by touching his feet or eating the leavings from his plate? What does it mean to believe that this power can be present in his ashes, or in the bed he once lay in, or the sandals he once wore, or his fingernail clippings, or the like? And what is the source of the power of his visage? How is it that looking at him can tap his power, a power so great that it can apparently be transmitted in some measure by his photographs? Indeed, *what* is this power that seems to be realized in some way in the interaction between a devotee and a person who, to all outward appearances, seems no different from other men?

2. Redemption in a Fluid World

The Role of Doctrine

There is an apparent inconsistency, even a paradox, in the Radhasoami attitude toward matters of the intellect. This tradition has little use for book-learning or abstract theories. Intellectual constructions are condemned as mere *bāchak gyān* (sophistry), and on many occasions my informants chided me for what they saw as the basic irrelevance of my many queries about theological fine points. In the end the only thing that really matters is soteriologically relevant experience of a type that is entirely beyond the intellectual capacities of human beings to appreciate or understand.

And yet the tradition has been a virtual cornucopia of writing. At one level the books of the tradition are ceremonial paraphernalia. In the Soami Bagh satsang, congregational observances center on the singing of verse and the recitation of prose from the various texts venerated in the Soami Bagh tradition. These stanzas and sentences, however, are not just ceremonial noises. Many of the Radhasoami sant satgurus were men of erudition and great mental energy. Although the Radhasoami tradition disparages intellectual systems, the writings of the gurus constitute a vast intellectual system. The apparent paradox dissolves away once it is understood what doctrine is, and is not, in this tradition.

The highly distinctive Radhasoami world-view incorporates images of the human body, the cosmos, and cosmic history in a truly comprehensive interpretation of the human situation. It is to be found in varying degrees of completeness in the texts of the movement, and can be described, at least in outline, by informants. But this world-view is not a 'theory' of the world, or at least not in the usual meaning of that term. That is, it is not a discursive intellectual construct responsible to purely intellectual imperatives. For example, Radhasoami teachings 'fit together,' but this does not mean that they are always logically consistent with each other, or even that consistency is very important. Nor is it clear that these teachings are, at root, intended to be 'intellectually convincing,' since intellectual conviction is little valued in the Radhasoami tradition.

Rather, Radhasoami assertions about the nature of the world are meant to be received and understood within a very special context, outside of which they have little meaning. This context is the relationship between a devotee or devotee-to-be and a sant satguru. Thus a common Radhasoami assertion claims that the writings of past gurus are not fully intelligible unless read under the influence of a living sant satguru (an obvious difficulty for the Soami Bagh congregation). The relationship between guru and devotee is the beginning and end of all Radhasoami teachings. Salvation is made possible only by entering such a relationship, and salvation achieved through such a relationship is, in theory, the sole aim of the devotee. All else, including doctrine, is subordinate to this fundamental goal.

At the very heart of the matter is a question of identity. In the Radhasoami view the beings of this world suffer from a case of mistaken identity: we are not the persons we think ourselves to be. However, experiential realization of our true identities is attainable by means of special contemplative techniques. Only contact with a sant satguru makes this recovery of one's true self possible. The doctrinal system of the Radhasoami faith is probably best interpreted as a supportive ideological medium for self-revelatory experiences. Its persuasiveness is, therefore, not so much a matter of how well it makes sense of the world, but of how well it portrays a world in which these crucial experiences make redemptive sense. It will be to those for whom the sant satguru's persona has redeeming power, experienced as such, that these images of the world will speak. In other words, intellectual convincingness is at the trailing edge, not the leading edge, of the Radhasoami understanding of the world.

Physiocosmology

The imagery with which Radhasoami doctrine surrounds the issue of identity is a blend of cosmology, physiology, and history. According to Radhasoami teachings, the true self of the person, completely hidden under a cover of mind and body, is an entity called *surat* (or *rūh*). This self is an 'emanation' or 'part' (*ansh*) of the Supreme Being, whose name is rādhāsvāmī. Innumerable births ago the self became separated from its lofty source and descended to begin a career of transmigrations in the material world. This is our predicament. The object of Radhasoami teachings and practices is to foster an awareness in us of our true situation, and to provide the means for us to recover our true identities by leaving this 'alien country' (*pardesh*) and returning to our 'own' or 'true' home (*nij ghar*) with the Supreme Being.

The self in the world is an historical self. When it descended from above, it began a transmigratory career in a world of change. Oddly, however, the principal condition of the self's existence in time is forgetfulness. Even though it must experience the consequences of its actions (*karmas*) in previous existences, the embodied self cannot remember its former lives. Such memories come only in the intervals between death and rebirth; that is, they come only when the self is momentarily withdrawn from the historical process. And, of course, the self remembers nothing of its real identity. When it descended to this world, it became so encased in gross matter that it forgot, in effect, its own existence. To be an historical being, in sum, is to forget; having forgotten, we think we are of this world when in fact we are not.

This portrayal of the situation of the temporal self can be seen as a doctrinal formalization of something truly central to the Radhasoami outlook—namely, an attitude of deep alienation from the world. Before anything else, a Soami Bagh informant told me, one must learn to 'hate the world.' This attitude is expressed vividly in the poetic literature of the movement. In Soamiji Maharaj's verse (*S. B. Poetry*) the *jīva* (the transmigrating self) is depicted as a homeless nomad that 'eats delusion' as it wanders blindly about in the 'alien country' into which it has descended. The self inhabits a body likened to a 'leather water bag,' and it roams in darkness and desolation, knowing nothing of what or where it is. The waste through which it wanders is vast. The self has fallen into what is called *chaurāsī*, a word meaning 'eighty-four,' and referring to the eighty-four forms of existence (more commonly said to be 8,400,000)[1] through which the transmigrating self must pass. Through all of the 'four *khāns*' (the four classes of living things: womb-born, egg-born, vapor or sweat-born, and earth-born) it must wander for age upon age.

The enemy of the self is Kāl, the archfiend of the Radhasoami

---

[1] In the Hindu tradition the number of forms of existence is usually said to be 8,400,000. For reasons obscure to me, the Soami Bagh tradition reduces the number to eighty-four. It seems to make little difference. If the mosquito is one such 'form'—as an informant said to me—there are many different kinds of mosquitoes.

universe whose name means 'time.' He personifies time and death, which time brings to all beings. Assisted by his minion, Māyā (in this context, delusion personified), he spreads the 'net' of worldly attachments in which the self is entangled and bears the noose that drags the self from birth to birth. He is the 'devourer' of selves; therefore, to exist in this world is to be 'eaten' by time and death.

This image of the human situation is embedded in a wider cosmologic-cosmogonic scheme best characterized as spatio-moral.[2] We are 'down here,' while our true home is 'up there.' Down here it is dark and evil, while up there it is bright and good. However—and this is a vital point—the concept of good and evil deployed in this imagery is quasi-physical, being based on a contrast between 'subtle' (suksham) and 'coarse' or 'gross' (sthūl). Subtle is upward-staying and good while coarse is downward-tending and bad. The result is something approximating a sedimentary theory of evil. The higher one goes in the universe, the more subtle the material of which it is made. The universe culminates in the Supreme Being, who is the purest and most subtle substance (chaitanya, 'consciousness') and the source and climax of all value. Conversely, the lower one goes, the coarser the constituents of the universe. At our level the universe is made almost entirely of base, inert 'matter' (jar, and also known as māyā). This matter (together with man, 'mind,' which is contaminated with matter and entirely distinct from the self) is our prison. The self, as a 'part' or 'ray' (kiran) of the Supreme Being (and thus constituted of his substance) is actually pure and subtle, but it is trapped under layers of coarse (and 'unconscious') matter and so completely buried that it is totally unaware of its own existence.

The cosmos was created long ago. There was once only the Supreme Being; then, by his mauj, the cosmos came to be. The word mauj carries the meanings of pleasure, delight, whim, and wave; his creative mauj was a 'current' or 'flow' (dhār) of desireless, 'sportive' will-as-pleasure taking the form of a current of sound energy (shabd). This divine sound had (and has) something of the character of fluid substance (cf. Inden 1976, 16). This substance flowed downward, and as it descended, a process of discrimination and increasing differentiation occurred. Subtle constituents were kept back, while coarser elements, characterized as relatively dense 'covers' (gilāph), were sent further

---

[2] My sources for what follows are mainly the discourses and writings of the gurus of the Soami Bagh line (esp. S. B. Prose, Babuji Maharaj 1972, Huzur Maharaj 1973, and Maharaj Saheb 1973) as supplemented by conversations with informants.

downward. Thus, as it descended, this current generated ever-baser precipitates, of which the matter in our immediate world is the final residue.

Although this cosmogony ostensibly concerns events in the very remote past, it should be interpreted as an assessment of the present human situation expressed in a spatio-temporal idiom. It is really the story of the self's fall into mind and matter. Because of the precipitative nature of the creative process, the universe is stratified into many layers, each with its own presiding deity. This stratification locates the human predicament on a cosmic map. Within the wider movement there is some disagreement, particularly between the Agra and Punjab wings, about what this map actually looks like.[3] Here I present the Agra (Soami Bagh) version in which the cosmos is divided into three main levels, each of which is further subdivided into six sublevels (see Figure 2).

The topmost main level, known as *dayāl desh* (the Region of the Merciful), is composed of the subtlest substance. It participates directly in the nature of the Supreme Being. This level was/is both 'at the beginning' and 'out of time.' It is at the beginning in the sense that this was the first level of the cosmos to be formed, and also in the sense that it is the 'true home' of the wandering self, its place of far away, long ago, and long forgotten origin. The topmost level is out of time in the sense that it is changeless, and thus deathless; therefore, to return to this realm is the ultimate goal of the Radhasoami devotee. According to the Agra tradition, dayāl desh is further divided into six sublevels; the highest of these is known as *rādhāsvāmī dhām* (the 'abode' of *rādhāsvāmī*, the Supreme Being), and this is the final goal of the devotee.

The middle region is known as *brahmānd*. This is the region of 'mind' and subtle matter. Here divine substance is contaminated by an admixture of coarse matter; that is, it participates less directly in the Supreme Being's nature. It is 'in time,' but not fully. Here there is change, but minimal change. The beings who inhabit this region are not subject to the cycle of chaurāsī, nor do the four *yuga*s (the four ages of universal, cyclical history) pass here. However, this middle region is subject, as the topmost is not, to periodic dissolution (*pralaya*). According to the Agra tradition, this level is also divided into six sublevels that are reflections of the six sublevels of dayāl desh.

---

[3]   For a Punjab interpretation see, for example, Puri 1972.

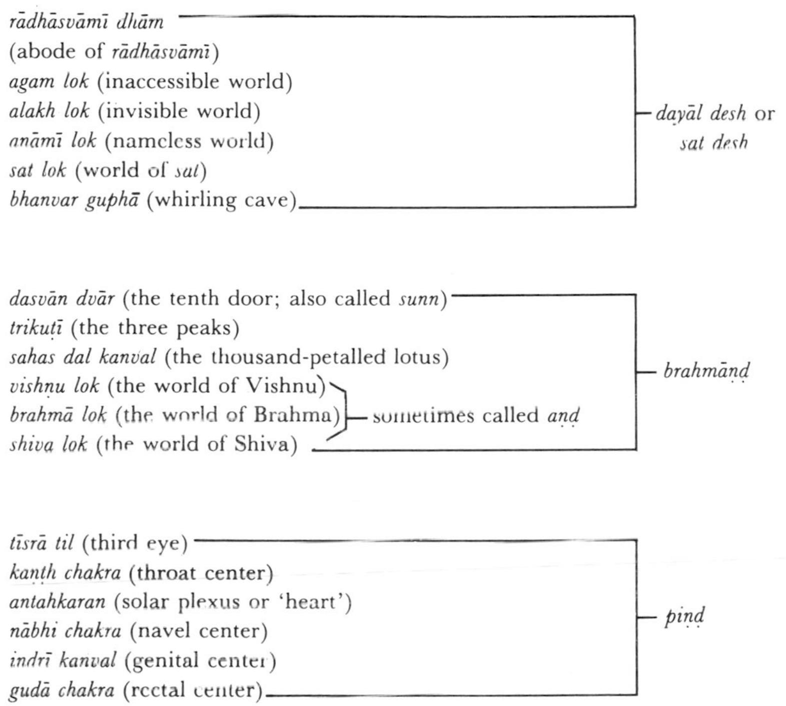

rādhāsvāmī dhām
(abode of rādhāsvāmī)
agam lok (inaccessible world)
alakh lok (invisible world)
anāmī lok (nameless world)
sat lok (world of sat)
bhanvar guphā (whirling cave)
— dayāl desh or sat desh

dasvān dvār (the tenth door; also called sunn)
trikuṭī (the three peaks)
sahas dal kanval (the thousand-petalled lotus)
vishnu lok (the world of Vishnu)
brahmā lok (the world of Brahmā) — sometimes called aṇḍ
shiva lok (the world of Shiva)
— brahmāṇḍ

tīsrā til (third eye)
kanṭh chakra (throat center)
antahkaran (solar plexus or 'heart')
nābhi chakra (navel center)
indrī kanval (genital center)
gudā chakra (rectal center)
— piṇḍ

Figure 2. Cosmic Map: Soami Bagh Version
Sources: Maheshwari 1963, 28–29; Maharaj Saheb 1973, 196 ff.; Mathur 1974, 75–77.

There is a peculiar ambiguity about the third and lowest level. This region, our prison and the world of all our normal experiences, is known as *pind*, or 'body,' and is the domain of gross matter. This is the world of chaurāsī, the four yugas, and all individual world-careers under the complete domination of Kāl. On the one hand, it is the entire visible universe, consisting of sun, moon, and other celestial levels, totalling six, of which the earth, our astronomical location, is one. But, on the other hand, pind is also the actual physical body of the individual, a 'bag' of corruption and the trap of the embodied self. In this body there are six *chakra*s, or centers, corresponding to the six levels of the visible cosmos, and to the six levels each of the invisible brahmānd and dayāl desh. The highest of these is the *tīsrā til*, or third eye, located between and behind the eyes.[4] The remaining centers, in descending order, are those of the throat, heart (or solar plexus), navel, genitalia, and anus, and each of these has a specific function in the body's economy.

Gross matter, when devoid of more subtle substance, is inanimate and incapable of maintaining itself in an ordered condition. When a person is born, the self—a current of subtle substance originating from regions above—flows downward into pind, that is, into the body. From its 'true seat' (*asal baiṭhak*) at the third eye, it sends animating currents of itself outward and downward throughout the body. The flowing of these currents is the body's life. As this flowing takes place, there is a continuous process of discrimination and separation; according to their fineness or coarseness, currents are distributed to the various centers of the body from which they flow forth to perform the functions of physical life. Three main streams issue from the third eye: one each to the pupils of the right and left eyes, and one downward through the spinal cord to the rest of the body. During sleep these currents are partly withdrawn, and when this happens, the body loses animation and the person loses awareness of the body. In death the self and the currents emanating from it are withdrawn completely, exiting upward and outward from the body through the aperture of the third eye. In its absence the body 'dies' and decays into chaos.

Desire holds the self in pind and will ultimately draw it back after death. Desire arises in the 'mind' (*man*) as a vital current directed toward the organs of sense or action appropriate for its fulfillment.

But compare Puri 1972.

This current takes the form of a kind of wavelike surge (*hilor* or *tarang*, wave and also whim) that flows out of the body and 'engages' (*lag jānā*) in the desired act or object. Therefore, all sensual and active interaction with the external world involves the extrusion and 'expenditure' (*kharch*) of value-laden current originating in the self. The self's predicament, then, is that desires keep pulling it downward into the body and 'draining' it off into the outer world. The solution must be to master desire in such a way that these downward and outward currents can be 'reversed,' allowing the self to withdraw from pind and ascend to its true home above.

But why must we be trapped in the world at all? This has never been an easy question for the tradition to answer. In Soamiji Maharaj's poetry and discourses there are multiple responses. He suggests that without experiencing the tribulations of life under Kāl's regime, the self would have no respect for the Supreme Being (*S. B. Poetry*: 26.1.78). However, he also portrays the self as having been sent into the world to see and admire the 'show' (*tamāchā*). Like a child at a fair who becomes so enthralled by what he sees that he loses his father's hand (a common Hindu image), the self then became separated from the Supreme Being and totally lost in the world (*S. B Prose*: II, 42). Elsewhere Soamiji Maharaj gives still another interpretation. Kāl once performed a great service (*sevā*) for the Supreme Being, and demanded and received the self in payment. He then bound the self to the world, causing the self to experience both happiness and sorrow (*S. B. Poetry*: 26.1.38–41).

There are two particularly notable features of the Radhasoami cosmic scheme. The first is that the imagery underlying it is not mechanical but hydraulic or riverine. The Supreme Being is here no watchmaker, nor is the cosmos a watch. The cosmos originated in, and is sustained by, the surging, fluid, wavelike current of the Supreme Being's mauj, a flowing forth of divine substance. This current coursed, and continues to course, downward, halting and forming 'reservoirs' (*bhandārs*) at each of the levels of the cosmos. As it descended—and continues to descend—it divided from itself, eddied, and flowed ever-downward until, as pind was created, it congealed into the relative immobility of matter. The entire universe is simply the result and continuing 'going on' of all this flowing. The self is merely a part of the subtlest element of the original and purest current that has found its way all the way 'down here,' and has become imprisoned in the coarsest sediments of the world-cascade.

The second conspicuous feature of this scheme is closely related to the imagery of currents and flowing. This is the idea that the body and the universe are microcosmic and macrocosmic versions of each other. There are many obvious formal homologies. Babuji Maharaj, for example, compares the three domains of creation with the head, trunk, and feet of the body (1972, 240). The topmost region, as the region of subtle substance, corresponds to the head, where the 'seat' of the self is located in the human body. Brahmāṇd, as the region of 'universal mind' (*brahmāṇdī man*), corresponds to the thorax, which is the region of the mind in traditional psychophysiology (see Kakar 1982, 240–41). The lowest region, piṇḍ, obviously corresponds to the lowest and basest extremities of the body.

Furthermore, just as there are six centers in the human body, there are—in the Agra tradition—six sublevels each in brahmāṇd and dayāl desh, and there are apparent functional analogies between some of the corresponding sublevels of the three domains. For example, the lowest level of brahmāṇd is *shivlok*, the world of Shiva (a Hindu deity). Shiva is, among other things, a god of destruction, which corresponds to what is characterized as the 'destructive' function of removing wastes (Maharaj Saheb 1973, 76) in parallel with the role of the anus in the body's economy. In this respect the anus has an implicit homologue in the lowest level of dayāl desh, which is *bhanvar gupha*, the 'whirling cave.' As a portal, it is not only an aperture of entry for the surat rising into dayāl desh, but also an orifice of exit for the flowings responsible for the creation below. The third eye at the top of the body is both the seat of the animating self and a portal of exit and entry. As portal it corresponds to *dasvān dvār*, the 'tenth door,' which is the uppermost level of brahmāṇd. As seat it corresponds to rādhāsvāmī dhām, the topmost level of dayāl desh, and the 'abode' of the Supreme Being.

The microcosm of the human body and the macrocosm of the universe are thus similar in structure and functioning. Radhasoami cosmology is therefore best understood as physiocosmology. The universe is one body, three bodies, and all bodies, through which enlivening and ordering currents flow continuously downward. The universe 'lives' through a universal process of alimentation in which subtle material is discriminated from coarse. The world of our normal experience is simply the residue of the entire process, that which is left when the maximum value has been extracted and retained. Therefore, our world, having its implicit analogue in the matter expelled from the rectum, is a world truly worthy of hate.

Finally, within this physiocosmological scheme, spatial relationships are understood in a rather striking way. We are down here and our true home is up there. In this sense our origin and goal are very far away, with an entire domain of creation (brahmānd) intervening. But at the same time they are very close, because in this image of the world there is a kind of klein-bottle inside-outness to spatial relationships. Every region of the universe, including the highest, is accessible from within the human body. In the gray and white matter of the brain, just above the eyes, there are orifices where the 'essences' (*jauhars*) of all the subregions of brahmānd and dayāl desh are located. If these orifices are awakened, the self can ascend to any region at all, and such ascent is the aim of the Radhasoami devotee.

Physiocosmology and the Errors of the Past

Radhasoami physiocosmology expresses in physical images a concept of the situation and salvationary prospects of the beings of this world. It supplies a rationale for a sense of alienation from the world and a basis for hope of salvation. But this is not all; the image of the universe given in Radhasoami teachings is also linked with, and supports, a particular rationale for the existence of the Radhasoami faith itself. On this point, however, there are quite fundamental disagreements between the Agra and Punjab wings of the movement. The idiom in which the argument is conducted is historical, and its true issue is the legitimacy of lines of succession to guruship.

Leaving aside the Radhasoami account of the creation (which occurred 'outside' the framework of world-time), the Radhasoami vision of history is essentially a variation of the Puranic theory of the four yugas (ages). This theory, which seems to be nearly omnipresent in the Hindu world, visualizes history as a series of endlessly repeating cycles of moral and physical degeneration. Each cycle consists of four yugas. The first, the *satyug*, is a golden age of virtue and perfection, and the last and present age, the *kaliyug*, is an era of shortened life span, vice, suffering, and struggle. The entire cycle is usually held to be immensely long, but ultimately it ends in dissolution, after which the world is recreated and the cycle begins anew.

The version of this story held by the Soami Bagh branch of the Radhasoami movement departs from the Puranic original in one important particular. There is the same emphasis on the physical and moral decline of the world, but the values that are assigned to this sequence are partially inverted. The kaliyug is indeed an age of depravity and suffering, but it is also seen as an era of unique opportunity. Only now is true redemption possible for the beings of this world. In support of this idea, the history of the world is frequently compared with the life cycle of the individual. Just as spiritual proclivities become more marked with a person's advancing age, so too the world becomes more receptive to spiritual opportunities in its advancing decrepitude.

According to Soami Bagh teachings, spiritual progress was possible to some extent in ancient times, for then there were adepts who had discovered methods of ascending within and beyond the body. Most never rose beyond the 'third eye,' the topmost of the six centers of piṇḍ, but a few of the very best of them, known as *yogeshvar gyānīs*, succeeded in raising themselves as high as *trikuṭī* (the three peaks), which is the celestial sublevel second from the top of brahmāṇḍ. And of these a tiny fraction managed to reach dasvān dvār (the tenth door), which is the apex of brahmāṇḍ. But all of these adepts were completely deluded. They thought they had reached the ultimate level and the Supreme Being, each regarding the level he had attained as the final goal; but in those days the existence of the highest region of all, and true 'final goal,' was not even suspected Because they had succeeded in ascending to only one or another of the levels of brahmāṇḍ, even the greatest of these adepts of the past will be subject to the dissolution that occurs at the conclusion of the cosmic cycle. Thus, death and rebirth will inevitably claim them in the end.

Moreover, the methods employed by these sages of old (mainly breath control) were both physically dangerous and far too difficult for ordinary people. For this reason the worship of deities was instituted as an aid to inner concentration for the spiritually weak. This, in turn, became a golden opportunity for priests (never admired in the Radhasoami tradition) and other mountebanks, under whose self-interested guidance the entire world became mired in pilgrimage, temple-worship, and other empty ceremonialisms. Such practices were inefficacious and worse, and therefore the world languished in ignorance and delusion. As opposed to sant mat, all the religions of the past were *kāl mat*, the 'creeds of Kāl,' as are their descendants, the various religions of the present era.

True redemption, according to this interpretation of history, became possible only in the kaliyug. In the course of innumerable births and deaths the heavy load of karmas (actions and their effects) with which the beings of this lower world are burdened had lightened to some degree, and a few beings had developed a deep aversion for the world and had thus become 'fit' (*adhikārī*) for salvation. The tribulations of the kaliyug were actually beneficial because they hastened disillusionment with the world. It was therefore at this late historical moment that the Supreme Being appeared in human form. At first came sants (who had been in the world in previous yugas, but incognito) such as Kabir, Nanak, Paltu, Dadu, and others (including certain Muslim divines). They were only forerunners, giving hints of disclosures not yet fully made; but in contrast to the sages of old, they knew of the highest regions of the cosmos, from which, in fact, they had come. At last the formless Lord appeared in the person of Soamiji Maharaj in Agra. 'When I saw you in pain,' the Lord says (in *S. B. Poetry*: 26.1.42), 'I felt pity and I came.'

According to this account, when Soamiji Maharaj arrived in the world, a totally new factor entered history, completely altering the redemptive economy of the world. For those who can recognize this factor for what it is, true salvation is possible for the first time. The path, moreover, is an easy one, unlike the difficult and dangerous yogic techniques of the past. It begins at the 'third eye,' where most of the adepts of old ended their quest, and it ends in regions never dreamed of before. There are even hints that Soamiji Maharaj's next coming will result in salvation for all before the end of the kaliyug. The sufferings of this age will ultimately weaken everyone's attachments to the world. In the distant future Soamiji Maharaj will be reborn in a 'royal family,' with Huzur Maharaj as his son, to complete the work begun with his advent (Maheshwari 1971a, 148).

This portrayal of religious history is closely connected with the Soami Bagh version of Radhasoami physiocosmology. While at one level the Radhasoami cosmic map is a representation of the predicament and opportunity of the salvation-seeking individual, at another level it is a cosmographic justification for the enterprise of sant mat as such. In fact, in Radhasoami physiocosmology the special status of sant mat is expressed as a feature of the cosmic map. The existence of a newly-revealed 'highest' region (dayāl desh), a true final goal beyond all previous 'final goals,' establishes sant mat as a radical departure from all other forms of religion, and justifies its claim to unique and transcendent value. Adepts of the past may even have merged with Brahm, but Brahm is only Kāl, Lord of brahmāṇḍ and all that lies below. Only sants know of the true final goal, and thus their teachings supersede all previous teachings. The map therefore establishes the uniqueness of sant mat as a function of 'altitude.' What is stratified is not only the cosmos, but also the spiritual incompletions and errors of the past.

But as we have already noted in the last chapter, the Agra (from Soami Bagh sources) and Punjab wings of the movement disagree fundamentally about the meaning of Soamiji Maharaj's advent and the nature of his teachings. These differences are also expressed as features of each group's own version of the cosmic map. The fine points of the dispute (see Maheshwari 1970; Puri 1972) are extremely abstruse, and will not waylay us. But the general issue involved is instructive, because it illustrates well how firmly doctrinal considerations are tied to the truly bedrock issue in the Radhasoami tradition, which is the recognition of sant satgurus and lines of succession to guruship. More specifically, if the map in general is a rationale for sant mat, then differences concerning its details rationalize and support the internal differentiation of the Radhasoami movement.

As already indicated, the Agra view is that dayāl desh, the highest region and the one known to sants alone, consists of six sublevels. The highest is rādhāsvāmī dhām (also called *anāmī*), the abode of rādhā-svāmī, and the lowest is bhanvar guphā, the whirling cave. The truly critical feature of this scheme is the existence of rādhāsvāmī dhām. According to the Agra view, prior to Soamiji Maharaj no sant had either reached or taught a method of access to this level (although Kabir is said to have alluded to its existence). Soamiji Maharaj's teachings were, therefore, not only a decisive departure from all previous religions, but also a critical augmentation of the teachings of the sants of the past, and this would also be true of the teachings of those whom the Agra tradition holds (variously) to be his legitimate successors. This is why Agra accounts of the movement focus on the revelation of the name 'rādhāsvāmī' (*rādhāsvāmī nām*) as the axial event of Soamiji Maharaj's career on earth.

Lekh Raj Puri (1972, 175–95), reflecting the views of the Beas branch of the Punjab wing of the movement, presents a significantly different version of the cosmic map (see Figure 3). Here the topmost four sublevels of the Agra scheme (rādhāsvāmī dhām, *agam lok, alakh lok,* and *sat lok*) are brought together as one upper domain called *sat lok*. Below sat lok are four more levels (bhanvar guphā, dasvān dvār, trikuṭī, and *suksham jagat*), and below these are the six centers of piṇḍ.

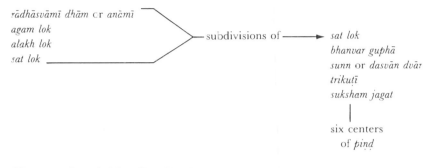

Figure 3. Cosmic Map: Beas Version
Source: Puri 1972, 175–95.

The critical feature of this scheme is the exclusion of rādhāsvāmī dhām from special status as a 'final goal.' According to the Beas view, 'rādhāsvāmī' was simply a new name that Soamiji Maharaj gave to *anāmī purush* (the nameless being), who is the Supreme Being (ibid., 23). Rādhāsvāmī dhām is merely another name for the level known as anāmī (nameless), which is not fundamentally different from the other levels in sat lok. According to this interpretation, Soamiji Maharaj did not teach the single name 'rādhāsvāmī,' but rather 'five names' that are keys of access to the five regions above pind. These regions were known to the sants of the past (ibid., 21), and therefore Radhasoami teachings are sant mat, and nothing else. Furthermore, the Beas view claims that sants have existed in every age, and thus Soamiji Maharaj belongs to a deeply ancient spiritual lineage continued today in Punjab. This view also strongly implies that because they have fetishized the name rādhāsvāmī, the Agra groups are not truly heirs to this tradition.

Agra adherents, on the other hand, maintain that in Soamiji Maharaj's satsang there were a few individuals who did not have the requisite spiritual 'fitness' (*adhikār*) to develop responsiveness (*bhāv*) to the name rādhāsvāmī (see Babuji Maharaj 1972, 315–16). Because they could neither hear nor understand the secrets (*bhed*) of this name, Soamiji Maharaj taught them the secret of ascending to sat lok only, and prescribed the repetition of 'five names.' From doing so they derived some benefits, but since Soamiji Maharaj's advent, it has been impossible to achieve full salvation without taking rādhāsvāmī as one's goal (*isht*). By this interpretation the Punjab gurus are excluded from the genuine Radhasoami tradition.

The texts can be made to support either view. Soamiji Maharaj's poetry often refers to 'five names' or 'five *shabd*s,' but these coexist with a strong emphasis on the unique power and significance of the name rādhāsvāmī. His last utterances are no more help. His brother, Chachaji Saheb, reported that on his last day he said: 'The Faith that I had given out was that of Sat Nam and Anami. Radhasoami Faith has been introduced by Salig Ram (Huzur Maharaj). You should let it also continue' (Chachaji Saheb 1978, 138–39). This quotation can be interpreted, as it is in the Agra tradition, as clear sanction for a Radhasoami faith as such, and for the legitimacy of Huzur Maharaj's succession. The Punjab side, however, sees the remarks as evidence of Soamiji Maharaj's wish to separate his own doctrines from the focus on the name rādhāsvāmī, which, from their view, seems to originate with Huzur Maharaj, not the master himself.

Ascending to Higher Regions

Despite its highly elaborated vision of the cosmos and its intricate and subtle doctrinal disputes, the Radhasoami faith is not a path of knowledge. Its true heart is the quest for salvation in the context of guru-devotee relationships. Doctrine, as such, will not bring a devotee one step closer to the final goal. Doctrine cannot even be fully understood except against the background of a direct experience of the reality to which doctrine only indirectly points. Experience (*anubhav*) is the key to the Radhasoami outlook, and the experience in question is portrayed as quite different from those we have in normal life. This extraordinary experience depends on a sustained relationship with a sant satguru, and can be cultivated only by means of special spiritual practices.

The actual method of salvation seeking taught by Soamiji Maharaj and his successors is usually called *surat-shabd-yoga*. A secret technique, involving a special posture and other esoteric details, the method is taught only in initiation (*updesh*). For this reason it is inaccessible to a non-satsangī observer. Nonetheless, the literature of the movement gives a good idea of its general outlines, and—perhaps even more importantly—provides images of what is believed to happen to its practitioners as a result of their efforts.

The purpose of the technique is to enable the practitioner (*abhyāsī*) to elevate his or her (but in this tradition mainly his) true self, the surat, to successively higher celestial levels (accessible within the body) without severing connections with the body completely (which would result in death). At first the self and the mind (*man*, regarded as completely distinct from self) leave the body behind as they rise into brahmāṇḍ. Later the self leaves mind behind as it ascends into dayāl desh. The journey begins with a gathering and concentration of the devotee's awareness at the third eye. Then the devotee mentally ascends, and while doing so sees and hears the characteristic sights and sounds of each of the levels through which he or she passes. The experience is described as a blissful one, the joys of which are quite beyond the comprehension of those who have not had it. Afterwards the devotee returns to his or her body, which has been seated all the while. The devotee's ultimate goal is the highest level of all, rādhāsvāmī dhām. Having reached the self's true home, the devotee knows that he or she will dwell eternally in a state beyond change and death, in the 'company' of the Supreme Being. At this highest stage the self realizes its primordial identity with the Supreme Being.

It is not possible for most people to achieve the final goal in one lifetime, but for those who begin the process, full redemption is guaranteed within four. Moreover, for such persons the pain of death will be greatly lessened. This is because the currents of self will not have to be ripped away from the body, being partly disengaged already. After a brief sojourn in brahmāṇḍ, such a self will be reborn in an earthly situation in which further progress upward will be possible.

The idea of the self's ascent is fully embedded in the imagery of flow so fundamental to the Radhasoami vision of the world. Normally the embodied self flows downward and outward in the economy of worldly life. But this flowing and wasting of the self can be reversed and pulled upward and inward to the third eye. Here the self can be engaged with the *ur*-current of sound energy, called shabd, that always flows downward from the Supreme Being. Shabd is an extremely subtle sound (an *anhad*, 'unstruck' sound) reverberating everywhere and in every being. The sound can be caught by the self by means of a special kind of 'listening' in the context of full concentration. Having caught it, upward the self goes, 'Like a fish swimming against the stream. /Like a spider ascending its web' (*S. B. Poetry*. 10.2.19).

Implicit in the Radhasoami imagery of salvation seems to be a powerful urge in the direction of stasis. As long as the self is in the lower world, it is trapped, as a small 'current,' in an oceanic realm of ceaseless flow.[5] In its own flowing state the self mingles, therefore, with the currents of a world in endless flux. In this context it is hardly surprising that identity becomes a major issue. But the self's final destination is imaged as fixity. The redeemed self will be at the 'feet' ot the Supreme Being, on firm ground as it were. Flowing will cease, time will stop, and never again will the self return to the eternal movement of this world. In a sense this is a soteriology of liquid beings (see esp. Marriott 1976), for whom the establishment of stable identity must necessarily be a process something like shutting off a faucet or damming up a stream.

As a technique surat-shabd-yoga has three basic elements, each of which involves its own principle of connection with the saving power of the Supreme Being. Two of these elements represent a preliminary phase to achieve focused concentration. These are *sumiran*, the repetition (or, more properly, remembrance) of name (*nām*), and *dhyān*, contemplation of the Lord's form. The third element, called *bhajan*, is the fulfillment of surat-shabd-yoga. It consists of listening to the sounds of higher regions.

In the Soami Bagh tradition, sumiran refers specifically to the internal or mental repetition of the name rādhāsvāmī (rādhāsvāmī nām). It is an exemplification of the widespread Hindu pattern of repeating *mantra*s, sacred syllables or utterances whose repetition awakens magical or spiritual powers. The outer or oral repetition of rādhāsvāmī is itself regarded as highly beneficial. Therefore, satsangīs employ the word in salutations and other everyday contexts. But the internal repetition of the name is of greatest value, and this is its proper use in spiritual practice. Internal repetition concentrates attention at the level of the third eye, and brings the devotee into contact with the redeeming power that will draw him or her up to regions beyond.

According to the teachings of the Soami Bagh group, the name rādhāsvāmī is an oral-auditory realization of the underlying and unifying principle of the cosmos. The sound of '*rādhā*' is said to be an imitation in speech of the true sound of the primal current that issued forth with the creation. *Svāmī*, the 'lord' of the current, is a speech imitation of the reservoir of sound energy that gave rise to this current. Therefore the name *rādhāsvāmī* is the name of the Supreme

---

[5] The predicament of the person in such a world has been well described in a wider context by Marriott (1976). The broader implications of Marriott's views for the interpretation of these materials will be dealt with in chapter 9.

Being, and as such represents a 'sound' that is in direct contact with, and indeed embodies, the true foundation of all reality.

The audible word, however, is not the actual sound itself. To understand why this is so, we must know something of the rather subtle Radhasoami theory of the metaphysics of sound. According to the tradition, characteristic sounds reverberate in each of the upper levels of the cosmos, and these sounds can be represented orally and in writing. The syllable *om*, for example, is a human representation (the *varnātmak*, or written and spoken form) of the 'real' sound (its *dhvanyātmak* form) that can actually be heard emanating from the region of trikuṭī by a fully awakened inner auditory sense (Maheshwari 1967, 269–70; also 79–80). To repeat this or any similar sound orally is of some benefit, purifying and concentrating the mind. But the spoken or written name is only a kind of crude auditory indication of the real sound that actually reverberates in a given region.

The name that is 'resounding' (*dhvani ho rahā hai*) at each celestial level is the 'root' or essential sound (*mūl shabd*) of that level and the basic name (*mūl nām*) of the deity (*dhanī*; wealth-holder, lord) presiding there (Babuji Maharaj 1972, *bachan* 67). An essential concord exists between this deity and his name, such that if one performs the sumiran of that name correctly, he or she can gain access to the benefits of that level of the cosmos.

As already noted, in the Punjab wing of the movement the emphasis is on the sumiran of five names that correspond to what these groups take to be the five levels above the third eye culminating in sat lok. In the Soami Bagh tradition, however, the emphasis is placed decisively on the name rādhāsvāmī. Possession of this name is deemed to supersede the necessity to rely on any other. It is the key to 'true redemption' (*sachchā uddhār*) and the *param mantra*, the supreme sacred utterance that encompasses and includes all others.

In the Radhasoami tradition the term *dhyān* refers to the contemplation of the Lord in the form of the sant satguru. As in the case of the repetition of name, such contemplation has inward and outward forms. The contemplation of the physical form of the guru with the outer eyes is itself highly beneficial. Such contemplation is necessary in order to develop love for his form and also leads to a kind of intimate communion between devotee and guru (which will be discussed in chapter 3). Therefore, devotees gaze at the bodily form of the sant satguru and, short of that, greatly value his pictorial representations. But the sant satguru's true or own form (*nij rūp*), seen within, is most important. One who has the requisite love for the guru's outer form will be able to see it inwardly while engaged in spiritual practice. This inner image is seen at the third eye, and exercises an attractive force on the devotee, concentrating awareness at that point and pulling him or her upward. This form is said to be like the physical form of the guru, but radiant. As the practitioner moves upward from level to level, he or she is accompanied by this inner form. At each stage the form of the guru becomes more radiant and subtle.

Bhajan, the third element of spiritual practice, is the most difficult. The word refers to an intent, focused, inward 'listening' to the sounds that emanate from the celestial levels above. Sumiran and dhyān are said to lay the internal foundations for this practice, and devotees who are unsuccessful in bhajan are advised to concentrate on sumiran and dhyān alone, or even sumiran by itself.

The sound that is heard is the current of sound energy (shabd) that has its ultimate origin in the Supreme Being at the apex of the cosmos. This sound takes different forms as it descends—that is, as the 'true' (dhvanyātmak) names resounding in the various regions. The specific names of these levels are disclosed to the devotee at the time of initiation. By listening to these subtle sounds (in a prescribed, and secret, posture) he or she is brought into direct communion with the levels from which they emanate, and is drawn upward as a result. This is surat-shabd-yoga, properly speaking. It is the very essence of spiritual practice, and the ultimate realization of the salvationary promise of the Radhasoami tradition.

The tradition distinguishes two ways of putting these methods into practice: external and internal satsang. External satsang is keeping the 'company' of a sant satguru, and more specifically refers to congregational observances ideally taking place in his physical presence. Satsangīs gather before the guru who sits on an elevated seat. They deliver offerings to him, and if he permits it, they touch his feet with their hands or foreheads. He may bless devotees in return by placing his hand on their heads. Texts are recited and the guru may deliver a discourse. Central to satsang is *ārati*, which in this context refers to a visual interaction in which guru and devotees gaze intently at each others' foreheads and eyes. At the conclusion, devotees partake jointly of the guru's prasād, his food leavings.

In the absence of a living guru, members of the Soami Bagh congregation nowadays conduct satsang in the presence of photographs of the past gurus of the Soami Bagh line, and the main focus of the event, as already noted, is the recitation of texts. Lines of poetry from *Sār Bachan* and *Prembānī* (Huzur Maharaj's poetry) are sung in concert, and then passages from the discourses of the gurus are read aloud. Food offerings are exposed to absorb the atmosphere of the occasion, and are then distributed to participants as prasād at the conclusion.

But internal satsang is, at least in theory, the highest expression of the Radhasoami faith. Internal satsang is keeping the inward 'company' of the current of sound energy emanating from on high, and the *nij* (own, true) form of the sant satguru. Its method is sumiran, dhyān, and bhajan, as described earlier, and its object is ascent to higher regions. External satsang is portrayed as a kind of preparation for its internal realization. The devotee's mind is purified and focused. By taking the guru's leavings, he or she absorbs something of the guru's superior inner nature (which will be discussed in greater detail in chapter 3). External satsang also fosters love for the sant satguru and the eradication of the devotee's egoism, both of which are indispensable for genuine spiritual progress. In the end, however, all culminates in the ascent of the self, and this is realized only against an inner landscape.

Of the actual experiences to which these practices lead we can know nothing at all. The testimony of the movement is that they cannot be understood by those who have not had them. What can be reported is the imagery of the movement's poetic literature. The devotee is said to take his or her 'seat' at the third eye. There the devotee has a vision of the guru and/or a brilliant flame, and hears the sound of a conch and bell. The devotee then ascends to *sahas dal kanval*, the 'thousand-petalied lotus' (third level from the top of brahmāṇḍ; the bottom three are skipped). Sounds come from the left and the right. The devotee rejects the sound from the left (Kāl's work) and concentrates on that from the right. Then, in the company of the guru he or she is pulled further upward. The ascending devotee sees marvelous sights—suns, moons, skies beyond the sky—and hears the sounds of bells, thunder, musical instruments, and sounds quite unlike anything we know in this world. The devotee has visions of the deity presiding over each of these celestial levels. At the end of the journey—that is, if the end is reached—the devotee has a vision of the Supreme Being himself, who is the object of this vertical pilgrimage. This is the climactic vision. The beauties and grandeur of this region surpass everything seen before. The form of rādhāsvāmī 'is without limits and beyond description. /To what could I compare it? It is beyond all measure' (*S. B. Poetry*: 5.2.35–36). The journey is now over: 'I have gained a dwelling place in the feet of rādhāsvāmī. Pure bliss is now forever mine' (ibid., 6.8.26).

Living in Lower Regions

The real lives of devotees, of course, do not take place in heavenly regions. They must make their way through the social institutions of this world, and this means that the movement has had to develop a strategy for dealing with the requirements of earthly existence.

Because the Radhasoami faith is supposed to be a path for house-holders, the tradition does not consider what is called a devotee's *paramārthī* (spiritual, soteriological) interest to be radically at odds with the requirements of worldly life, although a dim view is certainly taken of excessive worldly attachments. As we have seen, with the exception of Buaji Saheba, all Soamiji Maharaj's successors in the Soami Bagh line were men who supported families and earned their livelihoods in normal forms of employment. Since the time of Maharaj Saheb the religious recluse has had no role in the religious life as practiced by this congregation. Clearly, though, at some level the Radhasoami tradition exists in a state of tension with the world, which, after all, is portrayed as a trap and a prison. In general terms the resolution of this tension has taken the form not of sharp opposition to the world, but rather of a somewhat narrow definition of religious interests as such. These are jealously guarded within a context of more general accommodation to the obligations imposed on the individual by worldly institutions.

The question of a devotee's relations with his or her family is obviously a critical one. It is fundamental to the Radhasoami faith that the essential 'unit' to which religious interests adhere is not a collectivity, but the individual. In Hindu India, however, individuals have deep ties to collectivities, and of these the most important are likely to be families. Yet even if an individual is a satsangī by virtue of birth in a satsangī family, his or her relationship to the sant satguru is portrayed as a purely dyadic one. Such a person is an individual who had the requisite 'fitness' (adhikār) to benefit from contact with a guru, and for this reason was born into a satsangī family. In other words, each individual finds the guru on his or her own. It is thus clear that ties with guru and ties with family are understood to pull at an individual from two quite different directions.

Therefore, although the movement encourages family life (or at least does not discourage it), it regards the family as a potentially grave spiritual hazard. An informant, whose views were quite representative, put the matter as follows (I paraphrase): 'You have no control over those people [family members]. You just have a temporary responsibility for their welfare, an obligation you must meet. But you have no way of insuring their love for you. Your son will leave you; if not now, then some time. So don't waste your energy worrying about your family. Discharge your duty toward them, but don't hook yourself to them.' An even less sanguine view of family ties is given in Soamiji Maharaj's poetry. Family and kinsmen are like 'snakes' and 'robbers'; one is 'lost' in the 'company' of mother, father, son, and wife (*S. B. Poetry*: 14.9.3–4; 18.4.14; 19.16.2; and elsewhere). Their company is a source of bondage, and temporary in any case; therefore, says the master, you must seek a guru's company instead. On the other hand, in apparent acknowledgment of the force and legitimacy (in worldly terms) of family bonds, and in contradiction to the primary emphasis on the individual, it is also said that the benefits resulting from spiritual practices can be transmitted along lines of kinship. 'When I perform ārati with love,' says the poet, my kin and family are redeemed' (ibid., 18.6.15). This idea is repeatedly expressed in the texts.

A critical question is that of how a satsangī is to represent the Radhasoami faith to non-satsangī kin, particularly those with whom he or she lives. The satsangī is advised to explain the Radhasoami faith patiently, but if they fail to understand or adopt it, he or she is not to press the matter, and is certainly not to feel hostility toward them. He or she should pursue the faith quietly and with fortitude, and accord due respect (though not belief) to the views and customs of others.

As far as gender is concerned, it should be noted that there is a detectable element of misogyny in this tradition.[6] The true self is present in men and women alike, but it is sometimes said that a woman's self cannot rise above dasvān dvār (that is into the highest region). This does not, of course, preclude her salvation in later births, but many hold that she must be born in a man's body first. Women are said to be dangerous distractions from spiritual practice for men. In congregational satsang women are frequently segregated

---

[6] On this point, however, it should be acknowledged that Huzur Maharaj (see 1973, 387–95) took a very sanguine view of the spiritual potential of women and disapproved strongly of many traditional practices that inhibited women's freedom.

from men, behind a screen or in an adjoining room, where they can hear the recitations without being seen. Otherwise, an informant remarked in explanation, 'You'll be thinking of nothing but having intercourse with them.' Nothing is more dangerous to spiritual progress than women, this same informant went on to say; woman next to man is like a flame near a piece of cotton. The tradition does not discourage sexual relations in the context of marriage, but it does counsel moderation.

The Radhasoami movement has rejected caste distinctions from the start; caste exclusiveness is simply another of Kāl's traps. But it should be understood that what is really meant by this is that caste distinctions are irrelevant from a paramārthī (spiritual) point of view. Members of low castes are uncommon in the Soami Bagh congregation, so far as I was able to tell.[7] Moreover; this congregation has never fostered anything resembling crusading zeal for the amelioration of caste injustice, or for that matter injustice of any other kind. A dim view is taken of social reform in general. The world itself cannot be reformed; that is, the world is utterly benighted, and efforts to improve it will simply lead to further fatal attachments to it in the end (see Phelps 1947, 112–44). Philanthropic activities are not positively condemned, but are certainly not encouraged. Politics is likewise regarded as spiritually hazardous.

The domain of potential conflict between a devotee's spiritual interests and his caste's or community's customs and obligations is relatively narrow. Radhasoami spiritual practice does not arise as an issue. Daily meditation and weekly congregational satsang (Sunday morning for Delhi devotees) are not likely to put an individual into conflict with caste or community rules. Devotees are required to abstain from meat and alcohol, but this is not a problem for devotees belonging to nonvegetarian castes (such as the Kāyasthas, who are very prominent in the Soami Bagh congregation) because vegetarianism and teetotalism are not status-lowering. Informants told me that difficulties sometimes arise when satsangī women marry into non-vegetarian (non-satsangī) households. As we have seen (in the case of Huzur Maharaj), the custom of taking a sant satguru's food leavings is in potential conflict with caste rules. I do not know how often this has arisen as a problem.

While satsangīs would like to have their children marry into other

[7] By contrast, untouchables are quite important in the Beas congregation. See Juergensmeyer 1982.

satsangī families, many marriages—perhaps most—seem to be governed by traditional caste, family, and financial criteria. Informants said that satsang-endogamy is made difficult by the fact that other kin, likely to be non-satsangīs, have an interest in the match. There are exceptions. During the period of my contact with the Soami Bagh congregation, a prominent marriage occurred that was not only satsang-endogamous, but also intercaste and inter-regional (Marwar-Bengal).

The festivals and rites engaged in by the wider community are treated as social obligations devoid of religious meaning. Participation in occasions like *divālī* or *holī* is not prohibited. A satsangī may participate in such activities in the interest of concord with his or her caste-fellows and others. While engaging in outward participation, though, he or she should meditate on the name rādhāsvāmī internally. The tradition has tried to sublimate certain common Hindu festivals into what is viewed as their inner and true form. Thus, an informant told me that the real meaning of holī is that the syringes are one's eyes, which are turned around and discharged at the form of the guru within, and that a satsangī should think about this as he plays holī with others outwardly (the source of this idea is *S. B. Poetry*: 39.5).[8]

Major life-cycle rites usually appear to be conducted in the manner customary in the caste or community of the individual concerned, but frequently with a Radhasoami overlay consisting of the recitation of Radhasoami texts and the sponsorship of special satsangs and *bhogs* (food offerings). In theory a marriage can be finalized between a satsangī boy and girl by the simple exchange of garlands in the presence of the sant satguru (and/or symbols establishing his presence). In his day Babuji Maharaj personally solemnized the marriages of many couples by garlanding them. The one marriage by garland-exchange I saw was followed by a full Hindu-style marriage ceremony, complete with Brāhman priests. Even during the standard rites, however, pictures of the Soami Bagh gurus presided. Funerary observances are likewise governed primarily by caste and community custom but with Radhasoami emphases. In one instance with which I had direct contact, the brother (a *satsangī* and chief mourner) of a deceased *satsangī* woman engaged in daily recitation of *Sār Bachan* in parallel with the standard Hindu rites. After the final Hindu death

---

[8] *Holī* is a Hindu festival associated with the deity Krishna. Participants 'play' holī by sprinkling each other with colored powders and spraying one another with colored water.

ceremonies of the twelfth day, he sponsored a special satsang and bhog to which fellow satsangīs were invited.

The world of work is very important in the Radhasoami value system. It is an arena in which to discharge what the tradition regards as basic obligations of family support, and is also seen as a potentially valuable training ground for the cultivation of spiritually important features of character. A male satsangī should earn his own livelihood, as all of the gurus (save Soamiji Maharaj and Buaji Saheba) in the Soami Bagh line did themselves. As noted earlier, the mendicant is little admired, and the general tone of the Soami Bagh congregation reflects the situation and outlook of active men in (mostly) middle-class service occupations. The ideal is a balance between work and spiritual practice, and work itself is deemed to have a steadying influence on a man. The object of employment should be subsistence for one's self and one's family on a modest scale. It is said that the best kind of employment is of the sort that requires submission to authority (see Phelps 1979, 106). This fosters humility and a willingness to accept guidance from superiors, both of which, as we shall see in chapter 3, are values central to the pursuit of redemption as the Radhasoami tradition defines it.

The Promise

Among my acquaintances in the Soami Bagh congregation was a man who seemed to exemplify Radhasoami virtues with something close to perfection. He was a Kāyastha and a family man who worked as an office manager in a New Delhi firm. He entered the congregation in middle age, apparently during a period in which his career had taken an uncertain turn. Since then the Radhasoami faith had become his constant preoccupation outside working hours. Unlike many of his fellow Soami Bagh satsangīs, he had a living guru, for he was one among a number of people who regarded one of the senior satsangīs at Soami Bagh as sant satguru (a guruship not officially recognized by the Soami Bagh congregation). At every possible opportunity he would go to Agra to meet his guru and engage in his *sevā* (service).

While in his guru's presence he was a changed man. In this context his demeanor reflected what can only be described as perfected humility. No remark of his guru was inconsequential, and no service too onerous or demeaning to be performed. And yet he did not engage in regular spiritual practice. In some embarrassment he confessed that he would go for long periods without daily meditation, to be followed by bouts of guilty catching-up. When I asked him if he had experienced the wonders of higher regions of the cosmos, he responded that in his case such experiences had been minimal, and that the closest he had ever come to hearing celestial sounds was actually before his initiation. Often, he said, such experiences are authored by Kāl to lead one astray in any case.

My informant's unusual candor pointed to what seems to be a rather puzzling feature of the Radhasoami movement. As we have seen, the ultimate goal and raison d'etre of the Radhasoami faith is the cultivation of soteriologically significant experiences of higher regions of the cosmos. There is little doubt, moreover, that many devotees do indeed have such experiences. But it is by no means clear that all devotees have them, nor is it certain that having such experiences is a necessary precondition for deep commitment to the Radhasoami faith. This, however, is a very difficult point to establish. My informant's frankness was exceptional. Devotees are not supposed to discuss their 'spiritual progress' with anyone but a sant satguru. It is widely held that doing so will decrease the efficacy of spiritual practice. This belief may be an important ingredient in the credibility of the movement's promise. But the fact that a significant number of informants did not, in any sustained way, engage in the actual practice of surat-shabd-yoga, combined with many warnings against inflated expectations in the gurus' correspondence and discourses, suggests that if 'experience' is what the movement is all about, it is not, for many devotees, the experiences of upper regions described so vividly in the movement's literature.

And yet Radhasoami teachings imbue the salvationary situation of the devotee with a kind of now-or-never desperation. In the movement's texts the devotee is portrayed as one who has wandered for age upon age in a world that is alien to the self's true nature. At last, after an immense journey, he or she has acquired a human body, the only body in which salvation is possible (a common Hindu idea), and has met a sant satguru. The devotee's 'fortune' (*bhāg*) has at last 'awakened.' The texts warn that against the experiences of tens of millions of past lives, the pleasures of this life will last but 'four days' (an image repeatedly used in this context). The devotee could die at any moment. His or her 'capital' (*pūnjī*) is very little, and is wasted with every breath. One must, therefore, seize this priceless opportunity to make one's brief human life 'fruitful' (*suphal*). Those who fail to do so will wander in chaurāsī for ages more.

What lets the devotee off the hook is his or her relationship with a sant satguru. It is said that nobody (except a guru) really knows how much spiritual progress any individual has actually made, but for those who enter a relationship with a sant satguru, those who take his 'shelter' (*saran*), full salvation is guaranteed within four lives. Hardly anyone can attain salvation in one life, for the ties that hold the self in bondage are strong. Still, one should not be discouraged. No matter how little progress a devotee has made, if he or she is truly devoted to guru, then such a person's case is in the guru's hands. Those who have taken a guru's shelter may be sure that they are at least in the first stage of a pilgrimage that can last no longer than four lifetimes. They know that death will be relatively painless, and that they will not fall back into the cycle of chaurāsī. In lives to come they will again inhabit human bodies and resume progress where they left off before. And, many say, such devotees will also enjoy greater happiness in life itself.

A 'fruitful' life, in sum, is mainly one that is shaped by one's relationship with a sant satguru and led in resignation to the guru's mauj (will-as-pleasure). In such a life, the tradition proclaims, even misfortunes are salutary, being placed in one's way by the Lord for one's own ultimate good. Those who lead such a life are, in effect, already redeemed, whether or not they have actually experienced the highest celestial regions.

We find, therefore, a curious transposition of the question of identity at the heart of the tradition. The Radhasoami faith supplies a conception of the lost self's true identity and a contemplative technique for its personal realization. But in the end, the discovery and realization of one's true identity is totally dependent on establishing and maintaining a relationship with someone else, the sant satguru. Once a sant satguru is found, and once the devotee enters his 'shelter,' the problem of his or her own identity becomes, in a sense, moot. The devotee at least knows that he or she is the beloved of the Supreme Being, and that his or her destiny is guaranteed. What this amounts to, however, is not a solution to the problem of identity, but a shifting of its focus. Since everything now depends on entering a relationship with a sant satguru, all now hinges on the question of who is, in fact, a sant satguru. To recognize himself or herself, in other words, the devotee must first learn how to come into relations with, and above all to recognize, a sant satguru.

Obviously the relationship between devotee and guru, whether enacted with a living guru or the relics of past gurus, is charged with a very special kind of energy. It is a saving relationship. But what makes it so? What is there in this relationship that has the potential to instill in the devotee a sense that he or she is realized, or on the way to being realized, as a different kind of self than he or she has seemed to be before? And how does the devotee know that the relationship he or she has entered is truly one of this special type? How, that is, can the devotee recognize a sant satguru as such? In the next chapter I examine more closely what takes place between devotee and guru with these questions in mind.

3. Identity and Recognition

Intimate Contact

As described in chapter 1, the great samādh is a theater for certain distinctive behaviors. Displayed prominently at the central altar are wooden sandals used by Soamiji Maharaj during his lifetime. Devotees touch these with their hands and foreheads, and some informants report having spiritual experiences when they do so. Outside, in the shadow of the samādh, stands a well. Because the water from this well was once used by Soamiji Maharaj to wash his feet and rinse his mouth, it is greatly venerated by devotees. They call the water *charanāmrit* (foot nectar) and *mukhāmrit* (mouth nectar), and they believe that drinking it confers great religious benefits on the drinker.

More extended observation of the life of this congregation reveals that these are not isolated instances. In fact, they are merely conspicuous examples of a ritual gesture that is fundamental to Radhasoami devotionalism. The tradition gives great emphasis to patterned contact between a devotee and a sant satguru's body, especially, though not exclusively, with the guru's mouth and feet.

The same pattern, for example, is very strong in congregational satsang. When members of the Soami Bagh congregation living in Delhi hold their weekly satsang (on Sunday mornings), they invariably do so in the presence of a framed sheet of paper on which are impressed Babuji Maharaj's footprints in red ink. Attending devotees bow before this, symbolically placing their foreheads at or on this guru's feet. Moreover, during these observances food is displayed and is then eaten at the conclusion. Its consumption is beneficial because during the service it has become the prasād (food leavings) of the gurus of the Soami Bagh line, who—although not physically present—symbolically preside over these and similar ceremonies, and are visible in the form of prominently displayed pictures.

Of course these behaviors are only substitutes for the actual contact that occurred between devotees and these gurus when they lived. All the past gurus distributed food leavings to their followers. Devotees also avidly sought contact with their gurus' feet. As an extreme example of this, Chachaji Saheb reports that one of Soamiji Maharaj's most devoted female followers would suck his toes 'for hours,' regarding the 'nectar' that flowed therefrom as 'mother's milk' (1978, 81). Devotees also sought and greatly prized articles that had been used by the gurus, particularly if they had been used in intimate ways. During his last years, for example, Babuji Maharaj made a daily practice of distributing to his devotees handkerchiefs with which he had wiped his face. After his death numerous articles were sanctified by being touched to the cadaver's feet.[1]

This pattern is not unique to the Soami Bagh congregation. In the Punjab wing of the movement prasād is also distributed at the conclusion of congregational observances. I am told that Maharaj Charan Singh (guru of the Beas group) does not like people to take actual leavings from his plate, but he sometimes makes exceptions. An informant recalled with delight how the master gave his (my informant's) brother an ice cream cone from which the master had taken a single bite, a sign of his special favor. Some devotees, the same informant told me, furtively scrape up street dust over which Charan Singh has walked, which they consume as prasād.

Intimate contact of this sort is also an extremely powerful theme in the literature of the movement. In Soamiji Maharaj's poetry the ideal devotee is portrayed as loving the guru's feet and longing for them. 'I lick his feet,' the poet says, 'with my tongue' (S. B. Poetry: 3.5.40). And not only are the virtues of the guru's foot leavings greatly praised, but in two unforgettable lines on the subject of sevā (service) the poet says: 'He [the devotee] should help him [the guru] rinse his mouth with water, fill his hukkā [water pipe], prepare his bed, and supplicate him. He should take the saliva in a spittoon, and then drink it all' (13.1.26–27).

All these acts, real or expressed as poetic images, have at least two things in common. First, they involve some form of intimate bodily contact between devotee and guru, although it can be indirect (as in the case of relics and symbolic food leavings of gurus who no longer physically exist). Second, all these acts are, in the wider setting of Hindu life, suggestive of 'dirtiness' or 'pollution.' Moreover, this implication is explicitly acknowledged within the Radhasoami tradition.

---

[1] In allusive language Farquhar (1977) suggests that devotees once consumed their gurus' excrement. I know of no evidence supporting this.

Adherents recognize that to an unenlightened mentality a guru's foot washings or saliva may seem filthy. But to a true devotee these things are supremely 'pure' and value-laden. Indeed devotees try to establish contact between these things and parts of their body where they would normally never put filth, namely their own mouth and forehead.

In fact, these practices are sectarian variations on a theme of the most general importance in the Hindu world. They fall within a fundamental paradigm of interactions characteristic of relations between superiors and inferiors in the human world, and between deities and their worshippers. This pattern raises fundamental questions: What are the leavings or effluvia of an exalted being actually understood to be, particularly in the context of devotional worship? Are such things clean or dirty, pure or impure? Why should they be accorded such high, even soteriological, value, when in other settings apparently equivalent things and substances are regarded as the very antithesis of value?

These questions turn out to be a bridge to even more basic issues having to do with the very nature of the religious experience in the Radhasoami tradition, and possibly in the Hindu tradition more generally. The question of 'clean or dirty' is not just an outsider's question; it arises within Radhasoami discourse, too, and has crucial relevance to fundamental religious issues. The answer to the question depends on *who* you are—that is, it is a matter of identity, both social and, by extension, soteriological. Indeed, in relation to intimate contact between devotee and guru, questions of social identity and salvationary expectations become fused. The result is a situation in which an essentially social transactional symbolism can become the basis for a soteriological transformation of the individual. In chapter 2, we saw that a devotee discovers true identity in his or her relationship with a guru; in this chapter I hope to suggest how this process is manifested in guru-devotee interactions.

Exchanges

When the sant satgurus of the Soami Bagh line were living, offerings from devotees to their gurus were a central feature of the congregation's life. Although there was no compulsion in the matter, money offerings were expected of all satsangīs. They were given during personal encounters with the guru, during satsang, and in connection with the major feast-days of the congregation. They were also presented on such special personal occasions as the birth of a child, a death in the family, a success (or failure) at some task or enterprise, and so on. Sometimes offerings were made for designated purposes—for example, to help pay for food offerings to be distributed as prasād at a satsang or feast-day, or to support the construction of the great samādh. Offerings could be sent by mail or presented personally. Although the money, and any property purchased with it, was understood to be the property of the sant satguru, in fact it returned to the congregation in the form of food distributed as prasād and the other accouterments of satsang life, including the great samādh itself. This same pattern of giving continues today, with the council and the trust acting on behalf of the physically absent sant satgurus.

Much else was offered too. Food, garlands, furnishings, clothing, and physical objects of every description were given to the gurus. Generally, though not always, they were given back, either to the donors or to other satsangīs. Food was presented to be touched or tasted by the guru, and then returned. A devotee might offer a garland, which the guru would touch, or even wear for a brief period, and return. It was very common for a devotee to present the guru with any recently acquired item (jewelry, clothing, etc.) which would be touched in blessing and then restored to the giver. These gestures, too, continue to be a feature of the life of the Soami Bagh congregation. Food offerings are fundamental to congregational satsang, and I have been present when recently acquired objects have been presented to, and then blessed and returned by, one of the unofficially recognized gurus of the congregation.

Things given to the guru are supposed to be given selflessly, without any thought of reward. The paradigm for this is the widespread Hindu idea of the ideal devotee's sacrifice of 'body, mind and wealth' (tan, man, dhan) to God. The point is, a true devotee gives everything, including himself or herself. But this is combined with the notion that the things given can come back to the giver. This does not contradict the ideal of selfless giving, because the things in question, once given, belong to the sant satguru. They may be used by the devotee, but they are not really his or hers. In fact, the ideal devotee's 'body, mind, and wealth' are actually return gifts, having been accepted by the guru and returned 'in trust.' From this standpoint, everything in the life of a devotee is really the guru's prasād.

An implicit idea in this pattern seems to be that what a devotee gives the guru carries something of himself or herself with it. This is suggested by Soamiji Maharaj's remark that he who feeds a *sādh* (an accomplished devotee) without true feelings of love may derive some benefit thereby, but the sādh will be harmed (*S. B. Prose*: II, 74). It is also of a piece with the ubiquitous belief that a sant satguru can actually assume the load of harmful karmic effects carried by devotees. Babuji Maharaj, for example, suffered from a mild case of leukoderma, which he is said to have taken onto himself from a female devotee.

In accord with this general idea, an offering to a guru would appear to be, among other things, a possible vehicle through which the offerer can deliver up impurities, his or her 'sins,' which are taken by the guru into or onto himself. This concept has a deep paradigm in Hindu mythology. When the gods and demons churned the ocean in order to obtain ambrosia (a great primordial act of discrimination), Shiva swallowed the residual poison, holding it in his throat and thus becoming the 'blue-necked' god (O'Flaherty 1975, 273–77). When the infant Krishna killed the stinking demoness Pūtanā—who had tried to kill him by offering him a poison-smeared breast—he did so by sucking her life from her body. When her body was burned, the smoke was sweet in smell; she was purified, for in sucking away the poison, Krishna had destroyed her sins (ibid., 214–17). Likewise, Soamiji Maharaj describes offering food to the Lord, who then (says the poet) 'instantly ate Kāl [whose snare is really our own impure desires] and *karma* [binding action and its effects]' (*S. B. Poetry*: 42.4.3). This is why the guru does not always accept offerings, or accepts them only in degrees. The burden of impurities might be too much for the frail human frame of the guru to bear (though not, of course, for the Supreme Being who, in his true majesty, 'devours all' [ibid., 42.4.4]).

The essential principle underlying these notions seems to be that the worldly objects and acquisitions with which we engage as desirers, acquirers, possessors, and users ensnare and bind us through the currents of desire and action that connect us to them. These binding factors are in some sense taken over by a sant satguru when he accepts something as an offering. By accepting selflessly given offerings—that is, offerings given out of nothing more than pure love of guru—the guru enables the devotee to become rid' of soteriologically harmful attachments. Giving all to the guru enables the devotee to live in, and with, the world while being in some fundamental way free of attachment to it; all having been offered up and returned, the devotee's life has been blessed and 'purified.'

Offerings that have been accepted and returned by a guru are therefore regarded as changed and improved; 'value' has been added. The imagery through which this notion is understood, however, focuses on physical intimacies between guru and devotee; the idea of enhanced value is assimilated to the concept of purifying or improving flows or currents emanating from the sant satguru's body. Food offerings are the clearest example. One may offer a box of sweets to the guru, which he may touch and return. Having been touched by the guru, the food is said to have paramārthī (spiritual, soteriological) value. But this value is greatly enhanced if the guru actually eats from the box. Not only does his consumption of the food signal the relative 'fitness' of the donor, but it also charges the food with virtues inhering in the guru's saliva. His redeeming 'favor,' in other words, is intensified with the availability of his intimate body juices. Similarly, the guru's mouth rinsings or the contents of his spittoon are more valuable yet. Likewise, one may offer a garland to a guru, which will have spiritual value if accepted and returned. However, this value is enhanced if he actually wears the garland prior to return, because then it has become infused with the detritus of his body.

The same principle is evident in honorific gestures, such as foot touching, in which no specific offering has been given beforehand. Touching the guru's feet is of value to devotees (and to be *allowed* to touch his feet is itself a sign of his favor). More valuable yet is drinking the water in which the guru's feet have been washed, since this water conveys the accretions and residues of his feet directly into the mouth of the devotee.

The theme of all this is intimacy of a very particular kind. In each of these transactions the devotee digests or takes in something coming from the guru's body. The more that is taken, and the more intimate the taking of it, the better. The Radhasoami tradition provides a well-developed interpretation of these transactions. The sant satguru's body, particularly his feet and mouth, are sources of a flow or current of chaitanya (*chaitanya kī dhār*). In this locution *chaitanya* might be translated as 'consciousness' or 'awareness'; satsangīs frequently render it as 'spirituality' in English. It is the sant satguru's inner 'spiritual' nature that is available to devotees in a substantial 'flowing' form. Therefore, by receiving things touched or worn by the guru—especially his food leavings, mouth rinsings, or foot washings—the devotee can assimilate the guru's true nature, which is a current-manifested power of awareness. This assimilation enhances the devotee's ability to achieve salvation. Soami Bagh devotees also believe that this flow is still present in the relics of the gurus of the past.

This entire image is directly informed by Radhasoami physio-cosmology. The body is conceived as a hierarchy of centers in which enlivening currents flow and separate into coarser and finer constit-uents, with the coarse residues tending outward and downward. The body's outer covering has orifices that provide points of egress for flows emanating from within. It is these currents, issuing from the guru's body, that the devotee takes into himself or herself. But, of course, the currents cannot be ordinary body-flows, because the sant satguru is not an ordinary man. The highest, subtlest, and most valuable of all currents is that which flows from the Supreme Being at the top of the cosmos. By the time this current reaches here, however, it is covered, encased, and difficult to sense and grasp. Since the guru is himself the Supreme Being, the flows that issue from his body are of exceptional value, even though they are coarse in relation to his apparent body. They are pure divine nature, a current of chaitanya, unadulterated by a value-extracting transit through the intervening levels of creation. Thus, they afford a direct link with the Absolute.

Given the premises of Radhasoami physiocosmology, there is a strong implication that offerings made to the guru (that is, to the Supreme Being in the guru's person) are, in a sense, 'digested' by him (cf. Hayley 1980; Parry 1980). The transformed results are then made available in a 'current-charged' form to the devotees. In the body, and in the cosmos at large (the body of the Supreme Being), there occurs a continuing process of discrimination, separation, retention, and downward discharge. As the Supreme Being, the guru is the universal alimentary actor, the 'eater of all' and the ultimate separator of fine from coarse and good from bad. He is, in other words, the most transformative of all beings (Inden 1976; Marriott 1976). Thus, the flow issuing from him is that which is left when all of the evil of the universe has been separated out and discharged elsewhere; moreover, the flow that inheres in offerings accepted and returned by him is a kind of distillate of the offering, the final result of a process in which coarse and world-binding accretions, the offerer's 'sins,' have been digested away. Hence, in *Sār Bachan* the poet-devotee can say, 'When I got Radhasoami's food-leavings, he purified me' (*S. B. Poetry*: 3.5.44).

Since true devotees offer all of themselves—including their mind and body—they themselves are 'digested.' Their true selves, their highest natures, are separated and retained from their prison of coarse matter and karmic residues. It should also be noted again that Kāl 'devours' embodied selves. He, however, does not discriminate and transform as the Supreme Being does; therefore, having been 'eaten' by Kāl, the self once again sinks under the coverings of the material world, even more bound than before. On the other hand, the Supreme Being is said to 'eat' Kāl and karma.

To summarize, all of these transactions seem to involve what might best be characterized as a 'physiological engagement' between devotees and the Supreme Being in the person of the sant satguru. The result is the closest possible intimacy, tending toward self-transformation of the devotees. That is, by 'feeding' themselves to the Supreme Being, and by (in effect) drinking his currents into themselves, devotees achieve what Marriott (1976) has called a 'biomoral' gain. They radically improve their own natures by shedding 'impurities' and by mixing their own internal substances with those flowing from the Supreme Being. This process, therefore, effects a union of devotees with the object of their devotion, and thus furthers their realization as uncontaminated, awareness-enhanced selves, which are of the same essential nature as the Supreme Being.

Given the liquidity of these encounters, it is not surprising that metaphors of thirst, drinking, soaking, and the like are nearly omnipresent in Radhasoami poetry. Devotees are compared with the *chakor*, a moonbeam-drinking bird, and also with the *papīhā*, a bird who cries out in a thirst that can only be assuaged by the *svānti* rain that comes but once each year. Devotees 'drink' divine 'nectar' (*amrit*), they are 'fish' in the ocean of guru, the 'pots' of their selves are filled, their bodies are 'bathed' in bliss, they are 'dyed' in the 'color' of guru, and so on.

But if these transactions establish and sustain a kind of fluid intimacy, it is humble intimacy, having powerful implications of hierarchy.[2] Each of the flow-taking gestures in question implies, in the wider context of Hindu culture, the subordination of the receiving party and does so in the idiom of relative 'coarseness.' This coarseness is usually characterized as relative 'dirtiness' or 'pollution.' For example, to accept the mouth rinsings of another person is to accept something that is, from the standpoint of the mouth-rinser, crude, residual, or dirty. Thus, the devotee is acceding to relatively lower status as 'filth accepting,' which is to say, as 'more filthy.'

---

[2] On the mutual consistency of hierarchy and intimacy, see Marriott 1978.

These hierarchical implications of such transactions are recognized by the Radhasoami tradition and, in fact, are invested with high religious value. The self is bound to the world by desire arising from egoism. Accordingly, a vital prerequisite for the self's liberation is the devotee's cultivation of humility (*dīntā*). This notion is a basic behavior-informing value of the Radhasoami faith. Devotees in the presence of one whom they regard as guru enact this value; their demeanor is humble and apologetic, and they jump at the guru's every command. Serving the guru, obeying him in all things, being his slave (*kinkar*), and accepting his inferiorizing body-flows are all gestures that 'banish egoism' by expressing humility and surrender.

Moreover, the hierarchical dimension of guru-devotee interactions is also linked with one of the most important concepts in Radhasoami doctrine—and in devotional Hinduism more generally—namely, the idea of saran. The term *saran* (or *sharan*), meaning 'shelter' or 'protection,' is a common noun in Radhasoami literature and discourse. The beings of this world are regarded as absolutely helpless on their own, totally unable to extricate themselves from the meshes of Kāl's net. Therefore, they must seek the saran of a powerful being, and in order to get such protection, they must surrender to that being. As Wadley (1975) has pointed out, acts of homage in Hinduism draw upon a fundamental social pattern in which devoted service to the great and powerful imposes on them the protective obligations of *jajmānī* patronage (and, we must add, of parenthood). By surrendering and 'clinging to the feet' of a superior being, the devotee becomes the child-client of a parent-patron and is thus entitled to his protection.

Intimacy and homage, therefore, appear to be the main themes of interactions between devotees and gurus. At first glance it is a rather striking juxtaposition, involving apparent contradictions. One 'rises up' by bowing down, and one purifies oneself by consuming 'filth.' Of course the contradiction is more apparent than real: if the sant satguru is the Supreme Being, then his body-flows cannot be inferiorizing in the same way as those of an ordinary man. But the matter does not end here. The very fact that the guru has the form of a human being—that he *looks* like an ordinary man—suggests additional complexities in the act of taking his flows. The very ordinariness of the guru's form is, in fact, a kind of spiritual opportunity. It makes possible perceiving the ordinary in an extraordinary way.

Flow and Self-Transformation

Flow taking obviously raises questions of identity. Because of its hierarchical implications, only certain kinds of persons can appropriately take flows from certain sorts of persons or beings. Because of its implications of intimacy, those who take flows become like those from whom flows are taken. Therefore, such transactions can signal relative identities. But can they actually establish and sustain an inner sense of self-transformation? I believe that in the Radhasoami world guru-devotee transactions do indeed have this potential.

In order to show what I mean by this it will be necessary to examine in greater detail the inner logic of guru-devotee interactions. Thus far we have looked at the surfaces of these transactions, their ostensible meaning in relation to visible, and often doctrinal, assumptions about the nature of the world, the body, and hierarchical relations. There is, however, a deeper substructure involving some of the most basic questions of identity as a function of ego-other interaction.

The basis for my analysis of these principles is the writings of Babuji Maharaj, the last sant satguru of the Soami Bagh line. Even though the Radhasoami tradition strongly devalues what it regards as mere bookish knowledge, the tradition has been highly productive of texts. In some of these texts, most notably the prose discourses of Huzur Maharaj and his successors, the doctrines and practices of the movement have been subjected to the most intense analytical scrutiny. The result is what might be characterized as an indigenous subtradition of cultural analysis. Here crucial practices and ideas are interpreted with extraordinary clarity and penetration. A good example of this analysis is a discourse (1972, *bachan* 20) in which Babuji Maharaj clarifies the meaning of the celebrated lines in Soamiji Maharaj's poetry, quoted earlier in this chapter, in which the devotee is enjoined to drink the contents of his guru's spittoon.

The guru explains that what a sant satguru's prasād actually *is* depends entirely on the internal disposition of the receiver. To most people the leavings of a sant satguru are abhorrent and valueless. However, on one whose self is awakened, these same leavings will bestow benefit and 'bliss.'

According to Babuji Maharaj (I am here paraphrasing throughout), the leavings of a guru are but an 'outer accretion' (*ūhari phuzlā*) on a subtle divine current. There is a current of phlegm (*shleshmā kī dhār*), which is actually a current of nectar (amrit), that drips into the body from above and helps maintain the body by cooling the process of digestion. It becomes ordinary mucus only after it passes outward through the vessels of the body, but even in this form the original and more subtle current remains in it, though obscured within the coarser vehicle. In ordinary human beings this current comes from the upper gateway of piṇḍ, but in sant satgurus it originates in the highest regions. This latter current of pure divine nature is what devotees take when they ingest the guru's leavings.

In ordinary life, the guru says, there are many examples of situations in which people take positive joy in 'filthiness' (*mal, gilājat*). For example, when the 'flows of attachment' of mother and child meet, they experience pleasure and do not even see the dirtiness (what the guru regards as such) in the relationship. Likewise, to one filled with lust there is no question of filth in the object of his or her desire (ibid., *bachan* 15). Just so, the guru says, if love for the sant satguru is present in the recipient, then the guru's leavings will not seem to be dirty or coarse (*sthūl*). In other words, though such things may appear to be dirty, they suggest nothing of the kind to the devotee with the right attitude.

But not everyone has the right attitude. Some people, Babuji Maharaj observes, are simply impervious to the 'love' of a guru's leavings. They cannot derive its benefits, or at least not its full benefits. Moreover, an understanding of the meaning of prasād is not sufficient; it is not enough, in other words, merely to assent to the idea that the guru's leavings contain a current of divine substance. One must actually feel love for the leavings of a guru. If there is any 'disgust' (*ghrinā*) in the mind, the receiver is not really taking prasād at all. Therefore, only the gurumukh, the perfect devotee, will derive full benefit from taking a guru's leavings. Only such a devotee feels full love for the guru's leavings. Others feel such love too, but in lesser degrees, and they will gain benefits from prasād according to their level.[3]

Are the guru's flows pure or impure, clean or dirty? Obviously this is a relative matter. It depends on who you are, and this, in turn, depends on who the guru is thought to be. The sant satguru looks like an ordinary man. But the guru's devotees see him, according to their level, for what he really is—namely, the formless Lord in human

---

[3] In this connection, however, it should be mentioned that it is said that a woman can secretly put prasād in her (presumably benighted) husband's food to good effect. I assume that the benefits of doing so are of a relatively low degree.

form. Seeing him thus, they see that his flows are not the filth they appear to be but rather the purest flows of divine substance. What is filth to the world is nectar to the awakened. Those who love the guru's leavings are in a special state of awareness or knowing; they are ones who 'recognize' the guru. On the other hand, according to the poet in *Sār Bachan*, Yam (Kāl) 'spits in the mouth' of those who have no devotion (*S. B. Poetry*: 38.2.18).

Persons who take the guru's leavings are known as *satsangīs*, or ones who associate with a sant satguru. Indeed a satsangī is, among other things, one who knows that a particular guru's leavings are actually currents of divinity. A satsangī is a 'lover,' and thus a taker, of the guru's prasād. Such persons keep 'good company' (*satsang*) as opposed to 'bad company' (*kusang*); those who keep bad company are like 'the mind,' who, says the poet, 'wanders like a dog from house to house eating the poison of falsehood' (*S. B. Poetry*: 31.1.2).

At one level, identity as a lover of guru's prasād is a social identity. As a result the practice of taking prasād can (as in the case of Huzur Maharaj) run afoul of caste identity. Those who do not believe that the guru is actually the Supreme Being will see his flows as filth, and the consumption of such as compromising the caste status of the consumer. On the other hand, those to whom the divinity of guru is evident will have in this conviction a basis for a conception of themselves as a community (a satsang) of cofollowers of the guru. As takers of his leavings they all share in his nature, and to this degree they all share in one another's nature as well.[4] Since this nature is the highest of all possible natures, theirs is the highest form of fraternity, superseding all worldly bonds of kinship and caste.

As it exists today, the Soami Bagh congregation is hardly a unified community. But ideally no differences should separate its members. Two dogs, a satsangī informant remarked to me (in the context of a discussion of prasād), will not fight if their master gives them a biscuit he has broken with his teeth. Satsangīs should be brothers and sisters in a transcendental family presided over by the sant satguru. 'One's true children and kinsmen,' said Soamiji Maharaj, 'are those who are one's company in paramārth' (*S. B. Prose*: II, 44).

But identity as a satsangī has an inward dimension too. The essential value of a guru's leavings is finally a matter of the taker's inner disposition. The prasād imparts its full benefits only to those

[4] On the wider context of this notion, see esp Inden (1976), Inden and Nicholas (1977), and Marriot (1976). On its place in the tradition of sant mat see Gold (1982).

who take it without disgust—that is, with genuine love. Since only those whose selves are to some degree awakened can do this, taking prasād without disgust and with real love is an indication that one's self is, to some degree, awakened.

Such a person is like the *hansa*s, the 'swans' who are said to inhabit the upper regions of the cosmos. In Hindu folklore the swan is much celebrated for its powers of discrimination, which are so acute that it can separate milk from water. The swan may inhabit filthy ponds, but it eats only pearls. Similarly, a devotee who takes the guru's leavings with love has high powers of discrimination. Within the guru's leavings the devotee can discriminate the essential divine current from its material vehicle. Such discrimination is possible because the devotee can differentiate in the guru's person between the Supreme Being and the physical body. In fact, the devotee's love *is* such discrimination, since without such discrimination there could be no love.

Therefore, the more a devotee feels love for a guru's leavings, the more his or her nature approximates that of the Supreme Being, whose leavings (as the devotee has come to know) they really are. Such a devotee does indeed drink in a higher awareness when taking prasād. Devotees become what they worship; by taking their guru's flows with real love, they enact, on a human plane, the physio-cosmological drama of the separation of good from bad and fine from coarse. As such they are ones who separate, within themselves, their true subtle selves from the matter that holds them down. If devotees are 'digested' by the Supreme Being, they also digest themselves, etherealizing themselves in acts of psychophysiological mimesis of the universal digester. The Lord has made of the devotee, the poet says, a 'swan' from a (carrion-eating) 'crow' (*S. B. Poetry* 3.5.6).

Expanded Vision

In the Radhasoami tradition the problem of identity is a matter of point of view: 'who' one is, as flow-taker, depends on one's perspective. In other words, identity is a matter of how the self, and the self in relation to guru and to the world, is 'seen.' This connection with seeing is not an accidental metaphor. The matter of vision is fundamental to the Radhasoami faith, as it is in the wider Hindu tradition as well.

Hindus want to see their deities. This is one reason why image worship is so basic to Hindu religious practice.[5] At a minimum one goes to a temple to see, to have the darshan (sight) of, the deity housed within. Deities sometimes emerge from their temples in procession, as kings and queens might come forth from their palaces, so that they may see and be seen by their worshipper-subjects. Moreover, short of temple visits, there are always pictures. Even though colored prints of deities may be relatively new on the Indian scene (Basham 1977, ix), there is hardly a more ubiquitous feature of Hindu life today. Virtually everywhere Hindus live or work there are pictures of the gods.

Less obvious is the fact that Hindus want to be seen *by* their deities as well. Perhaps nothing indicates this more clearly than the icono-graphic importance given to eyes. Even the crudest lithic representa-tions of deities are likely to have eyes, if nothing else in the way of facial features. Eyes, moreover, are associated with the life of the image, so that the consecration of an image is, in part, accomplished by the creation or opening of its eyes (Eck 1981, 5–6, 40). The implication is that if the deity is present, the image sees.

The Radhasoami tradition puts very great emphasis on seeing, and being seen by, the sant satguru. We have already noted the importance of seeing the guru's physical form in satsang, and of the internal visualization of his form during spiritual practice. These ideas are the point of convergence for an extremely broad range of behaviors and concepts. One should always seek a sant satguru's darshan. When one sees a true guru, one feels a surge of spiritual emotion inside. Devotees compete with each other for their guru's visual attention, and when a guru passes by, his followers gaze at him in hopes of provoking inner 'experiences.' When Maharaj Charan Singh (guru of the Beas group) visits Delhi, thousands of devotees obtain his darshan by filing by his seat in ten continuously moving lines. One informant told me that even if he seems to be reading his mail (which apparently he sometimes seems to be doing), he sees everybody, and can single out for admonishment those who have taken more than their one allotted turn. Even though Charan Singh has forbidden darshan except at appointed times and places, his devotees lurk around places where he is expected to be in hopes of getting a quick glimpse of him.

Devotees perceive the eyes and foreheads of gurus to be the most prominent feature of the face. In the Soami Bagh tradition devotees believe that there is a resemblance between all the sant satgurus of the

[5] For an admirable and far more comprehensive discussion of visual aspects of Hinduism, the reader is urged to consult Eck (1981).

past, especially in the eyes and forehead. Kāl has many tricks, but he cannot assume the eyes or forehead of a true guru. One can look intently into a true guru's eyes only if he permits it, and it is said that when large congregations are before the guru, he seems to be gazing at each devotee personally. When the guru looks at a devotee, he 'sees everything' within. I am told that Darshan Singh, one of the successors of Kirpal Singh (a distinguished guru of the Punjab tradition), claims that he obtained his master's power through his eyes. Kirpal Singh is said to have gotten his power from his predecessor (Savan Singh) in the same fashion.

The guru does not need to be physically present to grant darshan. Though his photograph is not the same as his real presence, it can preside over congregational observances in his absence. For the Soami Bagh tradition this is the only external darshan left (except in the case of unofficially recognized gurus). Dreams and waking visions of gurus are common among Radhasoami devotees and are greatly valued as signs of grace. It is believed, moreover, that at the time of death every true devotee has his guru's darshan.

It is not surprising, therefore, that when we turn to Radhasoami sacred literature, we find a rich visual imagery. This is especially true of the poetic compositions of Soamiji Maharaj and Huzur Maharaj. In these materials what takes place visually between devotee and guru is given special emphasis in relation to the Radhasoami version of the Hindu rite known as *ārati*.

In general usage this term refers to a ritual sequence associated with *pūjā* (worship) in which the worshipper or officiant circles a lamp (and sometimes other objects) before an image of a deity. While this takes place, bells are rung and those present often sing ārati hymns. In the Soami Bagh tradition, ārati is regarded as a visual encounter between a guru and his devotees. In the days of Soamiji Maharaj and Huzur Maharaj it was performed as an actual ceremony in which disciples and guru gazed at each other while ārati verses were sung. Informants say that this practice was discouraged by Maharaj Saheb and Babuji Maharaj. However, whether outwardly enacted or not, ārati has always been regarded as an essentially internal occurrence associated with the contemplation (dhyān) of the guru's form. The outer ceremony is a kind of provocation and guide. One closes one's eyes and concentrates on the form (*svarūp*) of the guru, especially the eyes, in effect sublimating the ceremony into mental images.

In the ārati hymns we find a complete poetic visualization of the rite. The devotee is described as prepared to perform ārati, 'adorned' for the occasion and looking beautiful. But since the true significance of the rite is internal, its paraphernalia are portrayed as aspects of the devotee's own being: 'My body and mind are the platter, my longing the lamp' (*S. B. Poetry*: 6.3.2). As in an ordinary act of Hindu worship, a food offering is present, but this too is inward: 'I made a bhog [food offering] of my devotion. I sang of my contemplation' (ibid., 6.12.3). But, above all, the devotee *sees* his or her guru: 'I got guru's darshan and sang his glory. I took into my eyes his incomparable appearance' (ibid., 5.5.3). The devotee is swept away by the vision: 'Every moment my love increases. The image of the guru looks marvelous. / I lose my eyes and breath. I lose my sense of body and mind / . . . to it [guru's image] I am as the [moonlight drinking] chakor to the moon' (ibid., 6.2.19–21). The ārati-performing devotee is then swept upward and sees the sights (and hears the sounds) of celestial regions.

An implicit theme in this imagery is the suggestion of a change in the devotee's own power of seeing: the cosmos, and especially the guru, come to be 'seen' in a new and spiritually significant way. The devotee begins by seeing the familiar form of the guru, and then he or she sees the presiding deities of the celestial levels, each higher than the one before. While the texts are not clear on this point, my impression is that these deities are actually successively higher visualizations of the guru. At the end of the journey the devotee has darshan of the Supreme Being himself. The point seems to be that the devotee's visual power is in some sense altered, increased, augmented—which may explain the poet-devotee's curious assertion that he employs a *durbīn*, a 'telescope' (ibid., 8.6.21). Seeing as never before, the devotee experiences a new cosmos. Most important of all, however, the devotee sees the guru with what may be properly called a much deepened insight; that is, the worshipper sees the guru as the Supreme Being that he truly is. This is the fulfilling darshan, and the devotee has now achieved his or her goal.

Another theme runs alongside this celebration of the expanding spectacle of the world and illuminated vision of guru. Not only is the sant satguru seen by the devotee, but the guru, in turn, sees the devotee in a very special way. 'We join glances as I stand facing him,' says the poet-devotee, and 'satguru casts on me his *glance of compassion* [*dayā drishṭi*]' (ibid., 30.4.5, my emphasis). This seems to be the crux of the matter. Devotee looks at guru, and guru looks back. The devotee, being a true devotee, is humble, 'surrendered.' The glance that the guru casts upon the devotee is one of 'compassion' or 'kindness' (the Hindi words *dayā*, *kripā*, and *mehar* are used interchangeably in this context). Furthermore, because the devotee is looked at *in this way*, he or she is able to achieve proper concentration and move upward to regions beyond: 'Guru cast his glance of kindness on me,' the poet says, 'and my mind became engaged in contemplation [dhyān] and shabd' (Huzur Maharaj 1972: 2.21.3). Elsewhere the devotee pleads for the guru's assistance, saying 'give me your glance of kindness [here *kripā drishṭi*] and swing me [upward]. Then the power of [mere] intellect (*buddhi*) will vanish' (*S. B. Poetry*: 30.2.7).

The idea that the drishṭi, the 'seeing' or 'glance,' of the guru aids the devotee in achieving deliverance seems to be a crucial aspect of the Radhasoami understanding of what is supposed to take place visually between guru and devotee. The idea is expressed succinctly in a passage from one of Soamiji Maharaj's prose discourses. The devotee, the master says, should have darshan of guru for a couple of hours; that is, 'with his eyes he should gaze at [satguru's] eyes.' The devotee should try to increase the duration of this every day, 'and on that day that [satguru's] glance of *mehar* [compassion] falls on you, your heart will be instantly purified' (ibid., 21, pp. 418–19). In other words, by joining glances with a true guru, the devotee can gain access to benevolent power that apparently emanates from the guru's eyes.

The āratī of the poet-devotee is a transposition of a common Hindu ceremony onto an internal landscape. The poet presents us with a certain conception of āratī, and one of the things he conceives it to be is an occasion for what psychologists call 'gaze fixation.' The worshipper sees an inner flame and hears a bell and conch (soteriologically significant, but also probably corresponding to the real flame, bell, and conch in an actual Hindu ceremony). But, above all, the worshipper sees—and is seen by—the guru, who in this context takes the place of the image of the deity in a normal āratī. As their gazes unite, the devotee's spirit is drawn upward.

The idea that 'looking' carries power is a commonplace of Hindu culture. It is widely believed that a person who is envious, or in some other way ill-disposed, can inflict harm, usually inadvertent, on persons or objects merely by looking at them. According to Maharaj Saheb (1978, 213–14), the 'benign gaze' of a sant or sādh is the opposite of this so-called evil eye. More generally, the guru's gaze is conceived as an eyeborne extrusion of benevolent power. Thus, for example, it is said that a true guru's mere glance can sanctify food as prasād. This imagery makes good sense in the context of other notions about vision. Huzur Maharaj (1973, 84 and elsewhere) speaks of a 'current of sight' (*drishṭi kī dhār*), a fluidlike 'seeing' that flows from the third eye to the two exterior eyes, and thence outward into the world. To fall under the gaze of a sant satguru, therefore, is to come into contact with a current emanating from his innermost and uppermost recesses. For a devotee to engage in eye-contact with him affords the most intimate kind of communion with the Supreme Being.

By 'turning' the pupils of the eyes, the devotee aims to reverse his or her current of sight (along with other currents), disengaging the sight from worldly objects, and pulling it back up to the third eye, from which point it is caught and taken to still higher regions. In the poetry devotees are portrayed as being pulled upward into a vision. They see the guru and more; what they see is beautiful, remarkable, and splendid. The vision pulls at their inner sight and concentrates their attention. They find themselves on a pilgrimage of insight, seeing and learning to see in a new way. But as they see, they are seen. The guru's glance of benevolence ultimately enables them to reach their goal. By mixing his superior seeing-flow into theirs, they come to see better. This mingling of seeings results in a visual consummation. As the devotee finally comes to see the guru for what he 'really is,' the devotee is seen in a way that confers benefits and effects (in theory) a kind of self-transformation.

We have seen that an implicit idea in prasād taking is that, as one might put it in English, 'you become what you eat.'[6] The same principle seems to be implicated in the confluent visual engagements that take place between guru and devotee—you somehow become what you see. This is quite clearly suggested in *S. B. Prose* (I, 54). Here the guru (Huzur Maharaj, who is the author of this part of the book) says that until the true 'searcher' obtains the *nij svarūp* (own or true form of the guru) within, he or she should regard the physical form of the satguru as that of the Lord and cultivate love for his feet. But when the searcher gets *nij darsnan* (true darshan) within, then he or she merges with the Lord, who is the perfect satguru, and assumes his form. Then, the guru concludes, the devotee's task is completed.

But there is another side to the matter. What the material on

---

[6] The same expression exists in Hindi: *jaisā ann, vaisā man.*

prasād taking suggests, and what the ideas surrounding visual engagement also seem to demonstrate, is that self-realization through the mingling of one's substances with those of a superior being is very much a two-way street—two identities are involved. If one becomes 'better' through an engagement with a superior being, it is only because one has learned to regard this being *as* superior, and has done so at the deepest levels of apprehension.

Prasād is redemptively useless (or nearly so) to those who cannot really love it, and the glance of mercy seems to depend on the devotee's own 'seeing' the guru in his 'true form.' To this must be added the phrase 'appearances to the contrary notwithstanding.' Just as the sant satguru's leavings seem like 'filth' to the unenlightened, so too the guru looks like an ordinary man. In other words, if the devotee's self-perception is transformed because of interaction with the guru, it is only because he or she sees the guru in a certain extraordinary way, a way that supplies something beyond mere appearances. That is, to the degree that he really redeems, the sant satguru's power to do so depends on his devotees' inner recognition of that power; indeed, their recognition seems to *be* that power.

Spiritual Mimicry and the Language of Succession

A truly curious feature of the Radhasoami tradition, as exemplified at Soami Bagh, is that sant satgurus do not claim to be such. Nothing is more important than the identity of the guru, and yet this identity is hedged about with uncertainty and indirection, or at least this is so on the surface. In a letter to a satsangī, for example, Huzur Maharaj said the following: 'To identify *me* with the Supreme Father is a mistake, but my Spiritual Father Radhasoami was really a manifestation of the Supreme Being Himself and from Him I learnt the secrets of the practice which can one day secure us the kingdom of the Supreme Father' (1952, 34). On other occasions he characterized himself as a mere schoolroom 'monitor,' there to keep order while the teacher (Soamiji Maharaj) was away. I have been told by an older informant that Maharaj Saheb and Babuji Maharaj discouraged the performance of their āratīs and the touching of their feet precisely because they did not wish to seem to be claiming the guruship. Indeed, as far as I am aware, the *only* time Babuji actually claimed to be sant satguru was when he was required to do so in court in order to refute the claims of the rival Dayal Bagh group.

How, then, does one know who is a guru and who is not? At one level the answer is easy: he is the successor to the previous sant satguru. The only exception to this was Soamiji Maharaj himself, who was a svatah sant (according to the Agra view) and had no guru. As we shall see, however, the criterion of succession hardly simplifies matters.

The Soami Bagh tradition possesses a well-developed theory of succession. It is based on a passage in *S. B. Prose* (II, 250) in which Soamiji Maharaj (in a letter dictated to Huzur Maharaj) says that a sant satguru 'enters' (*ā samāte hāĩ*) his appointed successor, if such is his will, and that devotees should therefore make no distinction whatsoever between them. Around this core idea has grown a highly elaborated conception of the transfer of guruship.

According to this view, the successor to a sant satguru, who need not be named in advance, is his gurumukh. The term *gurumukh* means 'one who faces the guru' (its opposite is *manmukh*, 'one who faces [the villain] mind'). He is, in other words, one who is fully surrendered to guru. According to this theory, the sant satguru himself does not descend into this world (that is, into piṇḍ, below the third eye), because the force of his divine current is so great that it would be disruptive to the order of this region. Accordingly, in order to redeem the beings of this world, the sant satguru must have a principal agent. This is the gurumukh, who does indeed descend fully into the world. Under the guidance of the sant satguru, the gurumukh achieves his own salvation, and in doing so acts as an exemplar to others, pulling them along in the direction of the sant satguru and their own redemption. In the texts the gurumukh is often likened to a camel driver, pulling the string of devotees along. He is said to be of the same essence as the sant satguru, his *nij ansh* (own emanation), though of course he seems to be different externally. At Soami Bagh it is held that Soamiji Maharaj originally brought four nij anshes into the world—Huzur Maharaj, Maharaj Saheb, Buaji Saheba, and Babuji Maharaj—each of whom became successor to the guruship in turn. There are and will be others, though who will be the next sant satguru is not yet known.

The career of Huzur Maharaj, as portrayed in the texts and lore of the Soami Bagh congregation, was a nearly perfect embodiment of this idea. Gurumukh is gurumaker, and that is precisely what Huzur Maharaj was. He was the perfected devotee of Soamiji Maharaj, and the tradition holds that the master did not reveal the name *rādhāsvāmī* or the secrets of access to the highest regions until Huzur Maharaj came on the scene. Only at the urging of a small group of favored satsangīs, of whom Huzur Maharaj was the foremost, did the master finally reveal the highest truths and open his satsang to the world. It was also Huzur Maharaj who first called Soamiji Maharaj by the name *rādhāsvāmī*, thus acknowledging recognition of the master's true identity. In other words, Huzur Maharaj was the indispensable agency by which Soamiji Maharaj's identity became disclosed and his redemptive power, otherwise hovering inaccessibly above the third eye, was made available to the beings of this world.

In the idea of the gurumukh-successor, theology and religious sociology converge. It is said (in disparagement) by some on the Punjab side of the movement that Huzur Maharaj was the actual creator of the (supposedly inauthentic) 'Radhasoami faith.' This contention is not far from the truth as understood in Agra, but in a sense very different from the one intended. It is historically probable that there would indeed have been no Radhasoami faith without Huzur Maharaj, but this likelihood is not a problem for Soami Bagh. The Radhasoami faith does not so much create guru-devotee interactions as it is created *by* such interactions. The gurumukh theory of the succession can be viewed as an implicit recognition, within the tradition, of this fact. The gurumukh is the ideal devotee, who, in his engagement with guru, causes the Radhasoami faith to spring into ever-renewed existence in every generation. He creates the sant satguru by 'recognizing' him for what he really is. As such, he is the model for what every satsangī should try to be. By a kind of spiritual mimicry, that is, they should try to become guru-creators too.

In accord with these notions, the hagiographic literature of the tradition attempts retrospectively to portray each sant satguru as having had a special kind of relationship with his predecessor. He was always the perfected devotee before he became an object of devotion himself. Thus, we are told at great length of how Huzur Maharaj brought water for Soamiji Maharaj, cut twigs for his toothbrush, spent income in his service, and so on (Chachaji Saheb 1978, 73–78). Maharaj Saheb, once a powerful athlete, dwindled away into a wraith of his former self after beginning his devoted and submissive attendance on Huzur Maharaj (Maheshwari 1971a, 50, and often repeated). In turn, Babuji Maharaj completely forgot his former friendship with Maharaj Saheb (once the latter became guru) and kept his eyes only on his 'feet' (ibid., 65). In the photographic and pictorial collections of the movement, each sant satguru (with the exception of Buaji) is portrayed as standing behind a seated predecessor with a fly whisk in his hand, a pose that is symbolic of humble service.

However, at the time of a guru's death, matters are never so clear. In the Soami Bagh tradition the transition from sant satguru to his successor has apparently never occurred quickly. The tradition deals with these uncertainties by holding that after the death of a guru the current that he embodies 'withdraws' somewhat. His gurumukh is 'shy,' and indeed may not even be aware of his exalted status. The current will still be present, but in an attenuated or somewhat less accessible form. Therefore, a period of 'interregnum' may ensue. It is, however, not a genuine interregnum, for the previous guru and the current he brought with him are said to be still at work, though not in bodily form. For this reason, in the writings of the Soami Bagh tradition the postscript 'so to say' is almost always added to the English word *interregnum*. Moreover, such a so-called interregnum is not without spiritual benefits. The absence of a fully manifested sant satguru gives rise to religiously salutary longings for his company. In the meantime, devotees can take comfort in the conviction that in the end a guru will appear, and that the line of gurus—if this is the Lord's will—will continue from guru to gurumukh to the end of the cosmic cycle.

When a new sant satguru becomes manifested as such, it is not as a result of any claim of his own, but rather because others come to regard him as guru. In other words, in the Soami Bagh tradition the true core of the idea of guruship is not prior 'designation,' but present 'recognition.' We are told, for example, that after Soamiji Maharaj's departure, 'Satsangis started paying obeisance to Huzur Maharaj and regarding him as guru, but Huzur Maharaj would not approve of it' (Maharaj Saheb 1978, 413). Even though Soamiji Maharaj may have obliquely sanctioned Huzur Maharaj's guruship (see 'Physiocosmology and the Errors of the Past' in chapter 2), the latter apparently took many years to 'manifest himself,' claiming all the while to be no more than a satsangī trying to serve his master and his fellow disciples.

The same was true of Maharaj Saheb, though he apparently did indicate his guruship by indirection. Once in response to the observation (made by whom is not clear) that devotees should try to touch the feet of one whom they consider guru, even if this makes him angry, 'Maharaj Saheb withdrew his feet and all the Satsangis present there flashed into smile' (ibid., 187–88). But it was Babuji Maharaj (thereby a gurumukh) who was the leader in recognizing Maharaj Saheb's guruship. An elderly informant told me that once during satsang Maharaj Saheb was sitting with others in a line, when Babuji Maharaj arose and motioned the others away, saying, 'the current is with us in Panditji [what Maharaj Saheb was often called].' This opened the way to more general recognition.

Apparently Babuji Maharaj, in turn, was being importuned to manifest himself as guru even before Buaji's death. A satsangī is recorded as having said to him in 1908: 'Do not conceal yourself any more. Who else is there besides you?' With an ambiguity typical in these matters, Babuji Maharaj responded by saying with a smile, 'The Supreme Father is more concerned than you' (Babuji Maharaj 1974, 21). A viable constituency for his guruship, probably never sought by him, finally emerged after Buaji's decease. It is quite possible that this distinguished satsangī represented an ideal rallying point for a congregation increasingly beset by challenges from the nascent Dayal Bagh group; but in any case, except in the context of the legal battle with Dayal Bagh, Babuji Maharaj persisted in portraying himself as nothing more than a faithful servant of sant satgurus, who tried to live in the expectation of his own salvation.

Who, then, is a sant satguru's successor? He is whoever is regarded and treated as such. The claims are made by others, not by him, since he never engages in self-advertisement. The Soami Bagh tradition proclaims that all sant satgurus live simple, inconspicuous lives. They do not perform miracles (though it must be added that a few miraculous occurrences are recorded in their biographies). The world does not and cannot see them for what they are. Indeed, the world will regard the claims made of them with contempt. This contempt is itself spiritually beneficial, serving as a barrier to keep the 'unfit' away from their company. The true signs of guruship are internal to the devotee, and must even pass the test of the guru's denial of his guruship. In a sant satguru's presence the devotee feels peace and 'bliss.' As the devotee takes prasād, his or her 'love' increases. The devotee derives benefits, known finally only to himself or herself, from external and internal contemplation of the guru's form. Thus 'recognition' grows.

In other branches of the movement rather different conceptions of succession prevail.[7] At Dayal Bagh there has apparently been a

---

[7] The following discussion of succession patterns in other branches is based on the invaluable description and analysis in Gold (1982).

somewhat greater emphasis on 'designation' (as opposed to 'recognition'). Sahibji Maharaj is held to have clearly indicated who his successor was to be (Gold 1982, 277–78). But the concept of recognition continues to play a role here too. The last succession was decided by unanimous election in an assembly of satsangīs (ibid., 178), apparently a somewhat bureaucratized and greatly accelerated application of the recognition concept. It may also represent a genuine alteration of the concept, which might, in turn, be related to a weakening of the idea of identity between guru and the Supreme Being that we have noted in connection with the Dayal Bagh–Soami Bagh dispute. The rapidity with which succession questions are decided at Dayal Bagh is probably necessitated by the intolerability of an uncertain 'interregnum' in a situation in which the material interests of a large and highly organized community are at stake.

The Punjab groups have developed a succession pattern of their own. Here the idea of the transfer of 'current' is given short shrift (see Puri 1972, 121–24). As already noted, the Punjab conception of the essential nature of the Radhasoami tradition is quite different from that of the Agra groups. For the Punjab groups, Soamiji Maharaj was not unique in history, but one in a long line of gurus stretching back into antiquity. Moreover, in contrast to the Agra belief in the essential oneness of all the sant satgurus, the Punjab groups seem to stress the idea of the gurus as a connected series of unique individuals occupying an 'eternal office' (Gold 1983, 287).

A devotee's bond with his guru is therefore also unique. A devotee need not, as at Agra, shift from inner contemplation of the form of one guru to that of his successor. In Punjab there also seems to be a decided bias in favor of the 'designation' principle of succession. The supporters of Maharaj Charan Singh, the present incumbent at Beas, maintain that he was named as successor in the will of Jagat Singh, who in turn was named as successor in the will of Savan Singh (Jaimal Singh's principal disciple). For his part, the late Kirpal Singh (a Beas rival) claimed that he had received 'verbal directions to carry on his work' from Savan Singh (ibid., 289). 'Internal signs' of recognition play a role in this tradition too, but the prevailing view seems to be that the departing guru finds among his disciples someone 'fit to take charge' and 'hands over the "Gaddi" to him' (Puri 1972, 124).

In light of the Radhasoami emphasis on the necessity to establish a relationship with the guru of one's age (*vakt guru*), the importance attached to relics at Soami Bagh may seem, at first glance, anomalous.

But however paradoxical, given the succession principles at work at Soami Bagh, the relics are probably a structural necessity. The great importance placed on 'recognition' in the Soami Bagh tradition—something that requires time to mature—means that periods of interregnum are inevitable. Such periods are all the more certain in view of the fact that the guru-to-be denies his guruship. Were succession determined mainly by descent or designation, this would not be so, nor would it be the case were the device of election by acclamation superimposed on the recognition principle. But where the principle of noncorporate, 'inward' recognition prevails, as at Soami Bagh, there will necessarily be periods of discontinuity. Because the relics are suffused with the 'current'—that is, evoking the same sentiments and attitudes as living gurus—they provide a physical bridge from one guruship to another. Given the uncertainties of transition, it is precisely *because* of the emphasis on synchrony in this tradition that relics of the past are important. The faith lives only in devotees' ongoing relationships with sant satgurus. In the inevitable periodic absence of recognized gurus, the relics provide a focus for otherwise objectless devotional energies. From the tradition's point of view, this has its dangers too; it can degenerate into the mere worship of object and place that the sant satgurus themselves condemn as idolatrous. This is precisely the Punjab interpretation of what has happened at Soami Bagh.

In addition, the relics provide the props against which the drama of legitimacy can be enacted. Because the relics are such potent sources of the 'current,' intimate connection with, or custodianship over, these objects can enhance the current-connectedness of a guruship. Moreover, in being the chief devotee and servant of such relics, a guru or guru-to-be can continue to act within the paradigm of gurumukh to his predecessors. It is not surprising, therefore, that the careers of the gurus of the Soami Bagh line have been intimately intertwined with the relics. Huzur Maharaj erected a samādh for Soamiji Maharaj's remains, Maharaj Saheb began the construction of a bigger one, and Babuji Maharaj spent decades presiding over its construction and protecting it from defilement by those whom he regarded as heretical schismatics. It is precisely because the Dayal Bagh group holds a similar view of the nature of guruship that these two groups came into such bitter opposition over the relics.

Interregnum

With schisms in every generation, and uncomfortable periods of interregnum, one is tempted to conclude that the Soami Bagh congregation has an intractable succession problem. There has never been an uncontested succession, nor has there ever been a fully resolved succession. New offshoot groups have emerged with every generation. But the materials we have seen suggest that the uncertainty surrounding succession, far from being a 'problem,' is close to the essence of what the Radhasoami faith, as understood at Soami Bagh, is all about.

The devotee seeks redemption in a relationship with a sant satguru, a redemption conceived as a realization of the devotee's long-forgotten true self. The experiential validation of redemption is the experience of higher regions of the cosmos under the sant satguru's influence and guidance. To this we must add, however, that the tradition has succeeded in blending this principle with another concept—namely, that a devotee's redemptive sense of self can be directly nourished by his or her engagement with the person of the guru.

In significant part, it is in a devotee's personal feelings about the sant satguru that are found the experiential rewards of the faith. The symbolism of the movement links these feelings tightly to questions of self-rediscovery and salvation. The real trick of this tradition, its implicit secret, is the conversion of the question 'Who am I?' into 'Who is he?' What it *is* to be a devotee is to be able to say of a particular and apparently human other, 'He is the Lord.' But it is not enough merely to say it. It is not enough, that is, for the devotee to know that he or she *should* love the guru as God; the devotee must *actually feel* such love for guru, and *actually see* that the guru is not what he seems to the world to be. Even in the teeth of a guru's denial that he is anything other than an ordinary man, the devotee must 'love' his leavings by ingesting them without disgust, and feel real 'bliss' in his gaze. The problem of who is and is not a true guru is therefore finally the devotee's problem, not the guru's problem. Only the devotee can feel the feelings that make a sant satguru; indeed, coming to feel such feelings is the devotee's main task. Put slightly differently, the so-called succession problem is really the process of redemption seeking by another name. To be on the road to salvation means asserting, on the basis of inner recognition, someone's 'true' guruship, appearances and the disbelief of others to the contrary notwithstanding.

Obviously, therefore, interregnum is a built-in feature of the soteriological style cultivated at Soami Bagh. Interregnum exists for any devotee who is seeking but has not yet found, and as such is a spiritual opportunity. Even to *seek* a sant satguru in the midst of the world's delusions is salutary, and a sign of inner fitness. In the meantime the relics take the edge off salvationary anxieties. But even more important, without uncertainty on the matter of guruship, there could be no *active* recognition, and it is recognition that underlies the tradition's salvationary promise. Recognition of a sant satguru in the context of apparent interregnum is, from this standpoint, a form of perfected devotion. Obviously there will be disagreements about who is the 'true' sant satguru. By its very nature, being a sant satguru is being the Lord in a form that cannot be recognized by all. Calumny, the tradition proclaims, is the 'watchdog' of faith. It is exactly in the gap between what others regard as obvious, and what the devotee knows to be the truth, that the path to redemption is found.

Admittedly the present interregnum at Soami Bagh may be, by some standards, overly prolonged, and in this there may indeed be a 'succession problem.' But if there is, it can be traced not to the tradition as such, but to the creation of the Administrative Council. I suspect the council was formed without full appreciation of the inconsistency between the idea of individual inner recognition of a sant satguru and corporate recognition by a preexisting group. Whether an already constituted group can ever achieve inner consensus on such matters is at least an open question, although the Dayal Bagh group may have succeeded in this at some level. For the present it seems unlikely that the Soami Bagh congregation will ever achieve such consensus as a whole.

And this may presage basic changes in the way the Radhasoami outlook is construed at Soami Bagh. The Radhasoami tradition is not one that valorizes pasts. What matters is the present, spent in the 'company' of the sant satguru of one's own time. But for the Soami Bagh community the emphasis seems to be shifting from a focus on 'now' to 'since then.' Individual surrender to a living guru has been largely superseded by recruitment by birth in congregation families. Increasingly visible are the outlines of a community, persisting through time, that periodically reconstitutes itself in the presence of symbols that recall a formative past. In this we see evidence that this congregation may well be on the verge of exemplifying what Daniel Gold has characterized as the movement from *paramparā* to *panth* (1982, 173).

But the congregation is not quite at that point yet, for in the meantime older images retain their energy. 'The current is still with us,' one is told, and there is no doubt that older members of the congregation are still able to preserve freshness in their 'inner' relationship with the last sant satguru. Furthermore, there have in fact been more recent gurus in the Soami Bagh ambit, albeit without official recognition. For other devotees congregational satsang, individual spiritual practice, and contact with the relics of the past continue to confer what are considered to be spiritual benefits. That, for now, is how matters stand.

In all events, these various usages define a distinctive form of religious life. Here we find a coherent definition of the human situation vis-à-vis the world, and a vision of redemptive possibilities. The devotee's object is to become fully realized as the emanation of the Supreme Being that he or she always was. With such realization comes release from the travails of existence in a world that is alien to the self's true nature—as defined, that is, by Radhasoami concepts of the self. Few indeed can expect salvation in one lifetime. But given Radhasoami assumptions about the nature of the world, the sant satguru's leavings, the water from the well at Soami Bagh, and the like are physical media through which devotees—if they learn to love them—can know themselves, in the most extended sense of knowing, as ones who will feel the pain of death but little and will surely find their way home again.

II. Amnesia and Remembrance among the Brahma Kumaris

4. Dada Lekhraj and the Daughters of Brahma

Doom

The end of the world by the combined means of natural catastrophe, civil strife, and (apparently) nuclear holocaust was predicted by an Indian religious visionary in the late 1930s. The prophet was an elderly Sindhi businessman of Hindu background named Dada Lekhraj. In what he took to be divinely inspired visions, he foresaw the destruction of the world in a series of vast calamities. His visions also revealed that following the great destruction a paradise will be established on earth. This paradise will be a world quite unlike the one we know now. Its population will be tiny, and there will be food in abundance for all. There will be no competition, and therefore no strife. Nature will be kind: never too hot, never too cold, each day perfect. Death will be a painless shedding of bodies to be followed by rebirth and resumption of perfect happiness. This will also be a world—and this was a point to which Lekhraj gave much emphasis—in which the sexes will exist in perfect equality.

The message was clear: prepare now for the end to come and the new world thereafter. The end, Lekhraj said, is imminent; preparations must be made quickly. All, or nearly all, of the vast population of the globe will be consumed, and only a small spiritual elite will be able to inhabit the heavenly world to come. Very few will hear God's warning. Fewer still will act on it. But for those who can truly hear the call, and who have the inner strength to 'purify' themselves and to persevere in the face of the world's disbelief and disapprobation, a heavenly kingdom is waiting.

Lekhraj's warnings and promises ultimately became the core doctrines of a Hindu sect that outlived its founder (who died in 1969) and flourishes today. They are known as the *Brahmā Kumārīs*. The group does not usually translate this name into English, but when they do, they prefer to render it as 'Daughters of Brahmā.'[1] It is regarded primarily as a women's movement, although it has many male adherents. The sect has adopted the institutional persona of an 'educational' institution devoted to the teaching of yoga and what is called spiritual 'knowledge' (*gyān*). In consonance with this image, its official name is *prajāpitā brahmākumārī īshvarīya vishvavidyālaya*, that is, 'The Prajapita Brahma Kumari Divine (or 'Godly' in their own English rendering) University.' The headquarters of this institution are at Mt. Abu in Rajasthan.

With a claimed membership of 100,000, the movement is not large by Indian standards. It is, however, a well-established and conspicuous feature of the religious landscape in urban India, especially in the north. It is particularly active in Delhi. In recent years it has been vigorously internationalizing, and movement centers now exist in Britain, Australia, the United States, and many other countries. It has also managed to become affiliated to the Department of Public Information of the United Nations, and the UN logo is displayed on some movement publications.

In urban India, as a result of its extremely energetic proselytizing, the movement has a visibility out of proportion to its size. As far as I am aware, no Hindu sect has ever sought converts with the single-minded dedication of the Brahma Kumaris. This activity is associated with an institutional style quite distinctive of the movement. They are inveterate sponsors of exhibitions, often associated with Hindu festivals, to which they give wide publicity in newspaper advertisements. These exhibitions are designed to bring outsiders into contact with the rudiments of the Brahma Kumari belief system as portrayed in displays of vivid poster-sized pictorial illustrations. These depict the destruction of the world, the paradise to come, and many other points of Brahma Kumari doctrine. Visitors are shown the pictures, encouraged to purchase literature, and urged to visit one of the movement's many local centers. The movement also sponsors elaborate conferences, often on the theme of world peace, for which

---

[1] In the Hindu pantheon Brahmā is the deity responsible for the creation of the world. His various attributes are described in standard works on the pantheon (see, e.g., Danielou 1964). As we shall see, Lekhraj is identified with this deity and is regarded as the 'father' of movement members. *Kumārī* can also be rendered as 'maiden' or 'princess.' As will be seen, these meanings are also consistent with the movement's teachings. A female member of the sect is a *brahmā kumārī*; a male member, a *brahmā kumār*. From this point forward I shall give the sect's name without diacritics, as they themselves do in their English writings.

massive publicity is generated. A common feature of these occurrences is the legitimacy-conferring display of Indian and foreign dignitaries and foreign members of the movement. Probably most people become aware of the movement's existence as a result of these and similar activities.

The true heart of the movement is in its local centers, of which there are said to be some eight hundred, large and small. The larger centers, usually called 'Rāja Yoga Centres' or 'Spiritual Museums,' are located at major urban concourses, and are readily identifiable as Brahma Kumari institutions. Facing the street is typically a large example of the movement's distinctive artwork and a sign identifying the movement center within. The central feature of such a center is likely to be a gallery of pictures, the 'museum.' During visiting hours movement members conduct visitors from picture to picture, explaining the points of doctrine that each picture illustrates. Congregational meditation and classes (discussed in more detail in chapter 5) are also held in the morning and evening. The purpose of the museum is to persuade visitors to attend the classes and meditation sessions, which are where the real life of the movement takes place. The center is also the residence of a few fully 'surrendered' movement members, typically women, who conduct the classes and maintain the building.

The Brahma Kumari movement is regarded with considerable suspicion by many in Indian society, which is probably not always fully appreciated by foreign adherents. When the sect was formed, it was bitterly opposed by outsiders and Lekhraj was considered by many to be a kind of evil magician whose main motive was to engage in sexual misconduct with his female followers. Similar attitudes continue to linger around the movement today. 'I am afraid of them,' the daughter of a recently converted elderly couple bluntly said to me, and in doing so she expressed what seems to be a widespread feeling. Most nonmovement middle-class informants with whom I discussed the Brahma Kumaris expressed negative attitudes.

At first glance it is not at all clear why Lekhraj's movement should evoke such distrust. On the surface the movement's symbols are very familiar ones in the Hindu milieu and are surrounded by a halo of highly conventional legitimacy. The Brahma Kumaris are advocates of yoga, which they say will bring peace of mind. They urge vegetarianism, abstinence from tobacco and alcohol, and celibacy. In none of this is there anything truly novel or objectionable. Yoga, or at least the idea of it, is deeply respected in Hindu India. Vegetarianism and teetotalism are practiced by millions for reasons of caste custom and/or religion. While celibacy has always been regarded with some unease in Indian civilization, it is nonetheless a time-honored religious value (though by no means, as some believe, a supreme value). Lekhraj's warning of imminent doom might be construed as bad tidings, but whether such a prediction is regarded as lunatic or merely realistic, there is nothing in it that touches especially sensitive nerves in the Hindu world.

The source of the tension, rather, is at a somewhat deeper level. It has to do with women. From its earliest days the movement has been mainly associated with women. This in itself raises no problems. In many ways women have always been the true custodians of what is called 'popular Hinduism.' However, the involvement of women in a movement that advocates celibacy is quite another matter. As we shall see, this constitutes a direct challenge to the prevailing imagery of who women are and what they should be in the social order. Dada Lekhraj characterized the present human situation as an 'emergency.' Doom is imminent, and every remaining moment counts; drastic measures are required by drastic times. In the little time left the only way to gain a place in heaven is by means of *radical* self-purification. Therefore, the celibacy that was in the past reserved for the *sannyāsī* (male world-renouncer) is now required of all who wish for true salvation, male and female alike. The result was, and remains, what many outsiders see as a kind of madness or worse.

Sind Workis

The cultural and social setting out of which the Brahma Kumari movement emerged was the 'Sind Worki' (*sindhvarkī*) merchant community of Hyderabad in the region of Sind (now part of Pakistan). Belonging to the Lohāna trading caste (on which see Aitken 1907, 185–86), the Sind Workis emerged as an elite class of merchants during the second half of the nineteenth century. They began as hawkers of Sindhi handicrafts ('Sind Work') in European settlements, and they prospered greatly. By the time the sect started to form, their businesses had taken them to other parts of India and overseas, where many had made quite sizable fortunes (Thakur 1959, 37–38). Informants characterize the Sind Worki men of those days as being rather conservative culturally, but because of business opportunities outside Sind, many were also quite cosmopolitan.

But if the world was wide for Sind Worki men, for their wives and daughters matters were very different. Their world was the household, within which most of them were secluded. Excursions beyond the house were customarily limited to family gatherings and ceremonials and visits to religious institutions. The education of these women tended to be desultory at best, and in general their lives were circumscribed by the many restrictions of movement and contact with outsiders characteristic of northern India's upper castes and classes.

There is some evidence suggesting that the women's world of household and family was a troubled one at the time the movement began. At the root of this was the commercial life of Sind Worki men. Because of business activities abroad, these men often lived away from home for years at a time, and the result was a pattern of absentee husbandship. The statistical incidence of this pattern cannot be determined from existing evidence, since the society in question was long ago dispersed by the migration to India at the time of the partition between India and Pakistan. However, the accounts of older Sindhi informants and the Brahma Kumaris' own portrayal of the period suggest that absentee husbandship was at least pronounced enough to have disrupted some families, and also to have generated strong negative stereotypes of the life-styles of Sind Worki men and of family life in the Sind Worki community more generally.

For example, at the time the movement began to form, popular belief held that absentee husbands formed extramarital unions while abroad.[2] Although a double standard of sexual morality was certainly nothing new in India, and although we have no way of knowing to what degree such allegations were true, it is reasonable to conjecture that these images of the lives of absent husbands could have been quite damaging to the morale of their wives and daughters, and also to the esteem in which they held the patriarchal family as an institution. This would certainly be consistent with the importance the idea of the libertine husband was to assume in the Brahma Kumari critique of the family.

Another stereotype of the time, reported by informants, is the sex-starved wife languishing at home while her husband has his good times abroad. This also might or might not have been the case, but judging by autobiographical accounts of the period, some women in this community were evidently quite dissatisfied with their lives in

[2] Informants presented such allegations to me as facts.

traditional families.[3] Women were expected to fulfill the usual obligations of wives and mothers in traditional seclusion. However, the families within which they were expected to do so were sometimes truncated because of the absence of key male figures. More importantly, rumor and local stereotype proclaimed that the men in these families were leading lives of sin when away and out of sight. Indeed, according to the Brahma Kumaris, these men were habitually given to vices of all kinds even at home.

The matter of male corruption seems to have been much on the minds of the women who composed the early core of the Brahma Kumari movement. What they stress in their depiction of the period is the moral hypocrisy inherent in the marriage relationship (see esp. Chandar n.d., 11). Husbands, they say, were supposed to be 'gurus' and 'deities' to their wives (this is, in fact, a standard Hindu usage), but their behavior was often brutish and quite ungodlike. They treated women as 'dolls' for sexual enjoyment, and were certainly unworthy of worship by their wives. The extent to which men ever really adhered to the rules of virtuous family life is another matter, but it is apparent that by the 1930s they were perceived by some women not to be playing by the rules, which called into question (for some) the legitimacy of the game itself.

Visions

Dada Lekhraj was a wealthy jeweler who was born in 1876 to a family belonging to the Kriplānī clan. His father was a schoolmaster in a village near Hyderabad, and Lekhraj himself was a reasonably well-educated man. He was fully literate in Sindhi, of course, and could read religious writings in Hindi with ease. He was also able to read the *Guru Granth Sāhib* (the sacred book of the Sikhs) in Gurmukhi, and could follow English newspapers. He apparently had a sizable English vocabulary, for his recorded discourses are peppered with English terms (though tightly embedded in Hindi constructions). His later notoriety seems in no way to have been foreshadowed by his life prior to the formation of the sect. He is said by older Sindhi informants to have been quite an ordinary man, just another rich Sindhi merchant.

It is probably significant, however, that his trade was jewelry.

[3] These accounts are preserved in Lekhraj's official biography (Chandar n.d.). The following discussion of the movement's history is based mainly on details given in this book, supplemented by conversations with informants inside and outside the movement.

A jeweler is a specialist in women's ornaments, and we may surmise that Lekhraj, therefore, came into more intimate contact with women who were nonkin than would have been normal for a man of his class and time. It is conceivable that this contact could have fostered a more than ordinary insight into women's problems. His business also brought him into contact with another group that seems to have played a major role in his revelations: royalty. According to his biographers (Chandar n.d., 12–14; *Pita shri* n.d., 1–2), Lekhraj was regarded with extraordinary friendliness and respect by the Rajas and Maharajas (Udaipur and Nepal are mentioned specifically) to whom he sold jewelry, and was even allowed more or less free access to their palaces, including the women's quarters. These accounts may exaggerate, but they do indicate that he probably had a fair degree of familiarity with some of the surface aspects of palace life. As we shall see later, royal symbolism is central to Lekhraj's conception of heaven, just as the life-style of worldly and cosmopolitan Sindhi merchants provided the foundation for his concept of hell.

Dada Lekhraj became a prophet late in life. Although he was a lifelong vegetarian and teetotaler (or at least is represented as such in the movement's hagiography), and a man of strong if conventional piety (apparently of Vallabāchārī background), it was only when he was about sixty years old that he began to acquire prophetic insight, which became manifest for the first time in a series of startling and totally unexpected visions (*sākshātkārs*). In sudden transports he saw Vishnu in his four-armed form, and also Shiva as a *jyotir lingam* (a column of light). But the most significant of all was a horrendous vision in which he witnessed the destruction of the world He reported that he saw civil strife, vast natural calamities, and monstrous weapons being used in a cataclysmic war. He saw tens of millions of the souls of the dead flying upward 'as moths flutter in the direction of a light' (Chandar n.d., 22)

Much jolted by these strange experiences he began to wind up his business affairs. After settling accounts with his partner in Calcutta, he returned to his native Hyderabad where he had further extraordinary visions. On one momentous day he quite suddenly rose from a congregational ceremony occurring in his house and retired to his room. He was followed there by his wife and daughter-in-law, who (they later reported) were astonished to see that his eyes were glowing as if there were a red light burning within his head. His face and the whole room, they said, were suffused with red luminescence. When at last he descended from what was clearly a trance of some kind, he said that he had seen a strange 'light' emanating from a vast power and a 'new world' where 'stars' descended to become princesses and princes. A mighty being, he said, was instructing him to 'make such a world as this' (ibid., 26).

In any case this is what we are told of Dada Lekhraj's earliest revelations. The problem, of course, is that all that we know of these experiences has been filtered through his own recollections and those of his followers. These recollections are certainly conditioned by the complex Brahma Kumari doctrinal system, which took time to mature, and in which they later became embedded. What Lekhraj made of his experiences at the time he had them (for there is little doubt that he did have visions of some kind) cannot really be known. In retrospect, the tradition represents Lekhraj as having been quite puzzled at first, but soon coming to a divinely inspired recognition of the meaning of what had been happening to him. He was being given *gītā gyān*, the true 'knowledge,' of the *Bhagavad Gītā*.[4] Its source was Shiva, the Supreme Soul (in the Brahma Kumari view), who had chosen Lekhraj to be his earthly medium (*sākar madhyam*). Like Arjuna in the *Gītā*, he had been shown the Lord's true form in both benign and terrible aspects. From Shiva he also learned that persons are really immaterial selves or 'souls' (*ātmās*), not the bodies they seem to be. The world that we now know is soon to be destroyed, sending these souls heavenward like the moths in his earlier vision. But some souls, the stars, will descend to rule a new and heavenly world. These lucky few will become deities in the world to come, and Lekhraj himself will become the deity Nārāyaṇ.[5]

These extraordinary occurrences and revelations must have thrown Lekhraj's household into a considerable uproar. We are told that family members at first could not understand what had come over him. His behavior was odd indeed (these details from ibid., 28ff.). He began saying to all of his friends and relatives, 'You are a soul' (*tum ātmā ho*); and then he began writing out 'I am a soul, Jasoda is a soul, Radhika is a soul,' and so on. For several days he remained in his house, and people began to come to sit and listen to his discourses. At

---

[4] The *Bhagavad Gītā* is an extremely important Hindu text—said to have been Lekhraj's lifelong favorite—that forms part of the epic *Mahābhārata*. Consisting of a dialogue between Arjuna and his charioteer, the deity Krishna, the text announces a theistic religion based on devotion to God and the renunciation of the fruits of action.

[5] One of the names of Vishnu, a major Hindu deity.

first came relatives and friends, and then strangers. Retrospection proclaims that they came because he had a 'hidden power,' that his discourses gave 'coolness' to the troubled heart, and that there was an 'unearthly light' in his 'gaze' (*drishti*) (ibid.). But of all the attractions, the greatest was almost certainly that under Lekhraj's influence others began to enter what they called *dhyānāvas'hā* (a contemplative state) and to have visions similar to his.

Most of those who initially came to Lekhraj seem to have been women from the wealthy business families of Hyderabad. This social class was his natural milieu, and that it was women whom he mainly attracted is not surprising. Women, particularly older women, often provide the principal constituencies of lesser saints and gurus.[6] From this standpoint Lekhraj was initially little more than just another minor religious visionary with a certain local renown. His followers called him 'Om Bābā,' and the group around him began to be known as the *om mandli* (*om*, a sacred syllable representing the Absolute; *mandli*, 'circle' or 'association'). This was the core of what was to become the Brahma Kumari movement. In 1937 Lekhraj established a Managing Committee of several women followers, with his principal disciple, a woman known as Om Radhe, named as 'In Charge.' In early 1938 he turned his entire fortune over to this group.

These events created an immediate sensation in the surrounding society. An elderly Sindhi informant, an adult at the time of the events in question, recalls his own impressions of what happened as follows (I paraphrase):

> Then we learned that he [Lekhraj] had given up his business. We heard that he had come into contact with some *yogī*, and started a religious organization known as *om mandli*. Furthermore, it was learned that young married women were going to his *āshram*. We also heard that there was a vow of chastity involved. Now the community, especially the merchant community, was not really ready to absorb this. These were men with a lot of money; they were interested in good living, and this included sex. There was a lot of resistence from husbands. There was a real 'hue and cry' both in the city [Hyderabad] and in the province as a whole.

Backlash

It is not clear when *brahmacharya* (celibacy) became one of Lekhraj's teachings, but it was apparently very early in his prophetic career.

---

[6] For a good discussion of this pattern in another region of India, see Roy's *Bengali Women* (1975).

What is clear is that this tenet provoked an immense uproar. Husbands would return from long stays abroad only to discover that their wives had made vows of chastity and wished to change their homes into 'temples.' Wife and husband, these men were told, should live as 'Lakshmī' and 'Nārāyan' and should love each other with pure 'spiritual love' (*ātmik sneh*), that is, with asexual love.[7] These and similar confrontations created great and painful disruptions in many families.

The result was a savage reaction. Husbands and their families frequently responded with beatings, wife expulsions, and lawsuits for the reinstatement of conjugal rights. Lekhraj himself was regarded with deep suspicion. Some accused him of sorcery, and many believed that he was a man of inexhaustible sexual appetite whose real motive was the seduction of his female disciples. One informant, a boy at the time, told of being ordered by his mother to avert his eyes from Lekhraj's āshram as they passed by. Irate and despairing relatives of movement members formed an 'anti-om mandlī' association, and the local press undertook a campaign against the sect. Families of members were threatened with caste excommunication, and some of Lekhraj's women followers were forced to eat meat and locked in solitude by their families. Street rowdies insulted and intimidated members, and in 1938 an angry mob set a movement building afire.

In actuality the issue was never simply the denial of sexual pleasures to men, which in itself, in the Hindu context, might well motivate, but could hardly justify, the ferocity of the backlash that greeted the movement. A more fundamental issue concerned the family and the position of women within the family. In the Hindu world for an as yet unmarried or married woman to renounce her sexuality is for her to express a radical and unacceptable autonomy. It means withholding her maternal power, which she denies in the first instance to her natal family, whose right it is to bestow that power on another family in marriage, and in the second instance to her conjugal family, into whose service marriage consigns her.

Because the Brahma Kumari movement began in such tumult, its initial consolidation occurred in a seclusion necessitated by the hostility of the surrounding society. In effect driven from Hyderabad, Lekhraj and his followers sequestered themselves in Karachi. Here there were further confrontations with hostile outsiders, but in the end they were left in relative peace to develop their own style of life as

---

[7] Lakshmī is the wife of Nārāyan (Vishnu), and the Hindu goddess of prosperity. According to the Brahma Kumaris, their union is chaste.

a religious community. Lekhraj and Om Radhe (later also known as Sarasvati) ultimately presided as surrogate father and mother over a predominantly female following numbering about three hundred. Money was apparently not a problem. Lekhraj's personal fortune was large, and although donations were not solicited from outsiders, sympathetic relatives of members (such did exist) must have contributed something. It is also likely that some converts brought wealth of their own into the movement.

Isolation and Reemergence

During the ensuing years the doctrinal system and subculture of the movement matured into their present forms. A major theme, one that informed practically everything Lekhraj said, was that of separation from the surrounding benighted world. He told his followers that in joining the movement they had undergone a 'death-in-life' birth (*marjiva janam*). They had 'died,' he said, to their 'worldly' (*laukik*) families, and had been reborn as children in a 'divine family' (*ishvariya kul* or *ishvariya kutumb*). He therefore gave them new (and divinely inspired) names. He characterized the movement as a fiery 'sacrifice' (*yagya*) in which members would purify themselves and acquire spiritual power, thus becoming worthy to inherit the kingdom to come. He also revealed that he himself was Brahma (the creator-deity of the Hindu pantheon) and the agency of the Lord's creation of the new world. Many other details (which will be discussed in chapter 5) were disclosed as well. Those among his followers who had the gift of 'divine sight' (*divya drishti*) also had visions in which they saw every detail of life as it would be in the coming paradise, and much else too.

This small and highly insular community was a first-class psychological pressure-cooker. Most members had little contact with the outside world, and within the community, life was rigidly ordered. Members would arise to the sound of recorded devotional music. Early mornings were devoted to the practice of yoga and listening to Lekhraj's daily discourses. These discourses were called *muralis*, in reference to the flute with which Krishna summoned the *gopis* of Braj. The remainder of the day was given over to the various daily tasks necessary to maintain the community, with some time off for rest in the afternoon. The evening hours were again devoted mainly to yoga and religious instruction. There were occasionally weeks of 'silence' during which some members would subsist entirely on fruit and engage in uninterrupted yoga.

The pressure to conform was evidently very great. The *sandesh putrīs* (message-daughters), as they were called, would often have visions of the secret delinquencies and hidden unworthy desires of other members. The guilty parties were openly confronted with such revelations. These visionaries also saw the divine punishments (to be inflicted by 'Dharmrāj,' the god of death as King of Justice) that awaited sinners, which they vividly described to the community. We are told that from time to time a 'court' (*kachehrī*) was held in the evening. Those who were guilty of some failure or infraction during the day were expected to confess their guilt to Lekhraj and Om Radhe before the entire community.

Under the circumstances it is scarcely surprising that, perhaps at the price of considerable personal anguish (of which we are told nothing), a community of extraordinary solidarity emerged. Had Lekhraj and his followers been left alone at the start (a cultural impossibility, given his teachings), the result might have been quite different. However, the reaction of the surrounding society forced Lekhraj and his followers in upon themselves in a condition of nearly windowless isolation. A community evolved that was deeply consensual and essentially indifferent to the disesteem of the rest of the world. Its image of itself was familial, and its discipline was quasi-military. The military reference is not farfetched; the Brahma Kumari movement often characterized itself as the *pāndav senā*, the 'Pāndava Army,'[8] engaged in nonviolent war with the vices and impurities that characterize life in the present world.

An important legacy of this period in the movement's development was doctrinal, for this was when the full systematization of the Brahma Kumari belief system occurred (though fine-tuning continues even today). But an even more critical legacy was the development of bonds among those at the core of the movement that were deep and lasting enough to enable the movement not only to survive, but later to enter a new phase of vigorous expansion. It is likely that the intensity of the Brahma Kumaris' communal life reinforced the plausibility of Lekhraj's vision of the future. As E. J. Hobsbawm has pointed out (1959, 62), in millenarian movements the believability of the idea of the complete transformation of the world is supported by

[8]   The Pāndavas are the five sons of Pandu, king of the Kurus, and the heroes of the *Mahābhārata* war.

adherents' perceptions of the utter changes the movement has created in their own lives.

In 1947 partition came, and Hindus began leaving Sind, which had become part of Pakistan. The Brahma Kumaris were unmolested, but finally in 1950 they moved to India and their present headquarters at Mt. Abu. By this time their financial condition was very precarious, but I was told by a movement informant that they were rescued by a large anonymous donation.

Following the move, they first resumed their former seclusion. Gradually, however, a change occurred in the general outlook of the sect. Lekhraj had previously stressed the image of the movement as an isolated 'sacrifice,' but now he began to emphasize active proselytization. It is likely that this resulted in part from the concern that he and his followers must have felt about the future of a movement of celibates. In part, too, he was probably encouraged by the fact that the movement no longer had to confront the entrenched prejudices of Sindhi society. In any case, he began to speak of the former seclusion, which he compared to the Pāṇḍavas' exile in the *Mahābhārata*, as a period of necessary preparation for the real mission of the movement. This was to be the awakening of the *bhakta*s (devotees, or in this case, nonmembers of the movement) from their ignorance and spiritual slumber.

To some degree Lekhraj had already gone public. He had published pamphlets almost from the start, and he was an inveterate writer of letters to important public figures (Gandhi, the king of England, and many others) in which he interpreted the meaning of contemporary events in the light of his revealed knowledge. He began to intensify all of these activities, and some of the most gifted movement members began to visit major Indian cities to spread the word. The first permanent 'Rāja Yoga Centre' was established in Delhi in 1953, with centers in other cities soon to follow. By the time Lekhraj died in 1969, the outer persona of the movement had changed fundamentally. What was previously a highly reclusive sect had become an aggressively proselytizing movement. Internationalization was begun in 1971 with the establishment of centers in Hong Kong and London, and by 1978 beachheads had been established in New York and San Francisco (Streitfeld 1982, 8).

A nonmovement Sindhi informant recalls reacting to all this with astonishment. For years, he said, Dada Lekhraj's om maṇḍlī seemed simply to have vanished, but then it suddenly popped up again under a new name, the Brahma Kumaris. And as if this were not enough, this once-despised group had somehow managed to become a world-wide organization.

Following Lekhraj's death the leadership of the movement was assumed jointly by two senior women members. As far as an outsider can tell, this arrangement has worked smoothly. There was apparently some confusion at first concerning authoritative access to divine commandments. Prior to his death, Lekhraj was the medium through whom Shiva, the Supreme Soul, spoke to the movement. I was told by a movement informant that in the immediate aftermath of his death there was an upsurge in visions and trances in various movement centers. In effect, this represented a potential dispersal of sacred authority. This threat was dealt with by stipulating that Shiva would only enter the body of one particular woman (a senior movement member), and would do so only during specified periods at Mt. Abu. I do not know how compliance with this injunction was gained. During the period of my contact with the group a warning against unauthorized trances was appended to one of the morning sermons that are distributed in mimeograph to all local centers from central headquarters at Mt. Abu. This suggests that centrifugal forces continue to be perceived as a potential problem.

Within the framework of this organization a religious subculture of remarkable uniformity has continued to evolve. A movement center in Madras or Bangalore can hardly be distinguished from one in Delhi. The uniformity of the movement has two foundations. One is the close ties that core personnel maintain with Mt. Abu, as reinforced by frequent visits there. The other is the complete standardization of the movement's teachings through the medium of the morning sermons. Dada Lekhraj is said to have produced a murali, a discourse, every day of his life subsequent to his enlightenment. Not all of these were recorded, but thousands exist, and are mailed from headquarters to local centers to be read to congregations on a daily basis during morning services. As already noted, after Lekhraj's death Shiva continued to speak to the movement through a senior woman member. These discourses are also distributed to be read at local centers. What is stated in the muralis constitutes the principal standard of doctrinal orthodoxy among the Brahma Kumaris.

Warnings

When seen in close juxtaposition, the Radhasoami and Brahma Kumari movements present a picture of radical contrast. Two contrastive features stand out with particular clarity, and each of these raises important questions to be pursued in the following two chapters. First, there is the matter of women. Radhasoami teachings are simply not of the sort that raise basic questions about the role of women in social life. In comparison, the Brahma Kumari sect is a genuinely feminist movement, although its feminism is expressed in a distinctively Hindu idiom. To put it mildly, whatever the Radhasoami tradition may be, it is by no stretch of the imagination feminist.

But there is another difference, which has to do with history and time. Radhasoami teachings are little concerned with the future. It must be noted in qualification that the Soami Bagh community does await Soamiji Maharaj's ultimate return as a svatah sant, but this is a minor theme, essentially submerged in the more fundamental emphasis on finding and interacting with a sant satguru of one's own era. Dada Lekhraj, on the other hand, was obsessed with warnings and promises of 'things to come.' He tried to force the world into an orientation toward a significant future that held both appalling and hopeful prospects. This orientation seemed to give life in the present—for those who could hear and understand his message—a special rationale.

Lekhraj's concern with the future raises fundamental problems. On the face of things there is nothing very surprising about such prophecies. Dire predictions about the end of the world, and hopeful promises about the world thereafter, have been heard many times before and since, and they express themes that are well known to students of religion as 'millenarian.' In Indic studies, however, this entire matter has a special import, for it has been suggested that South Asian religious culture is essentially inhospitable to the spirit of millenarian prophecy. E. J. Hobsbawm, for example, says that millenarian expectations are 'alien to such religions as Hinduism and Buddhism' (1959, 58). Yonina Talmon asserts that 'religions in which history has no meaning whatsoever and religions which have a cyclical repetitive conception of time are not conducive to millenarism.' 'Otherworldly religions,' she goes on to suggest, 'do not give rise to the vision of the kingdom of god on earth,' which explains why 'there is apparently no apocalyptic tradition in Hinduism and why it has not occupied an important place in Buddhism' (1965, 531). Obviously if Hobsbawm and Talmon are right, then Lekhraj's warning presents us with a puzzle.

At stake is an issue of broad significance. 'Is it true,' Norman Cohn asks, 'that those world-views (such as the Christian, the Jewish and the Moslem) which include the idea of divine will working through history provide a better climate for millenarism than world-views which know nothing of divine purpose and see history as an unending series of cycles?' (1962, 43). The answer would seem to be yes. Whatever else millenarianism might be, it is a way of taking history seriously. Where history is depreciated, devalued, or ignored, millenarian ideas would not seem to stand a chance of finding much intellectual or psychological foothold. The Indic world has often seemed to be a world in which history is in some sense devalued. For example, the point of Heinrich Zimmer's justly celebrated retelling of the story of the 'parade of ants' is that the Hindu theory of cyclical history empties historical occurrences of value; even Indra's apparently momentous conquest of Vritra is meaningless when it is revealed that infinite Indras have so triumphed infinite times before (Zimmer 1962, 3–11).

And yet Lekhraj's eschatology turns out to be far from novel in the Hindu world. The myth of Kalkin, the tenth *avatār* of Vishnu who will come to restore *dharma* at the end of the present age of evil (a theme echoed in the Soami Bagh idea of the master's return), clearly reflects millenarian ideas, and Steven Fuchs (1965) has found enough examples of messianism in India to fill a medium-sized book. It may be that Kalkin's image has been largely peripheral to the true core of popular Hinduism, and perhaps the movements described by Fuchs are mostly at the fringes of the Hindu world among tribals and the recently detribalized. Nevertheless, these instances at least indicate that, despite Hobsbawm and Talmon's conclusions, millenarian expectations can indeed arise in a Hindu environment.

The cloudiness surrounding this issue may result from overly narrow understandings of what Hindu views of time and history really are. For example, Wilfred Cantwell Smith (writing as an Islamicist) states that in the Hindu world-view 'history is not significant' (1977, 21). This opinion is not outrageously wrong, since in context it illuminates an important contrast between the Islamic and Hindu traditions, but it doesn't encourage alertness to subtleties. The real issue is not whether history 'is significant,' but rather *how* history matters. There is no reason to believe that history always matters the same way in the Hindu tradition. Consider the Western world, which has produced Hegel, Marx, and Toynbee, and accepts such disparate accounts of the world's origin as those of Genesis and the big-bang cosmology. This is a cultural universe that has no single theory of history. Why must we assume, then, that there is a single, basic Hindu account of how time passes or what history means? If there is evidence for distinctive *tendencies* in Hindu historical cosmology (and I hope to show there is), this does not mean there is consensus on everything. One of the most notable features of Hinduism has always been the adaptability of some of its most basic concepts and symbols. The same is true of Hindu historical cosmology. It is not a single view, but a range of possible views, in which different ideas can be handled differently for different purposes.

Lekhraj's warning is an excellent example of the malleability of the Hindu tradition. The great emphasis he gave to the imminence of universal doom is certainly unusual in this tradition, but it is far closer to other Hindu systems, including the Radhasoami system, than it might at first seem to be. We have seen that Lekhraj gave unusual attention to the future. To this, however, it is now necessary to add a crucial, and hitherto unmentioned, fact: when Lekhraj predicted the future, he also recovered a past. He believed that the coming destruction of the world had already occurred countless times before. From this standpoint Lekhraj's warning was not really 'prophetic' in the narrow sense, nor was it truly novel. The idea that the world ends in periodic calamities is common coin in the Hindu world (and is part of the Radhasoami belief-system). In this respect Lekhraj's warning was simply a retelling of a well-known tale.

But the matter does not end there. If the idea that the world ends in periodic catastrophes was not new, what Lekhraj did with it was quite innovative. He had found a way to invest the end of the world with a new and urgent meaning. This meaning could, among other things, bring a certain kind of social discontent, that of women with traditionally sanctioned feminine roles, into the sphere of Hindu soteriology. He achieved this remarkable result, in part, by adopting a deceptively simple expedient: he drastically speeded up the traditional historical cycle.

5. History as Movie

Souls

At the heart of Dada Lekhraj's teachings was the familiar problem of identity. Who are you? was the question he always asked his followers, and this continues to be the first question put to potential members of the Brahma Kumari movement today. The answer to this question was both simple and, considering Lekhraj's lack of theological sophistication, impressively complex. You are, Lekhraj said, not the body you seem to be but an immortal soul. You are a soul with a complex history. The principal message of Brahma Kumari teachings lies in what he meant by this.

According to the fully matured Brahma Kumari doctrinal system, the universe consists of two utterly dissimilar elements: material nature (*prakriti*) and a vast number of nonmaterial selves or 'souls' (ātmās).[1] Material nature constantly shifts and flows; it is incessantly in motion. This motion is the history of the world. Our bodies are made of coarse matter and belong entirely to material nature. But although we tend to identify with our bodies, we are actually souls. Unlike material things, souls are indestructable (*avināshī*). Each soul is a massless point of brightness and power, invisible to the physical eyes, that has been drawn into engagement with matter. Its location in the body is at the middle of the forehead. The soul's mistaken identity with the material body that it happens to inhabit is the root of the human predicament.

Souls have a 'true home,' and this is a region of perfect peace and absolute silence at the top of the universe known as *paramdhām* (the supreme abode) or *brahmlok* (the world of Brahm). As imaged by Brahma Kumari teachings, the universe has the shape of an egg (see Figure 4).

[1] My basic sources for the doctrinal details to follow are the 'classes' I attended (during which I took extensive notes) and informal conversations with movement teachers and lay members. This was supplemented by extensive reading in the movement's literature. Especially helpful was the movement's catechism entitled *One Week Course*.

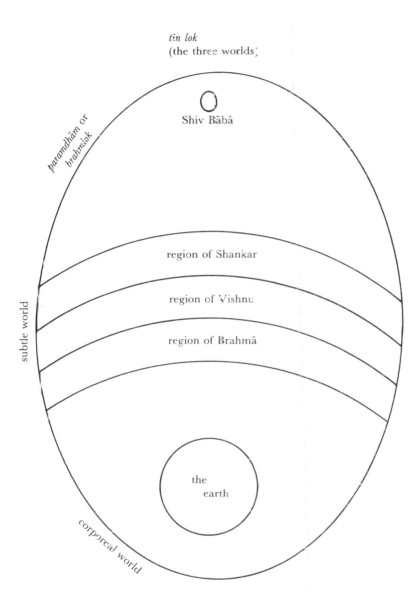

tin lok
(the three worlds)

Shiv Bābā

parandhām or
brahmlok

region of Shankar

region of Vishnu

region of Brahmā

subtle world

the
earth

corporeal world

Figure 4. The Brahma Kumari Universe (simplified from standard pictures)

At its apex is the Supreme Soul known as Shiv Bābā (the Hindu deity Shiva), and paramdhām is the region around him. This zone is silent, void of movement, and is suffused by a reddish glow. Beneath paramdhām is the 'subtle world' (*suksham lok*), which is the region of the 'subtle deities' (*suksham devatās*)—Brahmā, Vishnu, and Shankar,[2] who are responsible, respectively, for the creation, preservation, and destruction of the physical world below. In this subtle world there is movement but no sound. At the bottom of the universe is the material world of sound and motion. This is where history happens, and this is where we find ourselves. While inhabiting paramdhām, souls are in a state of dormancy, and although 'liberated' from the world, they are incapable of experiencing pleasure or pain. To experience anything at all, souls must engage with matter, and this is something all souls do sooner or later. When they do so, they descend from paramdhām to the material world to become encased in human (never animal) bodies and enter the process of history.

According to the Brahma Kumaris, history occurs in endlessly repeating cycles of world creation, degeneration, and destruction. Certain highly deserving souls enter the cycle at the beginning when the world is perfect, and they experience complete happiness in a condition known as *jīvan mukti*, or liberation-in-life. However, they must also experience unhappiness and pain later on when the world begins to deteriorate. Other less deserving souls enter history when the world is no longer perfect, and although they experience some happiness, it is less than the happiness of those who came earlier. All souls, whether they come early or late, must remain in history, transmigrating from life to life, until the historical cycle has finished and the world is destroyed, at which point they will return to paramdhām. This is our situation. We are souls that have descended from paramdhām into this historical process. In so doing, we have forgotten our true home (paramdhām) and our real nature as souls; falsely identified with bodies, we find ourselves wandering through the ceaseless flow of historical existence.

Presiding over this entire process is Shiva, or Shiv Bābā. He is also called the Supreme Soul (*paramātmā*) or the Supreme Father (*parampitā*). Like all other souls, his form is that of a point of light (*jyoti bindu*) and

---

[2] In complete disagreement with the conventional Hindu view, the Brahma Kumaris regard Shiva (Shiv Bābā) and Shankar as totally distinct beings. Shiva is the Supreme Soul; Shankar is a 'subtle deity' responsible for the destruction of the world.

power, of which the *linga*[3] is said to be a gross representation. He is omniscient and all-powerful, but not omnipresent, since he is entirely separate from material nature and the historical process peculiar to material nature. Yet he is concerned with the welfare of souls, his 'children.' Because of his love, a small number of especially deserving souls enjoy pure happiness at the beginning of history. At the end of the cycle—that is, in the present era—he imparts, to those few who will listen, 'knowledge' (gyān) concerning the human situation and what one may do to attain jīvan mukti. He does so by speaking to the world through the mouth of Dada Lekhraj, the founder of the Brahma Kumari movement. The Brahma Kumaris are simply those who receive this knowledge and act on it. In so doing they 'remember' who they are, and those who remember will inherit the heavenly kingdom to come.[4]

History

In radical contrast with the millions of years posited by more conventional Hindu theory, Dada Lekhraj taught that world-time lasts a mere five thousand years, with a maximum of eighty-four births possible for souls that descend to the world at the beginning of the cycle. This is standard Hindu historical cosmology, but run at high RPM. In most other respects his model closely approximated the Hindu yuga scheme from which it derived. Every historical cycle is an exact replica of all the rest, consisting of four ages or *yugs* (yugas), each lasting 1250 years. At first the earth is a paradise; then a decline ensues. Vice becomes more prevalent, the population of the world increases, strife becomes more general, and the human life span decreases. By the time of the kaliyug, our age, the world has become a sea of vices and a sink of misery.

The first era of the cycle is the satyug, an age of perfection and total happiness. Nature is benign, pain and disease are unknown, and food

---

[3] The phallic emblem in which form Shiva is usually worshipped. For reasons that will be clear later, the Brahma Kumaris strongly deny that the *linga* has any phallic significance.

[4] For the sake of clarity it should be noted that two quite distinct ideas of 'salvation' coexist in the Brahma Kumari belief-system. Every soul will achieve 'liberation' (*mukti*) in *paramdhām*. Only a relatively few souls, however, will receive 'liberation-in-life' (*jīvan mukti*) by means of rebirth at the start of history. *Mukti* is the final goal of most other Hindu systems; here it has become a kind of way station to the true final goal.

and wealth are available to all without limit. Death is painless; souls simply leave old bodies for new ones, and have visions of their future bodies before they die. There is no competition or conflict, and days pass in happy play and idleness. As one informant put it, conversations between the denizens of the satyug consist of utterances like, 'Do you like the way I've arranged my crown?' or 'See how many jewels there are in my shoes.' Each soul that descends at the beginning of the satyug will experience eight births during this era. Therefore, the average span of life will be about one hundred fifty years.

The souls that inhabit the satyug are entirely worthy of this paradisiacal world. They are absolutely pure, and because of their purity, they are *devātmā*s or 'divine souls,' which is to say, they are gods and goddesses. Among them there is no religion in the sense of supplication to deities, because they are deities themselves. They are *pūjya*, 'worthy of worship,' rather than *pujārī*, 'ones who worship.' These, in fact, are the very beings, dimly remembered through texts, who are worshipped by Hindus as deities today. And, of course, these deities still exist in the world; they are to be found among the membership of the Brahma Kumari movement.

At the onset of the satyug the population of the world is about nine hundred thousand, although this number will grow as new souls, less virtuous than the first-comers, descend from paramdhām. These fortunate individuals live in what is now India in the vicinity of Delhi. Their social order is highly stratified but completely harmonious. There are no religious divisions, since religion, as we now know it, does not exist. There is no political discord, because there is only one pair of sovereigns in existence at a time. The ruling dynasty is the *sūryavansh*, the 'sun line.' It consists of eight successive pairs of Lakshmī and Nārāyaṇ who rule the satyug jointly. Dada Lekhraj is himself the first Nārāyaṇ, and his foremost disciple, Om Radhe, the first Lakshmī. They will be succeeded in these statuses by other souls of very high rank.

In general, souls of the highest virtue will have the highest status and will belong to a 'royal family.' These are the princes and princesses that Lekhraj saw in his visions. Lekhraj's contact with royalty during his business career left vivid traces in this image of the paradise to come. The hierarchy of this age will be of a benign kind that merely reflects the innate capacities and dispositions of individuals. This concord of function and innate nature is exemplified especially in the principle of 'double-crowned' sovereignty that prevails in the satyug.

The rulers of the satyug are adorned with both crowns and halos, just as we see in pictures of deities today, symbolic of the complete coextension of sovereignty and virtue. This is a social order, in other words; in which inner nature and outer action are at one. There can thus be no conflict or competition, and social life is conducted entirely in accord with 'divine law' (*divya maryādā*).

One of the most important features of the satyug has to do with gender. Women and men are sexually distinct, as goddesses and gods are, but they are also entirely equal. Above all, there is no sexual intercourse, for this would be inconsonant (in the Brahma Kumari view) with the absolute purity of deities. Children are conceived within marriage, but by means of yogic power retained by their parents from spiritual practices undertaken at the end of the previous historical cycle. This is a matter to which we shall return.

Finally, those who enter the satyug do so in a state of innocence. By this I mean that they have no gyān, no 'knowledge' of their actual historical situation. Such knowledge is not necessary, since this is a time of reward, a time for the claiming of a rightful inheritance and a putting aside of 'efforts.' Those who live in the satyug have no memory whatsoever of paramdhām, no idea at all of the Supreme Soul, and no recollection of any previous state of earthly existence. This amnesia continues throughout the entire world-career of the souls, and is only ended, for a very few, when the Supreme Soul speaks through Lekhraj's mouth at the end of the cycle. The satyug is the beginning of history, and to be in history is to forget.

The next age in the cycle is the *tretāyug*. During the satyug souls of slightly less virtue than those who came at first continue to descend from paramdhām,[5] and the first-comers too lose some of their purity over time, apparently an inevitable consequence of life in the material world. As a result, by the end of 1250 years, the general level of purity has declined from sixteen degrees (perfect) to fourteen degrees (very pure, but less than perfect). At this point the tretāyug begins.

The beings of the tretāyug are still deities, although because of their slightly lower degree of purity, they are said to belong to the *Kshatriya varṇa* as opposed to the *devi-devatā varṇa* (the *varṇa* of goddesses and gods) of the satyug. In general, life in this era is very similar to that of the satyug: nature is kind and bountiful, and life is free from conflict and

---

[5] This is a somewhat cloudy point. In the literature I saw it never was quite clear whether the expansion of population begins at once or later in the cycle. I was told orally that it begins at once.

want. There are a total of twelve births in this age, yielding an average life span of about one hundred years. Women and men remain equal, and sexual intercourse is still unknown. The ruling dynasty of the tretāyug is the *chandravansh*, the 'moon line.' Twelve successive pairs of Sītā and Rāma rule jointly, with elite souls rotating through these statuses.

The next age is the *dvāparyug* in which twenty-one births take place. During the tretāyug souls continue to descend from paramdhām so that by the end of this period the population of the earth has risen to 330,000,000. The Brahma Kumaris say that this is why there are 330,000,000 deities in the Hindu pantheon. By now the general level of purity has declined to eight degrees, half that of the beginning of the satyug. At this juncture the dvāparyug starts.

In the dvāparyug the quality of *rajogun* (passion) prevails rather than the *satogun* (purity) of previous ages, and this is symptomatic of the transition that has occurred. 'Double-crowned' sovereignty is finished; mere power supplants true authority. There are now many separate political communities. Competition for wealth commences and becomes increasingly severe as the population, fed by new and increasingly vice-prone souls from paramdhām, continues to swell. This is the age when devotional religion (*bhakti*) originates. The deities who once lived in India now become 'Hindus.' No longer pūjya (worthy of worship), the inhabitants of the dvāparyug are merely pujārī (ones who worship). Other religions arise too: Buddhism, Islam, Christianity, and so on. Those who live in this age are no longer Kshatriya, but belong to the Vaishya varna, a low estate in the Brahma Kumari view, consistent with their fallen nature.

But the most important fact of all about the dvāparyug is that this is the age in which what the Brahma Kumaris call *deh abhimān*—'body pride' or 'body consciousness'—comes into existence. This development is a matter of historical necessity, because at the conclusion of the tretāyug, the yogic power hitherto used for human reproduction becomes exhausted. Coitus is now necessary; lust and other vices associated with it cause souls to sink into ever-stronger identification with the bodies they inhabit. As women become mere objects of lust, marriage becomes debased. With this development the subjugation of women begins. This is the fall of the world. With the advent of sexual intercourse the world changes from 'heaven' (*svarg*) to 'hell' (*narak*). All forms of violence, avariciousness, and exploitation arise from body consciousness. Thus with the onset of sexual reproduction the world begins an ineluctable slide into depravity and misery.

The trends emergent in the dvāparyug are simply continued and augmented in the present age, the kaliyug, comprising forty-two (generally short) births. This is an age in which all perfections are lost; it is a *vikār sāgar*, an 'ocean of vices,' and a time when harmful distinctions, contrasts, and conflicts run riot. The earth is now flooded with human beings, who are divided into thousands of linguistic, political, and religious groupings. 'Passion,' the predominant quality of the dvāparyug, now gives way to torpor and ignorance (*tamogun*). All people of the world belong to the lowest estate the Shūdra varna. In an inversion of Hobbes, life at the end of history is nasty, brutish, and short. This is our present condition.

The kaliyug is the nadir of history. At its conclusion the population of the world will rise to six billion, by which time all the dormant souls of paramdhām will have come to earth, and those who came at first will have completed eighty-four lifetimes of earthly existence. At this point the world will be destroyed. When the destruction will begin cannot be known exactly, but it will be soon.[5] This, of course, is the destruction that Lekhraj saw in his visions. When it happens, most souls will return to paramdhām, to await the renewal of the cycle.

Just prior to the end of the kaliyug, however, Shiv Bābā (Shiva) favors humanity with a remarkable act of grace. At this point, when human beings languish in the deepest alienation from their true nature as souls, Shiv Bābā speaks to the world through the mouth of Dada Lekhraj. For those who listen and heed what he says, the kaliyug becomes what is called the *sangamyug*, the 'confluence age,' so named because it is the age of transition from the kaliyug to the renewed world to come. Those who enter this fifth era are members of the Brahma Kumari movement, and their expectation is that they can become fit to be reborn in the paradisiacal phase of the next world cycle. By preparing his followers Lekhraj is, in effect, creating that new world, and thereby fulfilling the instructions he was given in his visions by Shiv Bābā. Because he creates the world in this sense, and because he dispenses gyān (knowledge), he is identified with the deity Brahmā and is called Brahmā Bābā within the movement.

[6] When I tried to pinpoint the date with a movement teacher, I was strongly discouraged. I was told that it might be around the turn of the century or sooner, but that, in any case, it would be long and drawn-out with no clear beginning. The movement has an obvious interest in quashing year-specific expectations, which I strongly suspect arise from time to time. I was told that at one time 1976 was rumored to be the year. It is quite likely, of course, that the world's continuing survival has required the movement to mitigate the concreteness of its expectations over time.

Remembrance

Shiv Bābā gives the Brahma Kumaris knowledge of who, where, and when they are. Therefore, at one level the Brahma Kumari movement is a kind of educational enterprise, and its self-portrayal as a 'divine university' is in no way disingenuous. One 'joins' the movement simply by beginning to attend 'classes' at one of the movement's centers. These classes consist partly of lessons on the nature of the historical cycle: what goes on in the four ages, how one should behave in the present era, and so on. Students sit in neat rows, women on one side of the room and men on the other, and listen quietly to discourses given by one of the resident 'sisters' of the center (less commonly a 'brother'). In the main these consist of Dada Lekhraj's discourses as they were recorded during his lifetime, supplemented by discourses delivered in seances by the medium who has acted as Lekhraj's surrogate since his death.

But lessons in themselves are not enough. Although knowing things about the history of the world and the nature of the soul certainly sheds light on the context and meaning of the human predicament, such knowledge cannot by itself ameliorate this predicament. At root our problem is 'ignorance,' but this ignorance, for which Lekhraj's 'knowledge' is the corrective, is not passive. It is an active, willed ignorance that arises from desire. It is ignorance of 'who we are.' We have forgotten that we are souls. In fact, attracted by material nature and its blandishments, we *want* to forget, and this forgetfulness has become an ingrained habit of mind.

At this level the Brahma Kumari vision of the human task converges with that of the Radhasoami tradition: mere understanding is not enough. What is required of us is not simply assent to the historical theory of the Brahma Kumaris, or to the proposition that we are souls, not bodies. We must undergo an actual change of self-awareness. In order truly to 'know,' we must eradicate 'body-consciousness (*deh abhimān*) and cultivate 'soul-consciousness' (*dehi abhimān*) instead. We must see ourselves, and our relationship with our bodies and the world in general, in a completely altered way.

In part the requirement is a matter of changing what we do, and in particular of avoiding behavior that is an especially dangerous source of further entanglements with the body and material nature. One should take only *sāttvik* (pure) things into the body; meat, alcohol, tobacco, and excessively spicy and passion-inducing foods (such as onions and garlic) must be avoided. One should eat only food prepared by someone who is 'soul-conscious,' since the physiomoral quality of food is influenced by the state of mind of the preparer. The proper way of beginning the day is arising between three and four o'clock in the morning for daily meditation. One's companions should be 'good company' (*saisang*)—that is, the company of the soul-aware (*yogīs* as opposed to *bhogīs*, those given over to worldy pleasures). And above all, sexual intercourse is forbidden. Lust (*kām vikār*) is the master vice. More than anything else, lust draws the soul into engagement with the body, thus entrenching the soul in further ignorance. Absolute celibacy is therefore the *sine qua non* of the virtuous life as understood by the Brahma Kumaris.

But even proper conduct is not sufficient to remove ignorance, although it is a precondition for doing so. True self-knowledge, rather, is achieved through a type of meditation the Brahma Kumaris call *rāja yoga* (*rāj yog*). If part of the curriculum of the Brahma Kumari 'university' is revealed knowledge, the other part is the teaching of this technique. Rāja yoga is said to 'burn away' the karmic effects of past misdeeds, to produce 'bliss,' and to result in a redeeming communion with Shiv Bābā in which the practitioner comes to remember his or her true identity as a soul. Put slightly differently, the object of rāja yoga is to achieve the swanlike discrimination we have already seen idealized in the Radhasoami tradition; the practitioner learns to distinguish the soul from the material nature with which it is normally confused.

The teaching of rāja yoga is standardized, and is easy to describe, at least superficially. It is an intensely visual experience, and vividly recalls themes that we have already encountered in our discussion of visual interaction between guru and follower in the Radhasoami tradition. It is usually taught to small groups or individuals. The student or students sit in a semidarkened room facing the teacher (usually a 'sister'). Just above and behind the teacher's head is a red plastic ovoid that glows from a lightbulb within; at its center is a tiny hole, which appears as a point of intense white light against the red glow. This device represents the Supreme Soul, Shiv Bābā. With devotional songs playing softly in the background, student and teacher gaze intently at each other, either in the eyes or at the forehead. While doing this, the student is supposed to think of himself or herself as a soul, as a bodiless (*asharīrī*) 'point of light and power,' as the 'child' of Shiv Bābā, as rising upward out of the body into paramdhām, as seeing the red glow that suffuses that region, as seeing Shiv Bābā as a point of light, as being bathed in his love, and so on. This may continue for fifteen or twenty minutes or more.

The central feature of this procedure appears to be a visual trans-action between student and teacher in which there is a kind of mingling of frames of reference. While sitting and gazing into the eyes of an adept, the student is instructed to think 'I am a soul; you are a soul.' As one who is already highly soul-conscious, the adept has the power to see the student for the soul he or she really is. The teacher has 'spiritual sight' (*ātmik* or *rūhānī drishṭi*), a power of seeing that enables souls to be seen. The object is for the student to come to share this point of view by opening his or her own soul-seeing third eye. That is, to know oneself as a soul, one must see as the teacher can see—seeing souls where others see only bodies. The student thus absorbs the teacher's soul-awareness. As in the Radhasoami tradition, you become what you see.

This mingling of frames of reference sometimes has a very vivid experiential basis. While staring at the teacher, many students experience visual hallucinations involving lights. Frequently a glow appears on or around the teacher's face and body. In my own case a reddish halo would appear around her face, sometimes followed by an undulating red brightness spreading over her features. Others whom I consulted reported similar experiences, although there appear to be many individual variations. For some the teacher's visage is replaced entirely by light. Some see white light, and for some the entire room lights up. Others experience themselves as the source of the light.

These startling effects probably result from the action of the glowing red emblem on the retina in semidarkness, but this is really a side issue. What is important is that members of the movement have such experiences, and that such experiences are within the realm of plausible expectation. This expectation, in turn, seems to rest on the assumption that a certain kind of reciprocal 'looking' conveys a soul-power that is manifested as light, and also as the ability to *see* that light. As in the Radhasoami tradition, this concept seems to involve a combination of 'being seen' and 'coming to see.' In the process the devotee is changed—that is, one perceives oneself more powerfully— by participating in a more powerful other's point of view.

The learning of rāja yoga may be seen, in part, as a process in which the making (or remaking) of self is simplified and formalized. One is supposed to renounce the old self by 'dying' to the world; that is, one becomes disengaged from interactions in which one was 'seen' in the old way. In what is, at least in theory, a vacuum of competing 'points of view,' one engages in the purest and simplest form of interaction—seeing and being seen—with a significant other. But as in the case of the Radhasoami guru, it is important that this 'other' be viewed in quite a special way. The procedure is most efficacious when the student can actually 'see' the teacher as a bright and powerful soul. If one's orientation toward the teacher is correct—'I am a soul; you are a soul'—then the arising of one's true self in the teacher's awareness becomes an aspect of one's own awareness as well. As one 'takes in' a superior power-of-seeing, one is 'drawn up' into a superior point of view. And for many devotees this superior power of sight, and through it self-identity as a soul, is actually validated by visions of light.

What I have discussed thus far is the teaching of rāja yoga as I experienced it in a movement center. But when one reaches a certain stage, the prop of visual interaction with a human other is said to be unnecessary (although congregational yogic sessions are usually led by an adept). The teacher is finally only a substitute for Shiv Bābā, the Supreme Soul. What is then left is pure interaction, through inner sight, with Shiv Bābā, whose form is a pure point of light-power. He is the ultimate 'other' to whom all rāja yoga is directed in the end.

In this relationship there are strong echoes of other themes we have previously encountered in the Radhasoami tradition. In one of the wall illustrations in the center I visited, a meditating devotee is portrayed as a swan into whose upturned beak rays are descending from red, egg-shaped Shiv Bābā directly overhead. In the movement's iconography Shiv Bābā's light-power is often represented as streaming downward (sometimes fountain-style, in the manner of the Ganges from Shiva's hair in a well-known pictorial representation) to earthly meditators below. They, in turn, drink this light-power through their now awakened inner vision. It is a subtle flow, pure divine power, to be visually imbibed by surrendered devotees, who have a metaphoric counterpart in the moonlight-drinking chakor bird of Radhasoami poetry. Moreover, it is said that the members of the movement are themselves Shiv Bābā's āratī, because, as practitioners of rāja yoga, they know themselves as souls. They see themselves as 'lights' in the eyes of each other, but finally and most importantly, in the perspective of Shiv Bābā. They see themselves and each other as the Lord sees them.

According to the Brahma Kumaris, having adopted this new outlook on oneself, one 'sees' everything differently. Living in the afterglow of periodic yogic experiences, one no longer feels bound to old friends and relations. One's attachments are entirely transferred to Shiv Bābā. With new powers of discrimination, one now sees all others, including members of the opposite sex, as souls, which means that lust disappears. In this state of awareness one is unaffected by the tribulations of life in this world. One knows in the most fundamental way that he or she is really a soul. On the basis of this insight one can achieve the detachment of a mere 'witness' (*sākshī*) to the activities of the body and the material world. Such a person possesses self-awareness as an 'actor,' playing a part in a 'vast drama' (*virāt nātak*); even while acting, he or she will be disengaged from actions, not merely believing, but *knowing* that actions are things of the body alone.

An obvious theme in all this is spiritual mimicry. Yogic practitioners become like Dada Lekhraj, reenacting his own self-discovery. As he once did, his followers discover Shiv Bābā. And just as he came to see himself and others as souls, so do they. For Lekhraj these insights opened a floodgate of revelation. He came to see the true nature of history and his role in it—that is, he was in his eighty-fourth birth, he was Shiv Bābā's medium, he would be reborn in the satyug to become its first king, and so on. In knowing themselves as souls, his followers achieve a similar self-revelation. Even if they do not know exactly what their world-careers are or have been, yogic practitioners are urged to cultivate the feeling that they are souls who were once in paramdhām, who lived in the satyug and tretāyug, who fell when the world fell, and who are now in their eighty-fourth birth. That is, they are encouraged to imagine their own world-lines as parallel to Lekhraj's. To the degree that this is really felt—which is to say, to the degree that one's conviction of its truth can be energized by the extraordinary experiences cultivated in meditation—one can live in expectation of rebirth in the paradise to come.

Among other things, therefore, rāja yoga is an experiential domain in which Dada Lekhraj's historical theory can be transmuted into a devotee's personal biography. One of the goals of yogic practice is to foster the inner conviction that the four ages of history are one's *own* ages. As in the case of Radhasoami doctrine, therefore, the elaborate Brahma Kumari theory of history is less a purely intellectual construct than an ideological medium for spiritually crucial experiences. The purpose of the historical imagery is not so much a portrayal of a world that makes theoretic sense as it is a portrayal of a world in which certain kinds of inner experiences can be understood as redemptively meaningful. This redemptive validity also extends to matters of gender role, but this is a matter to be taken up in the next chapter.

A practitioner of rāja yoga is characterized as one who 'remembers.' The Brahma Kumaris constantly employ the idiom of remembrance in discussing these matters. Rāja yoga is 'remembering father.' The soul has 'forgotten' its real nature and has identified with bodies. In yogic practice one should turn this upside down by 'forgetting the body' (*sharīr ko bhul jānā*) and 'remembering Shiv Bābā' (*shiv bābā ko yād karnā*). In this most fundamental act of recollection—that is, in cultivating awareness of the Supreme Soul—one becomes aware of one's own soul and forgetful of the body and the world. This remembrance is of a quite extraordinary kind. It is extrahistorical or trans-historical, a way of seeing the world and the self not from within history (where there is always amnesia), but from outside history, as Shiv Bābā does. Because he is never in history—that is, because he is never embodied—he never forgets. By achieving such a state of remembrance, one finds happiness (*sukh*), peace (*shānti*), and confidence in one's own destiny. Moreover, one who is body-forgetful will feel the pain of the coming destruction very little, being in the enviable position of a disinterested spectator.

Fate

Brahma Kumari life is pervaded by a sense of urgency. When the end comes, the destruction will extend over a period of many years. But nobody knows for sure when the destruction will start, and when it does, it will be too late to prepare. There is little time left; most people are now in their last birth. 'In the sangamyug,' I once heard in a sermon, 'every second has value.' The Brahma Kumaris sometimes say that one should not be in the position of a student who has to prepare for a final exam in the last hours. This perception of the imminence of final calamity is the principal source of the movement's energy, and is clearly the real point of the drastically shortened cosmic cycle.

In contrast, therefore, to what some theorists apparently believe, anxiety about 'last things' can indeed exist in the Hindu world, but the Brahma Kumari evidence suggests that such anxiety may flourish best in a Hindu world that is much speeded up. Strictly speaking, the precise numbers involved (Lekhraj's 5000-year cycles with yugas of 1250 years) are probably not that important. Although there is a numerical logic behind more conventional Hindu historical cosmologies (see Church 1971), these schemes seem to be at least as evocative as they are literally metrical. Very large numbers of years express a general disposition toward the world, devaluing history by mini-aturizing events in relation to almost unimaginably spacious vistas of time. What matters most about these numbers is just that they are very large.

Lekhraj's figures are best understood in this frame of reference. At one level they reflect an idiosyncratic twist on traditional numerical premises. The traditional date of the *Mahābhārata* war and the beginning of the kaliyug is 3102 B.C.—that is, about 5000 years ago. Lekhraj obviously accepted that date, and simply moved all of history into the time that has elapsed between then and now. But what is important is what he meant to say by doing so. What '5000 years' actually signifies is that the time ahead is much shorter than you think.

Exactly how or why Lekhraj formed this idea is difficult to say.[7] The role of women in the movement, however, almost certainly bears on this issue. As we have seen, most of Lekhraj's earliest followers were women, and although men belong to the sect today, in significant ways it remains a women's movement. Entering a movement of celibates is obviously a fairly drastic initiative for most people, and in India this is especially true for women. What Lekhraj and his followers most needed was a projected world in which behavior that was regarded as deeply unreasonable in Hindu society (indeed, acts of desperation for many of the women involved) would seem, after all, reasonable. A world on the brink of doom would be such a world, and a world in which there is little time left is most easily imagined, given Hindu historical-cosmological premises, as one of very short duration. If most of history has happened, and if history lasts but 5000 years, then there *cannot* be much time remaining.

Some other rationale for drastic initiatives could have been discovered within the Hindu tradition. As we have already noted, the Radhasoami faith has found support for a certain kind of soteriological

---

[7] It is, of course, quite possible that Lekhraj's vision of impending doom was inspired, at some level, by non-Indic examples. Given the thinness of the existing evidence, and the dispersal of the Sindhi society of those days, it is unlikely that this could ever be proven or disproven. In the present context it hardly matters anyway, for everything about Brahma Kumari historical cosmology, including the notion of historical urgency itself, is completely embedded in Hindu ideas.

urgency in the very long cycle of more traditional Hindu historical cosmology, but the Radhasoami path is basically for householders and does not require a truly fundamental break with the institutions of society. Lekhraj asked more, especially at first. Nowadays the Brahma Kumari movement declares its way of life compatable with family life, though as we shall see, this is at best a precarious accommodation. But in the early days Lekhraj asked his women followers to reject the world in a way that put them in direct and often painful confrontations with the most important social others in their lives. For many women, entering the movement involved all-or-nothing, bridge-burning conversions. This circumstance no doubt reinforced the need for a world outlook portraying the human situation in something close to desperate terms.

Whatever his reasons, when Lekhraj speeded up the cycle, he committed himself and his movement to a vision of cosmic history that differed from other Hindu versions not just in this particular, but in more comprehensive ways. For the Brahma Kumaris, history seems to 'matter' in a way that it apparently does not in the Hindu tradition more generally. As Zimmer (1962, 18–19) has pointed out, in the enormity of a timescape in which eons are but blinks of the creator's eye, it is difficult for events, as such, to carry ultimate values, no matter how momentous they may seem from a limited human perspective. But this is apparently not so when there is little time ahead. The point of the speedup is to invest the impending calamity with new and urgent meaning. This, in turn, seems to distribute new kinds of values, positive and negative, on other occurrences as well. They acquire significance as signs, anticipations, and finally, justifications of the horrors soon to come. History is not exactly an epiphany for the Brahma Kumaris (cf. Eliade 1971, 104). The 'facts' of history have their ultimate significance as features of personal biography, not as manifestations of God or his will. But history nevertheless defines the situation of humankind in relation to the things that matter most.

As a result, an almost obsessive historical-mindedness has become a deeply entrenched feature of the religious subculture of the Brahma Kumaris. It goes beyond the mere fact that much of what they teach is what they consider to be history. From the very start, Lekhraj's teachings and revelations incorporated a highly distinctive historiography that radically reinterpreted Hindu scriptures, thus 'setting the record straight.' For example, he said that the great war of the *Mahābhārata* is actually a hazy recollection of the destruction of the world at the end of the last cycle (complete, it was said later, with nuclear weapons). The deity Krishna is actually Dada Lekhraj before he became Nārāyan upon his coronation as king of the satyug and marriage to Lakshmī. This kind of reinterpretation of traditional history is a pervasive tendency in the movement's intellectual life. The contemporary world is also intensely scrutinized for occurrences that seem to vindicate the Brahma Kumari scheme. At the time of the disastrous Delhi flooding in the autumn of 1978, this event was cited to me as yet another indication of the imminence of universal doom.

An interesting and unforeseen consequence of Lekhraj's stress on historical imagery has been that the Brahma Kumari vision of the world seems to be on a collision course with the formulations of historians, archaeologists, and geologists in a way that may be quite unusual in the Indic world. This is partly a matter of the simple temporal proximity of the events of short-cycle history, but I suspect that more is involved than this. Given the historical emphasis of Lekhraj's theology, details of dating and historical sequence acquire a very special significance. For the Brahma Kumaris it matters vitally that the world was born just five thousand years ago, that sexual intercourse is only twenty-five hundred years old, and so on. It is not that other Hindu versions of history are any more consistent with the findings of modern science or historical scholarship, but such findings seem to be a far more direct challenge to what matters most about the world to the Brahma Kumaris.

As far as I am aware, for example, the radiocarbon technique of dating is of no interest or consequence to the Radhasoami tradition, but one of the theoreticians of the Brahma Kumari movement considers the matter important enough to have given me a lengthy and erudite lecture on the technical inadequacies of both this and the potassium argon method. The question of why no archaeological remains have been found from the satyug is also a matter of genuine concern to the Brahma Kumaris; defensive elaborations have, therefore, been added to their historical theory in order to forestall disconfirmation. It is said, for example, that because houses and buildings were plated with gold and studded with jewels during the first half of the cycle, no trace of them could remain today, all having long since been looted and converted into ornaments. How successful these defenses will prove to be in the long run is hard to say.

One of the most interesting consequences of Lekhraj's speedup of the historical cycle is what seems to be a heightening of a sense of historical-cyclical determinism. Such determinism is, of course, implicit in any historical cosmology based on the idea of recurrent cycles. If the cycles repeat themselves exactly, then anything that happens *must* happen as it has already happened before. Even so, in the wider Hindu tradition the possibility of the reiteration of individual world-careers does not seem to be much dwelt upon. Allusions to specific repetitions are apparently rather infrequent in Puranic texts (Zimmer 1962, 18), and as far as I am aware this is not an issue at all in the Radhasoami tradition. Here the question of why we have the experiences we do seems to be mainly the domain of karmic reasoning (with its implicit premise of free will) in the context of an encompassing conception of the Lord's will-as-pleasure (mauj). Things do not happen the way they do simply because they did so in previous historical cycles. It is as if cyclic determinism exists mainly as a latent possibility, an ideological empty space.

Among the Brahma Kumaris. however, with the shortening of the cosmic cycle, what is elsewhere a rather vague idea of determinism seems to have stiffened into what is felt to be literal fact. One of my informants reported asking Lekhraj whether a chip taken out of a stone would still be missing when he repeats the action the next time around. Lekhraj's answer—that his visions simply did not deal with such questions—is largely beside the point; what is important is that the question was asked at all. In the world as the Brahma Kumaris conceive it, the determinism implicit in the idea of repetition has become an insistent actuality that has to be faced.

The Brahma Kumaris in no way attempt to evade this implication. History, they flatly say, is like a 'movie'; the same film is screened again and again. Each person's 'part' is graven on his or her soul in the form of ineradicable *sanskārs* (inclinations). Those who enjoyed the earth as a paradise once will have the same experience in every cycle, and those who fail will always fail. Lekhraj has delivered the same warnings of the end to come countless times before, as he will for infinite times again.

One might suppose that such a strong determinism would lead to a fatalism that would be antithetical to the sense of spiritual-historical crisis so basic to the Brahma Kumari outlook. But this is no more true for the Brahma Kumaris than it was for the predestinarian Calvinists. Determinism, though absolute, settles nothing. It is permissible to take retrospective comfort in the inevitability of things as a way of putting past misfortunes into proper (and diminishing) perspective, but *purushārth*, or 'effort,' is necessary. Rewards await only those who strive, and if anything, the principle of repetition simply raises the stakes; those who gain the satyug will always do so, and those who fail will fail forever.

The apparent contradiction is resolved by a truly fundamental principle—historical amnesia. Brahma Kumari teachings provide highly detailed accounts of the passage of world-time and what happens in history, but the world-careers of individuals are another matter. Historical beings 'forget,' and although devotees are encouraged to think of themselves as ones whose world-lines approximate that of Lekhraj, the actual specifics of any individual's destiny (and/ or history) cannot be known—or so movement teachers told me— with certainty.[8] Or rather, there are only two personal destinies that are known and fixed: Lekhraj is to be the first Nārāyaṇ, and Om Radhe the first Lakshmī. Others must await the end to know for sure. There will be a 'final exam,' which souls will pass 'numberwise' (these terms are often given in English), according to their efforts. There will be a settling then of the *hisāb kitāb*, the account book. For now, however, we are in an odd sort of predicament; everything may be fixed, but from the standpoint of the individual nothing is settled.

Only a tiny minority of the earth's present population will inherit the satyug; most will receive *mukti* (liberation in *paramdhām*), but not *jīvan mukti* (liberation-in-life in the satyug and tretāyug). But the real issue is what one's status will be in the coming paradise. Will one be among the elite of the elite, a select 108 who are 'totally victorious'? Those of highest status will not only be the rulers of heaven, but will be close to Lekhraj throughout their world-careers. Or will one only be among the 16,000—those in the 'high royal families' of the heavenly world, but not at the top?[9] Will one rule, or will one serve?

---

[8]   I was told quite definitely that one's future cannot be known for sure, but this is obviously a matter with many complexities. There was probably greater certainty about individual destiny during earlier eras of the movement's history when visions were more emphasized. Many apparently saw their future selves in such visions, and being able to do so was one of the attractions of the movement No doubt this continues to be the case for some. I also suspect—though I have no evidence in support of this conjecture—that greater certainty exists in inner and higher circles of the movement. The doctrine of uncertainty is obviously consistent with the movement's hopes of attracting large numbers of converts. Why join up if the high places in heaven are already spoken for? It is likely that the estimate of the population of the satyug has expanded over time for the same reason.

[9]   There is apparently some concession to 'worldly' family ties here. I was told that family members (and friends) who had been in at least some contact with the *gyān* might be numbered among the 16,000.

Only at the very end of the cycle will everyone see visions in which their personal destinies will be fully disclosed. In the meantime, as a movement teacher put it to me, you can only know your destiny by knowing yourself. What this means is knowing yourself *as* someone whose characteristics match those of the denizens of the satyug. This is a matter of your own self-control; those who rule themselves will rule the kingdom to come. In this sense, effort 'counts,' even though effort in itself cannot alter one's destiny. Given the urgency of the present historical moment, the energy-potential of this idea is quite high.

But what kinds of effort count? Apparently not efforts to reform the kaliyug in accord with Shiv Bābā's will. The kaliyug is quite beyond redemption, and true reform is inevitable anyway, and soon to come. There is nothing *we* can do to change history, since the cycle is fixed. Moreover, it is far from clear that Shiv Bābā has a 'will' in the Judeo-Christian sense. He is a source not so much of 'commandments' as of 'disclosures,' for which Dada Lekhraj is the human medium. He is not a changer of history, because history cannot be changed; he is a revealer of history. Because he is never embodied (as we are), Shiv Bābā never forgets, and therefore at this critical juncture in history he can impart the knowledge that will enable those who receive it to redeem themselves, as they have already done time and again before.

What 'effort' really means is exemplifying Brahma Kumari values in one's way of life. This, in turn, has two aspects. The first consists of serving the movement and obeying its rules. Service (sevā) requires active support of the movement, especially by participating in its many proselytizing activities. Great emphasis is placed on the value of bringing converts into the movement, particularly converts who stick—since many do not. Following the movement's rules means striving for purity of life, through celibacy and control of diet. Purity is also a matter of thought. One's innermost attitudes and desires must pass muster in accord with the movement's almost inhumanly high standards. The individual alone is the best judge of how successful he or she has been in this.

The second aspect of effort, and the true fulfillment of Brahma Kumari life, is yogic introspection. Group sessions of rāja yoga are part of every movement gathering, and daily individual meditation is strongly enjoined on every member. This is the movement's most significant 'effort.' Ideally it leads to a transhistorical experience of communion with Shiv Bābā, which should instill confidence in one's salvationary destiny. One leaves the world of history in order to believe in one's reentry on favorable terms. Obviously there is a strongly millenarian theme in Dada Lekhraj's teachings. But if the Brahma Kumari sect is a millenarian movement, then it probably defines a distinctive species of the type. Lekhraj delivered a startling message of momentous things to come. However, his warning led not to confrontation with history, but flight from it.

Separation

There are basically two levels of membership in the Brahma Kumari movement. At its core are fully 'surrendered' women and men who have either left or never entered family life and reside in the movement's many centers.[10] A knowledgeable informant told me that there are currently some seven hundred surrendered sisters in the movement and a smaller number of men. At the center with which I became familiar there were usually six resident sisters and three resident men, but these numbers fluctuated over time. Most people with this level of commitment to the movement come from families with past movement connections. The depth of such prior connectedness varies, but in some cases among my surrendered acquaintances the links were with Lekhraj's original followers in 1937. On the basis of my own somewhat limited contact with this inner circle of the sect's membership, I have the impression that it is common for clusters of kin to be, as the Brahma Kumaris put it, 'in the gyān,' with some fully surrendered and others not.

Fully surrendered members are much needed. A knowledgeable insider told me that currently money is not really a problem for the movement, but there is an acute lack of qualified sisters to undertake the teaching and other spiritual tasks that are the heart of the movement's life. Full surrender is obviously a big step for anyone, especially a woman, and the matter is approached with great caution. The movement insists that recruits at this level must have a mature understanding of what they are doing and the permission of their families. A typical recruit will have been exposed to the highly distinctive atmosphere of the movement from childhood. She will be

---

[10] I am painfully aware of how little I know of the inner social life of the movement. My contact with the fully surrendered was at the relatively superficial level of teaching and being taught. A true ethnography of the movement would have to be written from inside.

required to undertake a trial period of residence for six months to a year at a local center. The trial period is to determine whether she really wants the life, and whether she has the intelligence and discipline necessary to lead it successfully. There was one such trial sister in residence at the center I attended. She was in her late teens and the daughter of a couple who had been lay members of the movement for many years; her elder sister had already surrendered to the movement in 1972. Some who surrender to the movement bring the equivalent of dowries with them. I do not know how great the sums involved are, or how common this practice is.

Surrendered women are the core personnel at all local centers. They do the teaching, conduct group sessions of yogic practice, and also do the cooking and housekeeping. Most of the resident men, apparently almost always a minority, maintain outside employment and function as indispensable mediators between the secluded sisters and the outside world. In the center I attended one of the resident men was a government bureaucrat, and another was an electrical engineer. A third, who was not always present, devoted his full time to the movement.

Surrounding this core is a much larger lay membership with varying degrees of commitment. Most of the daily attendees at the center I attended were men, but I was told that this is exceptional. Because of its location near middle and upper-middle class residential colonies of New Delhi, this center tended to attract members of government service families, but its constituency also included students, military personnel, and businessmen. The atmosphere of the center was strongly middle class. Attendees came from a variety of caste and regional backgrounds, but with North Indians greatly predominating.

Among the lay members at this center the distribution of time in the movement was strikingly bimodal. A minority of attendees had been members for many years, but at any given time most attendees had been in the movement for relatively short periods of weeks or months. This was so because turnover was very rapid. Many recruits do not really appreciate the personal implications of what the movement asks of its membership at first; with growing realization, enthusiasm cools. The movement is eager to hold on to recruits and to reclaim those who have fallen away. I once accompanied one of the resident brothers of the center on a surprise visit to a couple who had dropped out. The purpose of the visit was to rekindle their interest in the movement, but the overflowing ashtrays visible the minute we entered the sitting room suggested that this would be a fruitless effort, as it turned out to be.

Lay membership is not regarded as spiritually disadvantageous.[11] Lay members are those who live with their 'worldly' (laukik) families. While the movement expresses no positive enthusiasm for family life, it recognizes the family as an institutional reality, and sees in family life a domain in which virtues can be perfected. Families often participate in the movement as units, and although commitment to the movement by individuals has sometimes proven to be quite disruptive to families, the Brahma Kumaris claim that the quality of family life can be radically improved if members adhere to Brahma Kumari teachings.

Brahma Kumari families should be 'lotus like'; that is, they should be unsullied by the mire in which they grow (this is a common Hindu image). Every home should become an āshram, a hermitage. What this mainly means is that these should be homes in which celibacy is practiced. For this reason most of the converts in the center I attended seemed to be persons for whom sexuality was no longer an issue: widows, widowers, and—in the case of married couples—those in their middle years and beyond who had already had children. Simple loneliness was probably a motivating factor in many conversions. The Brahma Kumaris are *always* happy to see you, and for an aging widow or widower this can be an important attraction. The boredom of retirement was also a factor for some. 'It gives me something to do,' said an elderly retired diplomat.

Fully surrendered members of the movement belong to a community that is densely interconnected and highly solidary despite its spatial dispersal. Lay members, especially those whose membership is relatively recent, have a more atomic involvement in the movement. At the center I knew, most members in this category did not interact with each other very much. What little contact they had was in the context of the center itself. For them affiliation with the movement was essentially a matter of attending the center's various activities.

Within the center a very distinctive style of life is cultivated. One of its most striking features is the absence of overt signs of hierarchy. In day-to-day interactions there is little of the foot touching and other

---

[11] The private opinions of the fully surrendered may be something else again. Public doctrine, however, avers that merely living in a center does not, in itself, guarantee that a person is more self-controlled and soul-conscious than those who live with 'worldly' families.

symbolic apparatus of status distinction in evidence. Members greet each other with the words 'om shānti' (om peace). Resident sisters wear distinctive white saris, while lay members usually wear ordinary clothing. Diminutive signs with elevating slogans are ubiquitous: 'Are you remembering Shiv Bābā?' and 'He who is pure is like a diamond.' Such signs are printed against a bel-leaf background (the bel, or wood-apple, being sacred to Shiva).

Resident members arise at around three or four in the morning for their own meditations. Then follow congregational meditation and classes attended by lay members. As already noted, the central feature of the classes is the reading of the discourses that emanate from movement headquarters. At the conclusion of class, lay members are frequently asked to stand up before the assembled group to testify to their own spiritual progress or lack of it. Throughout the day there are further, more specialized classes, other spiritual activities, and housekeeping. The museum is open in the morning and evening after four o'clock. At four points during the day activities are interrupted by a few moments of recorded music, which is an opportunity for a quick session of individual yogic meditation.

At the center I attended there was an inconspicuous donation box located on the second floor of the building, a place where only regular attendees were likely to come. The movement is strongly committed to the idea that monetary donations should come only from members. Donations are voluntary and anonymous. Very occasionally members would be reminded of the high cost of the rent of the building (Rs 3000 per month), but such solicitation was low key. Members were not badgered for money in this center as far as I was aware.

In general Brahma Kumari life is not rich in ceremony. Their emphasis is on yogic practice and gyān, 'knowledge,' and on the words, writings, and didactic artwork through which knowledge is conveyed. An observer is therefore struck by the poverty of their ceremonial life when compared with popular Hinduism more generally. However, a Brahma Kumari ceremonial life exists.

Thursday is a special day in all Brahma Kumari centers, for this is the one day of the week on which bhog (food offering) is made regularly to Shiv Bābā. The ceremony occurs in the morning during congregational meditation. One of the sisters ascends a platform at the front of the room and sits in a yogic posture. She gazes around the room, making momentary eye-contact with all the other meditators in the room. After a few minutes of this, she closes her eyes and her body makes a slight jerk. She then sits with her eyes closed for ten or fifteen minutes. While her eyes are closed, the sister is visiting Brahmā Bābā (that is, Lekhraj in his 'subtle body') in the 'subtle world' above. She sees him there, floating and surrounded by white light. A food offering, usually fruits or sweets of some kind, has been stationed at the front of the room. The sister offers Lekhraj the food in 'subtle form,' and then engages him in conversation. Of course in doing so she is actually conversing with Shiv Bābā, whose medium Brahmā Bābā is. Because this is a world of total silence, they must communicate by means of gestures. Finally she leaves the trance, opens her eyes, and begins to tell the assembled group what he said. This usually takes the form of an admonitory sermon. He 'sees' the class, and notices that the 'children' in it have varying degrees of purity and commitment. He distinguishes between different types of children, and urges the dilatory to increase their efforts. After this, the food offering is distributed to all attendees as prasād.

Visions of this sort were apparently far more central to the life of the movement in the past than they are now. Currently only certain sisters have them, and then only under narrowly defined circumstances. The ability to have such visions is regarded as a *vardān*, a pure 'boon,' with no particular implications about the soteriological destiny of one so gifted. From informants I heard of occasions when such women have contacted the souls of recently deceased movement members who declared themselves 'with Bābā' and happy. I have never witnessed this. Nowadays the movement downplays trance activity for fear that it would be, as one informant put it, 'misunderstood by the public.'

As far as I was able to tell, the usual life-cycle rites are of little concern to the Brahma Kumaris. I was told by an informant that a marriage was once solemnized by Dada Lekhraj (obviously a celibate marriage), but I never witnessed anything resembling this. I was also told that when a member dies the usual rites will be performed by his or her 'worldly' family, but that the Brahma Kumaris will hold a commemorative food offering within twelve days of the death. Individuals sometimes sponsor food offerings (bhog or *brahma bhojan*) in celebration of some special event in their own lives. For example, at the center I attended an elderly gentleman sponsored such an occasion in celebration of his sixteenth 'birthday,' which was the sixteenth anniversary of his 'rebirth' when he entered the movement.

The Brahma Kumaris warily regard their members' participation in the ceremonial life of the surrounding society. To some degree their stance is confrontational. They have produced their own competing versions of certain major Hindu festivals, which members are expected to substitute for the rites of their own families and communities.

One of the biggest occasions of the Brahma Kumari year is *mahā-shivrātri*, the 'great night of Shiva.'[12] The rest of the world, they say, is engaged in an essentially false *shivrātri*. The real 'night of Shiva' is the dark night that has now descended on the world on the eve of its total destruction, during which Shiv Bābā comes down to disseminate redeeming knowledge. At the center I attended mahāshivrātri was celebrated by a morning food offering (with trance), followed by a special sermon on the real meaning of the occasion and the hoisting of a flag bearing Shiv Bābā's egg-shaped emblem in the front yard. Similar Brahma Kumari celebrations of *holī, bhaiyā dūj, rakshābandhan, dashehrā, divālī*, and other Hindu festivals are held at the appropriate points in the calendar. These festivals are invariably ideologized in the Brahma Kumari fashion. Bhaiyā dū (brother-second), for example, was enacted in a way that dramatized the siblinghood (as daughters and sons of Brahmā) of the members of the movement. The 'real meaning' of holī, I was told, is that 'we are spraying the nectar of knowledge [*gyān amrit*] on others.' Just as the rest of the world does on holī, my informant continued, 'we spray it on them whether they want to get wet or not.' There is also a special observance on the occasion of Dada Lekhraj's death anniversary in January.

As noted in chapter 4, major Hindu festivals are also occasions for the sponsorship of Brahma Kumari 'exhibitions.' During the year of my contact with the movement, one such exhibition was held near a major bus junction at Nehru Place on the eve of mahāshivrātri. Several hundred spectators were lured into a large tent by colorful advertising outside. They were then treated to a sound and light display illustrating major points of Brahma Kumari doctrine. Foreign devotees sang Brahma Kumari devotional songs, and various members gave speeches testifying to the value of rāja yoga and the importance of the movement in their own spiritual lives.

Special events of a nonceremonial kind were also frequently held at the center premises. A good example of this was a symposium entitled

---

[12] *Mahāshivrātri*, supposedly the darkest night of the year, is celebrated in the Hindu month of *phālgun* (February–March) and commemorates the marriage of Shiva and Pārvatī.

'Can Spiritual Education Help in Development of Self-Discipline?' The Brahma Kumaris invited a number of distinguished educators, most of whom, I think, had little idea of the real nature of the occasion. The visiting educators were first shown the museum and then seated amidst an audience consisting mostly of regular attendees of the center. They were then given a series of lectures on Brahma Kumari doctrine thinly overlaid with an 'educational' rationale. At one point the speakers (resident sisters and a couple of longtime lay members) began silently staring at the audience in the usual rāja-yogic manner. Most of the visitors seemed quite puzzled by this, but continued to pay polite attention.

In general the Brahma Kumaris' approach to popular Hinduism has been an attempt to reject what they regard as the dross and to assimilate the rest on their own terms. As we have seen, standard Hindu festivals are reworked to fit into Brahma Kumari formats. What cannot be absorbed is condemned and discarded. Thus, the usual holī revelry is rejected as a coarse accretion that has nothing to do with the real meaning of the occasion. And as we have also seen, there has been a massive effort to incorporate various aspects of Hindu lore and doctrine into the Brahma Kumari world-view. An example is a large image of the Hindu goddess Durgā stationed just outside the front door of one of the New Delhi centers. Over her head is a red egg, symbolizing the 'real' source of her power; under her feet are male figures, representing the 'five-vices,' whom she is slaying with her trident. Durgā has become a Brahma Kumari.

As already noted, the deity Krishna is regarded as Dada Lekhraj, imperfectly recollected from the beginning of history. Krishna's alleged 16,108 wives were actually his most favored followers, the elite of the satyug. The Hindu *mālā* (rosary) has 108 beads because this represents the 108 followers who were totally stainless. The Pāṇḍavas (in the *Mahābhārata*) are the Brahma Kumaris themselves; the Kauravas are the rest of the Indian population,[13] and the self-destructive Yādavas, with their fearsome weapons, are the Westerners and Western scientists who will destroy each other with nuclear bombs. The *shālagrāms*—the smooth, water-polished stones in which form Vishnu is often worshipped—are actually representations of the souls of those who became 'worthy of worship' (pūjya) by being 'washed in the stream of knowledge.' They are, in other words, the Brahma Kumaris.

[13] Who are said to use women 'for pleasure.' This is linked to Duhshasana's attempted rape of Draupadi as recounted in the *Mahābhārata*.

These rerenderings of Hindu tradition represent a vast and growing intellectual system on which I have merely touched. Its basis is the presumption that Hindu scripture, with the partial exception of the *Bhagavad Gītā*, is never really reliable. Existing Hindu texts, the Brahma Kumaris say, came to us by means of visions that occurred after the end of the tretāyug. In these visions things got blurred. Thus, Krishna was thought to be the source of divine knowledge in the *Gītā*, when in fact the real source was Shiv Bābā. Further distortions accumulated as scriptures were copied and recopied down through the ensuing generations. Divine revelation is now piecing the truth back together.

If there is a single theme that organizes Brahma Kumari religious life and characterizes their conception of who they are in the world, it is separation. Members are supposed to consider themselves 'dead' to the world. Having entered the sangamyug, one is *nyārā*, 'separate' and distinct from the rest of society. The condition the Brahma Kumaris seek to attain is, in fact, that interstructural, transitional, threshold state that van Gennep called 'liminal' in his celebrated analysis of rites of passage (1961). They say that they are neither of this world nor of the next, but *bīch mē*, 'in between.' Their sense of separation from the kaliyug is a powerful undercurrent in their outlook and behavior. They are encouraged not to form strong attachments outside the movement (even with nonmovement members of their own families), their white dress is distinctive, they refuse to take food prepared by outsiders (though fruit may be taken), and so on. They conceive themselves as having been reborn into a new kind of existence in which the most basic attachments of the old world count for little. And to this we must add that the behavior of the outer world toward them has sometimes massively vindicated their view.

The Brahma Kumaris say they have been reborn as 'Brāhmaṇs.' Each age has its own varṇa, and those who belong to the sangamyug are the 'true Brāhmaṇs.' The aperture of their birth is a mouth, the mouth of Dada Lekhraj, through which issues the knowledge that causes their rebirth. They are thus 'mouth-born Brāhmaṇs,' and Lekhraj can therefore be identified with the creative deity Brahmā (also classically a source of knowledge), since it is because of his utterances, inspired by Shiv Bābā, that the process leading to the rebirth of the world is begun. Having been reborn through his mouth, his children are therefore the daughters and sons of Brahmā.

There are elements of ritual logic in the Brahma Kumaris' stance toward the world. They see themselves as the agencies through which the world to come is coming into being; without their self-denial this world could never be born. Their object is nothing less than to stop and restart time, to recover the childhood of the world by becoming Brahmā's children. The malleability of time in religious thought is a notable feature of many cultures, as Eliade (1971) and others have shown, and it is especially within certain ritual moments that this magic is done. The Brahma Kumaris attack the problem of human bondage in history by conceiving the history of the world in the same terms as the history of the individual, and then applying the logic of rebirth. World and person are reborn together, as if in a rite of passage. To be reborn one must first be unborn, and so the Brahma Kumaris must die to the world and enter the liminal, or threshold sangamyug. In doing so they become ahistorical even as they continue—in some cases only marginally, and in others nearly fully—to live and act (while disengaged from action) in the historical world. For a time they are out of time, betwixt and between, but ultimately they will rejoin history at the rebirth of the world. Among the Brahma Kumaris the ritual sources of this reasoning have become sublimated and disguised. But when Lekhraj characterized the movement as a gigantic sacrifice, he knew very well what he was saying. The Brahma Kumaris are engaged in an extended and vastly magnified rite of renewal for themselves and for the world at large.

6. Otherworldly Feminism

Sexuality and Subjugation

Whether the Brahma Kumari movement is genuinely feminist is a very debatable question. That it was founded by a man is largely irrelevant. Lekhraj was in intimate and daily contact with his mostly female followers, and the content of his teachings certainly suggests the influence of a feminine perspective. But the mere presence of women, or even a woman's point of view, does not in itself establish the Brahma Kumaris' feminist credentials. What has to be shown is that the movement has produced a genuine critique of the social institutions that affect women's lives, and that it has generated at least some concept (its practicality is not at issue) of how the situation of women can be changed for the better.

I believe that it has. One of the goals of the movement, though certainly not the only goal, is the liberation of women from what is viewed as an oppressive social regime. This, however, is not an easy point to establish. The problem is that Brahma Kumari views on the situation of women are embedded in Hindu symbols, and are difficult to render into terms intelligible to Western feminism. They seek the liberation of women, but the *kind* of liberty they seek cannot really be understood except in the context of Hindu religious culture. Even their complaints about the institutions they consider oppressive are deeply colored by the outlook of the Hindu tradition.

This chapter shows how the Brahma Kumaris have expressed a will to be free as women by using Hindu religious concepts. For those who believe that a true feminism must seek radical change of existing social institutions, the Brahma Kumaris' beliefs will almost certainly seem misguided or futile. But, on the other hand, we might see feminism as the product of a transcultural motive that can be expressed in varied ways in different cultural settings. With this latter perspective the Hindu tradition itself appears as far more rich in possibilities than is sometimes supposed.

The place to begin is with Brahma Kumari views of history. These views are not only linked with an assessment of the present human situation in general, but also have directly to do with the position of women. The connection is the Brahma Kumari conception of the relationship between sexuality and the fall of the world. Readers will recall that the great transition between earthly 'heaven' and 'hell' occurs when sexual intercourse becomes part of the human scene for the first time. With intercourse arises 'body-consciousness,' the root of all other human evils and the primary cause of present miseries. At one level this is a general affliction affecting men and women alike; all have become bound to the body and to the misfortunes and pain of life in a world ruled by desire and passion. But it is also something that affects women specifically, because with the rise of body-consciousness women lose the equality they enjoyed during the satyug and tretāyug. Having become mere 'sex dolls,' they have fallen under the domination of men. The position of women thus emerges as a sharpened metaphor for the present human predicament. Women, more than anyone, are the principal victims of the human fall.

These ideas were not created ex nihilo. The notion that reproduction occurred without sex in the early phases of the cosmic cycle is an old one in the Hindu tradition (see O'Flaherty 1976, 27–29). Moreover, in the Indic world there is nothing remarkable about the doctrine that worldly passions and attachments are the principal causes of human bondage. Nor is there anything truly striking about the use of woman as a metaphor for the human situation, a concept with deep roots in the bhakti (Hindu devotional) tradition.

What is unusual in the case of the Brahma Kumaris is the incorporation of a critical point of view into this metaphor. Pervading the Brahma Kumaris' concept of the world and its history is an idea of human alienation that draws its strength from the image of women as victims of corrupt institutions. I certainly do not mean to imply that the Brahma Kumari movement can be reduced to a feminist critique of society, since this would violate the complexity of an intricate and multifaceted theological system. But a feminist motive is a discernable element in Brahma Kumari theology.

Though it is not to be found in any single place, a Brahma Kumari account of the situation of women in Indian society exists. Elements of it are scattered throughout Lekhraj's discourses (the muralīs) and the literature of the movement. When the pieces are put together, what emerges is a coherent and intelligible assessment of where women stand. Its focus is on the role of women in marriage.

As we have already seen, one of the principal Brahma Kumari complaints about the family and marriage, a complaint dating from the earliest days of the movement, is that women are subordinated to husbands who are unworthy of veneration. The question of the differential religious value accorded to the sexes is fundamental to this accusation. Men (it is said) are full of vices. Yet women are required to treat their husbands as deities, while they themselves are regarded as no more than the 'heel of the left foot' of man. And if this were not enough, to the degree that man has fallen, woman is regarded as the temptress who pulls him down. According to an adage attributed to the sannyāsīs (world-renouncers), woman is the 'door to hell' (*narak kā dvār*). The implication is that women are not so much the victims of world-binding sexual lust as they are its source. Put otherwise (although the Brahma Kumaris never formulate it quite this way), women are viewed not as true moral subjects, but rather as provocations for moral choices made by men.

All this, however, is but a surface manifestation of what these materials point to as the fundamental injustice—namely, that women are not conceived as soteriological agents. If man has fallen, he at least has the option of renouncing the world; he can become an ascetic in a culturally sanctioned (and highly esteemed) role, and seek what he believes to be his salvation. But sannyāsīs are men, not women. In the world as presently constituted, woman is not the renouncer, but (at least one element of) that which is renounced the 'door to hell.' Bondage is entanglement with the world; liberation is release from this. The implicit grievance in the Brahma Kumari assessment of women's condition is that women are not just bound to the world; they are also imprisoned in a particular concept of womanhood, one that envisions women as the bait in the trap of worldly life. And, in fact, at a more general level of Hindu symbolism the feminine is identified with māyā, the illusion that is the created world, and that draws the self into fatal bondage.[1]

[1] These attitudes reflect an interpretation of Hindu institutions and life that might or might not accord with the facts as others see them. There is good reason to believe, for example, that female sexuality is far more highly valued in Hindu culture than one might gather from the Brahma Kumaris, or for that matter, from many Western descriptions of Hindu life. For an excellent account of the positive valuations of the feminine, the reader is urged to see Marglin's *Wives of the God-King* (forthcoming).

Because the subordination of women began when sexual intercourse became a factor in human existence, sexual intercourse is at the root of women's inequality. In the world as it exists now, women must enter into sexual relations with men and live as sexual beings if they are to be married. This situation offers no real choice, since to be unmarried as a woman is to have no real status in society at all. Without the option of sannyās (world renunciation), women are trapped in 'worldly marriage.' Thus women are not merely housebound; they are bound absolutely to the world. But so are men; they are as bound by their passions as women are by evil conventions. And in the present age of degradation even the freedom of the sannyāsī, in the Brahma Kumari view, is finally a false liberty. The sannyāsī, indeed, is an abettor of present miseries, making orphans of his children and a widow of his wife. The Brahma Kumaris say that the sannyāsīs flee women precisely because of their own weakness; it is because they themselves are 'body-conscious' that women seem to them to be a threat. This is the great mistake; it is not woman, but lust itself, which is the 'door to hell.'

Marriage, or at least a certain kind of marriage, therefore becomes a paradigm for the human condition, with the sexual role of women its focus. And because reproduction requires sex (and reproduction is necessary until the sangamyug), ultimately the reproductive role of woman underlies her predicament. The Brahma Kumari version of this predicament, however, differs somewhat from the one portrayed by Western feminism. Consistent with the more general Hindu mistrust of passion, the Brahma Kumaris have concentrated on sexuality itself rather than the exigencies of childrearing and housekeeping as the significant factor maintaining women's subordination. More important, they have not viewed the present reproductive role of women as a biological given. Intercourse is necessary for procreation, but only in the 'hell' of our present world. Women *can* be free, and some women inevitably will be (though only a tiny minority among the world's women). Since the bondage of woman is the bondage of all, the world can be made free (albeit a much smaller world than the one we now know) through her liberation. But a free world will have to be a world without sex.

Sexuality and Power

Celibacy is the strongest and most inclusive value of the Brahma Kumaris. Their heaven is heavenly because of the absence of sex, and our present hell is mostly the product of sexual desire and the evils that flow therefrom. This does not mean that sexuality has an unambiguously negative role in the moral economy of the historical world. Intercourse is not only inevitable, but functionally necessary during the second half of the world-cycle. A movement teacher assured me that Dada Lekhraj himself, in the form of King Vikramaditya, aids and abets the spread of sexuality by causing erotic temple sculptures to be carved when the dvāparyug begins. Therefore, during the appropriate periods of the world's history, sexual life is at least tolerable since even those who were the goddesses and gods of heaven must lead this life after the world's fall. But now is *not* the right time for such a life. This is a time of 'emergency'; the end of history is almost here, and it is time for radical purification in preparation for the heavenly world to come. If an individual has produced children, then of course he or she must support them and see to their future. But sex must stop.

Hatred of sexuality is a pervasive theme in both the writings and the daily discourse of the movement. Sex, it is said, weakens the body and leaves it easy prey to disease. It produces children who are attachments in themselves, and whose existence leads to further attachments because of the necessity to earn money for their support. Sex is responsible for the overpopulation of the planet (a constant Brahma Kumari preoccupation) that has made a 'slum' of the world. Lust is a 'poison,' and indulging in it is like carrying a 'basket of rubbish' on one's head. Intercourse is compared to wallowing in a 'sewer.'

As the Brahma Kumaris conceive it, sexual intercourse has nothing whatsoever to do with 'love.' To love another person is to love what the other person really is—namely, a soul. But we are normally deceived by our undiscriminating physical eyes, and instead of souls we see male and female bodily forms when we look at other persons. Only those whose 'eye of knowledge' (the third, soul-seeing eye in the forehead) is fully opened are totally safe from this deception. Therefore, the only persons in the movement who were ever allowed to embrace members of the opposite sex were Dada Lekhraj himself and his main disciple, Om Radhe. From false vision arises lust, which, far from being love, is the source of interpersonal violence. In the daily discourses frequent reference is made to women being 'tortured' by demands for sex, and in one of the movement's booklets it is asserted that people who look on each other with lust 'do not make love, but actually commit criminal assault on each other' (*Purity and Brahmacharya* 1976, 14).

There is a crucial connection between the question of sexuality and matters of power. To be unfree is to be powerless; thus, the secret of freedom is power. The problem for women is that they are powerless in the present era. In part this is a matter of powerlessness within unjust social institutions—'worldly' families in which they are but the 'heel of the left foot' of man. But this in turn merely reflects a more basic kind of powerlessness. Sexuality, most of all, binds women, as well as men, to the world; precisely because we lack the power to conceive children without coitus, we are sexual beings. Moreover, our very sexuality augments our powerlessness, for sexual intercourse involves the expenditure and waste of vital power.

This point must be appreciated against the background of certain more general Hindu ideas about sexuality. In the Hindu milieu there is a close connection between sexuality and power. Intercourse is regarded as debilitating, because it rapidly drains vital energies that are slow to accumulate in the body (see esp. Carstairs 1961, 83–88). Conversely, sexual restraint is a method of concentrating and storing power. The deity Shiva is the preeminent symbol of this principle. Shiva is the ascetic of the gods, dwelling apart from society and, during one phase of his existence, gathering fiery energy within himself by means of chastity.[2] When the other gods once wished to rouse him from his trance of withdrawal to prevent him from absorbing all of the energy of the universe, they sent the unfortunate Kāmdev, the god of lust. Shiva, the 'enemy of lust,' then burnt Kāmdev to ashes with fire from his third eye.

The Brahma Kumaris seek the power to make themselves free in a world that they themselves, by means of their power, will make. Given Hindu ideas about the relationship between power and sexuality, this means that they must renounce sexual intercourse. Since Shiva is the divine archetype of the sexual renouncer, it is not surprising that he is the presiding deity of the universe as they conceive it. Like Shiva himself, the Brahma Kumaris 'destroy lust' by opening their own third eyes, the locus of their soul-seeing 'divine vision.' And like him they accumulate power, a power that is at once tapped, enhanced, and validated by the successful practice of rāja yoga.

Shiva was a very important deity among the Hindus of Sind (Thakur 1959, esp. 108–15), which no doubt provided the cultural infrastructure for the Brahma Kumaris' elaboration of his image in their own peculiar direction. However, the Brahma Kumaris' Shiva is

[2] Shiva's personality and attributes are analyzed in O'Flaherty's outstanding book, *Asceticism and Eroticism in the Mythology of Śiva* (1973).

a somewhat reduced or truncated version of the Puranic original. As portrayed in Puranic mythology, his character swings wildly (though regularly) between extremes of eroticism and asceticism (see O'Flaherty 1973). But there is nothing erotic about Shiva as the Brahma Kumaris picture him; he is a purely ascetic deity whose character fulfills the values of the movement. Nothing whatsoever (as far as I know) is said of his celebrated amours with his consort Pārvatī. Most Hindus worship Shiva in the form of the phallic linga. The Brahma Kumaris acknowledge the linga as a coarse representation of Shiva but adamantly deny that it is phallic in any sense. They themselves prefer to represent him not by the more conventional *yoni*-mounted linga, but—as we have seen—by a red, egg-shaped emblem. This is said to be a likeness of the halo of reddish light surrounding his real presence in the supreme abode. At the center is a tiny white dot (or hole, if the device is of the hollow sort with a lamp inside) representing the point of light (jyoti bindu) that is the locus of his immense power, forever retained by absolute chastity.

This emphasis on the connection between power and sexuality underlies what to Western feminists might seem a rather odd feature of the Brahma Kumaris' position with regard to existing institutions. Although they consider marriage, and thus the family, to be oppressive in the present age, and although commitment to the movement by individuals has sometimes proven to be quite destructive to marriages and families, they do not advocate the dissolution of either. Neither the family nor marriage vexes them as such. There will be marriage in the new world to come, and married couples (I was told by a movement teacher) will take care of their children much as they do here and now. As we have seen, moreover, many members are married and live in families. In itself, this arrangement is not regarded as an obstacle to achieving salvation. Rather, it is *worldly* marriage, marriage with intercourse, to which the Brahma Kumaris most object. Instead of directing the energies of the movement toward achieving the kind of institutional reforms sought by Western feminists, what they seek is purity (*pavitratā*) within the family. By purity they particularly mean chastity, which in their view is the virtue from which all other virtues arise.

Childhood

As a theme celibacy is probably susceptible to as many variations as sexuality itself. One may speak, for example, of postsexual celibacy, the renunciation of an already fulfilled sexuality. This is, in fact, the celibacy of many of the Brahma Kumaris' middle-aged and elderly converts (and, I should add, is not necessarily a virtue made of necessity). Celibacy might also be hypersexual, as in the tantric image of restraint within a context of erotic stimulation. But among the Brahma Kumaris, celibacy as a value seems to be conceived primarily as presexual, drawing for its imagery on what the West has learned to call the latency period of childhood. That this is so is consistent with the movement's concern with women.

In Hindu India, renunciation is one of the most important means for achieving liberation as religiously conceived. Unfortunately, in this tradition renunciation is not a value that applies very easily to women. While there is nothing in the idea of liberation through renunciation that necessarily excludes women, and while there are and have been female ascetics in the Hindu world, the fact remains that sannyās (world renunciation), conceived as a stage of life, is not for women, but for men. In the classical four-āshrama scheme (the four stages of life), a man's wife is permitted to accompany him to the forest in the penultimate stage of *vānaprasth*, but he becomes a sannyāsī, or full renouncer, alone. In this portrayal of world renunciation, the wife just seems to dwindle away.

But if the culturally dominant model of renunciation appears to exclude women, the Brahma Kumaris have exploited another possibility inherent in that construct as a way of developing a culturally legitimate conception of world renunciation for women. It involves an inversion of the dominant model: if men can become free through renunciation at the end of their lives, women can achieve a similar condition by recovering life's beginning. To some degree this idea is latently present in the concept of sannyās already. The full renouncer is, in fact, childlike in his asexuality and dependency on those around him. But the Brahma Kumaris have carried this idea much further.

The concept of childhood is a powerful theme in Brahma Kumari teachings. The satyug is not only the childhood of the world, but also an age of children. This is an era of endless springtime. There are no worries, there is no work, and above all there is no sex. It is a world of total innocence and perpetual play.

Likewise, there has been a rather distinct flavor of juvenility in the movement's subculture in the present world. Because of his advanced age at the time the movement began, and also in consonance with the general Hindu image of the deity Brahmā as a grandfather, Lekhraj's persona was in some respects rather grandfatherly. He was also then, and remains today, the movement's father. During his lifetime his followers were not merely his nominal 'daughters' and 'sons,' but were really treated that way. He was the pater familias of what was, in effect, an adopted family for committed members of the movement. He always addressed his followers as his 'children' or 'sweet children,' or by using other terms of parental endearment. He distributed prasād as a father might distribute sweets to his children,[3] and took his children-followers on seaside walks, picnics, and other excursions. One male informant very emotionally recalled to me being taken, as an adult, on Lekhraj's lap.

There were—and are today—other role-establishing symbolisms too. Lekhraj is not only imaged as parental-grandparental Brahmā, but also as playful Krishna, whose form he is believed to take as his first birth in the satyug. Here is a flute-playing Lekhraj. His discourses are called muralīs, which is the same word used for Krishna's flute. Thus, he attracts his followers as Krishna did the gopīs of Braj. Moreover, Lekhraj's identity also incorporates something of Kalkin's, who likewise comes at the end of history and who, like Lekhraj, is a teacher of women (O'Flaherty 1976, 30).

But the dominant image is parental. Whatever else members of the movement might be, they are Brahmā Bābā's reborn ('lost but now found again') daughters and sons, and this relationship continues through mediumistic seances today. When you 'die alive,' the Brahma Kumaris say, you become 'Bābā's child.' Nor is the image of movement members as children always strictly familial. Although the movement has chosen the institutional facade of a 'university,' in many ways the prevailing atmosphere is more that of a primary schoolroom with its emphasis on classroom decorum and mild scoldings for the disobedient.

But why should the Brahma Kumaris wish to be children? The answer seems to lie in their use of women's situation as a metaphor for the human condition. Brahma Kumari historical cosmology portrays the world as a paradise in its childhood; only when the world grows up (to its sexual awakening) does the trouble begin. The point is, a

---

[3] In the Hindu tradition generally the theme of child-parent love may be stronger in prasād-taking than is generally recognized. Parents are, of course, feeders. The 'special-treat' character of prasād, especially when it takes the form of sweets, may well evoke recollections of childhood feelings toward parents. A perceptive informant (not a Brahma Kumari) once said to me that in her view the real function of prasād was to inculcate 'positive feelings' (her words) toward the deity in children.

similar 'fall' is characteristic of changes a woman experiences over the course of her life cycle. Or this, at least, is the Brahma Kumari view.

The change in religious as well as social status that women in northern India undergo at the time of marriage is a matter of great symbolic importance to the Brahma Kumaris, and a subject frequently touched upon in Lekhraj's sermons. A *kanyā*, or unmarried girl, is considered a kind of goddess.[4] In northern India one of the main occasions for the worship of the goddess (in the generic sense) is a ceremonial period known as *navrātra* (nine nights). The Brahma Kumaris put great emphasis on the fact that one of the ways the goddess is worshipped during this festival involves the worship (pūjā) of unmarried girls, which is offered just as it would be to an icon of the goddess on an altar. But a woman is not worshipped in this way after marriage; then the husband, not the wife, is regarded as pūjya, 'worthy of worship.' A wife, by contrast, is merely pujārī, 'one who worships.' It is true that the Hindu world considers the new bride who enters the house to be an earthly Lakshmī, the goddess of prosperity. But according to the Brahma Kumaris, a woman cannot really be Lakshmī unless she lives in celibacy, and this is not possible in 'worldly' marriage. She cannot be Lakshmī, in other words, unless she is married to Nārāyan.

The analogy is obvious: just as the world falls with the advent of sexuality, so too the divinity (or at least the potential divinity) of women is lost when they marry. To regain divinity, or to ensure its perpetuation, the Brahma Kumaris must therefore become children; that is, they must be reborn as virgin daughters in the house of a new father.

Fatherhood may seem an odd idea for a group with an apparently feminist orientation to stress, but there is hardly a more pervasive concept in Brahma Kumari teachings. Dada Lekhraj was, of course, a father to the movement, a role he continues to play from beyond death's door. But even more important, the Supreme Soul—Shiv Bābā—is imaged as masculine and paternal; he is the Supreme

---

[4] This conception is very important in Sindhi culture. Thakur reports that 'a virgin or unmarried daughter is addressed as goddess ("Niani" or "Devi") and is considered equal to one hundred Brahmans . . . [who are] substituted in several rites by virgins. She is identified with sacred energy (shakti) as she symbolizes chastity which is potent with enormous powers . . . . She is frequently fed by the neighbors on various festivals including the Shradh festivities . . . . No fruit or vegetable of the season is eaten unless first offered to a virgin, whose feet are washed and homage paid whenever she is fed' (1959, 78). In this connection, it should be noted that Lekhraj also compares the worth of a pure woman to 'one hundred Brāhmans.'

Father (parampitā) who loves his children (the souls of human beings) with fatherly watchfulness and devotion. As we have already noted, the Brahma Kumaris characterize rāja yoga as 'remembering father,' by which they mean remembrance of our true father whose identity we forgot when we forgot our own.

The contrast between the idea of one's supreme and 'true' father (Shiv Bābā) and one's earthly or worldly (laukik) father is strong in these materials. The contrast is also explicitly linked with the issue of the structural exclusion of women from their natal families. This conjunction is deeply resonant with the life experiences of North Indian women. At the time of marriage a woman leaves her worldly father's home for an altogether new kind of existence. The Brahma Kumaris characterize this transition as a kind of rebirth. As a woman is reborn into a new family and a wholly new kind of life, her dominant identity changes from that of daughter to daughter-in-law. This change provides one of the staples of Indian folklore and literature, both traditional and modern, because of the potential for anguished separation and tragedy it carries. A married woman no longer enjoys the relative freedom that was hers as daughter and sister in her father's house. Her station as a daughter-in-law is low, at least initially. Also, according to the Brahma Kumaris, her role is largely one of onerous servitude. However, one need not ever be truly exiled from the Supreme Father's house, since he will always welcome his daughters back if they can but remember.

The life experiences peculiar to women are associated with what the Brahma Kumaris regard as distinctively feminine spiritual virtues. Lekhraj used to say (Pitā shrī n.d., 20–21) that it is precisely because women must leave their father's house at marriage to be reborn into a new life that they are uniquely amenable to the 'rebirth' that the spiritual life entails. Women are sannyās-minded, he said, because they are used to the idea of giving things up. He also said that the hardships that women endure tend to foster the humility and willingness to serve others that is fundamental to religious devotion. A good and pure woman is better than 'one hundred Brāhmans,' and such a woman can become a 'Ganges of knowledge.'[5]

---

[5] He also used to say that woman is not the 'field' (kshetra), but the 'field-knower' (kshetragya) (Pitā shrī, n.d., 24). In context this was a powerful assertion. In traditional theories of conception the woman is regarded as the mere 'field' (kshetra) into which man plants the vital seed (bīj). Lekhraj's statement is a double reference—to the famous field/field-knower (i.e., material nature/soul) distinction of the Bhagavad Gītā, and also to the aforementioned view of the feminine role in the economy of life.

In relation to the structural exclusion of women, another major issue for the Brahma Kumaris is inheritance. As Ursula Sharma has pointed out (1980, esp. 203–4), the inheritance system of northwest India is strongly masculine, and there is reason to believe that the hidden agenda of rules of exogamy in this region is to ensure the exclusion of women from the inheritance of land by exporting them as far from their natal families as possible. Sharma's analysis is probably valid for most areas of northern India, and is certainly consonant with what the Brahma Kumaris say. In the present world a daughter has 'no right' to her father's wealth (*Pitā shrī*, n.d., 21). The satyug, however, is an inheritance from the Supreme Father, belonging by right to the Brahma Kumaris as daughters who have proven themselves worthy of their claim.

But in a sense we, men and women alike, are *all* daughters who have become daughters-in-law. Subordination means living apart from one's father in worldly marriage; liberation, therefore, is to dwell with one's father as daughter of the house. The earthly hell into which we have fallen is simply worldly marriage, writ large. We have lost touch with our true father and have become 'lost children.' We must remember him and become his virgin daughters again, because only in his house can we find real freedom.

The idea of attaining autonomy and freedom by reclaiming premarital virginity has a special context in the symbolism of the Hindu pantheon. The image of the goddess in Hinduism is extremely complex, and since it has been explored in detail elsewhere,[6] I shall merely note a few relevant points here. Amidst the immense variety of forms the goddess takes, it is possible to discern two contrasting images. One portrays the goddess as the spouse of the gods. In these forms (as Lakshmī, Sītā, Pārvatī, and others) she is associated with such positive qualities as prosperity, nurturance, and fidelity. She is not a truly autonomous figure, since her identity is closely linked to that of her divine husbands. But when the goddess's marital connection is not stressed, another of her selves comes to the fore. Then she appears as a supremely powerful weapon-carrying killer of demons. In at least some of these forms, such as Kālī, she is portrayed as fearsome and even potentially dangerous, but these same powers can also be highly auspicious.

The autonomous goddess is an obvious symbol for a concept of woman as powerful and free. Her inherent power is unmodulated by

---

[6] See, for example, O'Flaherty (1980) and the essays in Hawley and Wulff (1982).

the restraints of marriage; she is a self-sufficient and self-directing force in the universe. Moreover, her status is not derived. Devotees worship her on her own account, since they believe that all other deities are subsumed in her. This independent goddess is the one virgin girls primarily represent in the rites of navrātra. This is also the goddess the Brahma Kumaris wish to emulate—autonomous, free, possessing inner powers protected by chastity, and worthy of worship like the virgins of the festival.

To recover childhood—and with it the virtues of premarital virginity—the Brahma Kumaris must die to old social roles (though they may continue to act them out) so that they may return to their true father's house. In their view earthly families are only temporary concatenations of material persons that have nothing to do with the souls that we essentially are. Thus, one must be reborn as a special kind of child in order to recover one's true identity in the eternal father's abode. Within this divine family (īshvarīya kuṭumb) the Brahma Kumaris believe they can achieve liberation from the injustices of this world and the promise of a liberated life, jīvan mukti, in the world to come.

Gender and Recognition

On the surface the Radhasoami and Brahma Kumari movements have little in common; millenarian and feminist tendencies seem to situate the Brahma Kumaris in an almost wholly different universe of religious thought and experience. But the differences seem less striking on closer inspection. What we learn from the juxtaposition of these two traditions is not simply how various the Hindu tradition is, but also how adaptable some of its most basic symbolisms and concepts can be.

Obviously the Radhasoami and Brahma Kumari traditions construe history quite differently. The Radhasoami image of the cosmos emphasizes temporal vastness, and finds in this idea support for a particular vision of the self's alienation from the world and salvationary opportunity. However, the celebrated cyclic déjà vu of Indic religions seems to play little role, if any, in this tradition. The Brahma Kumaris' scheme, on the other hand, emphasizes temporal finitude (in the context of infinite repetition). For them this focus provides a basis for a sense of crisis that has given them the courage to challenge the institutions of what they regard as an evil world. It is not, though, a motive to try to reshape the world directly. Differences of this magnitude between the two movements can be accommodated within the fold of the Hindu tradition, though not (in either case) under its name.

However, there are also similarities between these two constructions of time's passage. The most obvious likeness is that both schemes include a conception of history as cyclical. The materials we have seen suggest that in the Indic world this is a pattern that can be much modified, and even, as in the Radhasoami tradition, relegated to the status of a footnote, but it cannot be easily rejected. A focus on 'last things' may seem to be such a rejection, but in the Brahma Kumari case an emphasis on the imminence of the end of the world seems—paradoxically—to have accentuated a sense of historical reiteration: history becomes a movie, shown again and again. The end of the world can be made into a desperate fact by bringing it close, but it cannot be made unique. Moreover, any attempt to shift salvationary goals from the total otherness of transhistory must apparently be trapped by the cycle in the end. The Brahma Kumaris expect a heaven on earth, but the price they pay for this expectation is commitment to a paradise that cannot be forever.

In relation to interpretations of the human situation in history, another common theme is amnesia. The importance of this principle is far greater than its lack of visibility in many writings on Indic religion might suggest. Amnesia is central to the logic of karma as a response to the theodicy problem. If our experiences are the effects of the moral qualities of deeds done in past lives, then, given the capriciousness of fortune, faith in the justice of one's present experience makes sense only in a world in which the past can never be certainly known. This is undoubtedly one reason why the Brahma Kumaris, for all of their emphasis on their own peculiar brand of historiography, expect full memory (taking the form of full foresight) only when the books are closed at world's end when history stops. Full self-awareness has to be atemporal awareness.

By accelerating the cycle, Lekhraj made history matter in a very special way. But in the end this vision collapsed back into the black hole of transhistory. Lekhraj's warning was also a recollection, and all of his prophetic visions had this double aspect. The result was a pervading sense of present tense. What will be, was; all of history, in the final analysis, is. To the degree that history is known for what it truly is, it is known from a standpoint outside of history.

Nor is there any possibility of ameliorating history from within.

Because Lekhraj's thinking was based on the Hindu idea of cycles, and because the cycles are inevitable and fixed, it would have been nonsensical for him to have advocated trying to rescue *this* world by reforming its institutions. In this kind of world you cannot deal with things *in* history—you have to deal with history itself. And this means, at some level, escape from history. Therefore, although Lekhraj encouraged in his followers an urgent awareness of their position in history, the final result, at the level of praxis, was a renunciation of history by means of withdrawal into the liminal sangamyug and the contemplative disengagement of rāja yoga. Among other things, this meant that women—women greatly concerned about their position in a highly patriarchal society—ended up by meditating in semidarkened rooms.

On the matter of feminism, it must be stressed again that this is by no means the only concern of the Brahma Kumari movement. Although women's interests are a conspicuous element in their conception of the world and the human situation within it, they regard the tragedy of our present existence as a human problem, not specifically as a women's problem. Men have been involved in the movement from the beginning, and were in fact a majority among the daily attendees at the center in Delhi where most of my inquiries were conducted. Moreover, gender and sexual issues are muted in the movement's current persona, which has been deliberately focused on the culturally less provocative theme of world peace. All this said, however, at the very core of the Brahma Kumari view of the world there is an outlook that is feminist in the sense that it is based on a critical analysis of the position of women in Hindu society whose liberation it seeks, albeit in accord with what Western feminists might regard as a very queer idea of freedom.

It is possible, of course, that the Brahma Kumaris are in error about the relevance of their message to the women of India, or for that matter to anyone. Certainly their message seems to have very little general appeal. The sect has prospered greatly, but it still remains quite small in comparison with the size of the society in which it is situated. On the other hand, this may be an indication that its message is all too relevant. From its inception there has been nothing more striking about the Brahma Kumari movement than the uneasiness and distrust it has provoked in Indian society. This discomfort may reflect what men and women alike perceive as a powerful symbolic challenge to heterosexual relations in a highly patriarchal society—relations that may be more sensitive and fragile than is commonly supposed.

In this respect the Brahma Kumari movement is an excellent illustration not only of the richness of the Hindu tradition, but also of the ways in which elements of religious culture can be reordered to serve goals ostensibly quite remote from tradition. The indigenous roots of the Brahma Kumaris' teaching about women are plain at many levels. Their notions of the wrongs done to women, their concept of the power that liberates, their idea of how such power can be acquired, and their image of liberation itself are all in one way or another derived from the Hindu tradition. The result is a notable achievement: a Hindu feminism, radical in its implications, yet true to its own past.

But there is also an even deeper level of congruence between Brahma Kumari feminism and other Indic visions of the world. Here the striking contrast between Brahma Kumari concern with women and Radhasoami indifference to the same issue is a happy circumstance, since it points the way to true fundamentals. If the Radhasoami and Brahma Kumari traditions are visualized as the two arms of a 'V', widely separated at the top, then at their intersection we find that most basic of all religious problematics: identity. In both traditions the truly crucial question is that of who the devotee really is. The devotee is portrayed as lost, alienated from his or her 'true home' and real nature. Self-discovery is thus the devotee's task and challenge.

In both traditions, too, the resolution of the identity problem seems to involve very special kinds of interactions with identity-transformative 'others.' One transforms oneself by in some sense 'taking in' the superior nature of an exalted being. There are obvious differences of emphasis. Far more than the Brahma Kumaris, Radhasoami devotees are eaters and drinkers of the Lord's effluvia. Among the Brahma Kumaris the aperture through which divine-human interaction takes place is very narrow. By comparison with Radhasoami practice, there is relatively little prasād-taking; instead devotees ingest mainly knowledge in the form of the divinely inspired words for which Lekhraj was the human medium. Like prasād, these words were and are mouth-borne, but they are a somewhat more subtle medium for deity-devotee transactions than food and saliva. In addition, the visual medium, also crucial in the Radhasoami tradition, has become central to Brahma Kumari practice; in rāja yoga the Brahma Kumaris are visual drinkers of divine soul-light through awakened faculties of inner awareness.

But it is not enough merely to be a drinker, hearer, or seer. All depends on who the 'other' is. What is crucial seems to be the trick of recognition that supplies energy to the devotee's sense that his or her interactions with another really are self-transformative. This trick of recognition requires seeing the other in a way that transcends mere appearances.

For the Brahma Kumaris, as a devotional congregation, what was first necessary was the recognition of Lekhraj himself as a special being, 'appearances to the contrary notwithstanding.' The Brahma Kumaris stress that outwardly he never seemed to be anything more than a perfectly ordinary 'old man.' Recognition dawned for his first followers when their 'divine eyes' were opened and they saw light and power in his visage. This formative recognition continues to be enacted on a weekly basis when sisters enter trances to visit him in his subtle form. These visual visitations are exactly analogous to the ideal Radhasoami devotee's vision of more refulgent forms of the sant satguru in his or her ascent to regions above. It is also enacted, on a different level, in rāja yoga. When a student learns the technique from a human teacher, he or she is learning, in effect, to know himself or herself as soul by coming to see another as soul—that is, by coming to see the other in a way that departs completely from appearances. Having learned this, the student can then enter unaided relationships with the totally nonphysical Supreme Soul. In all of these cases the other is essentially an identity-transforming mirror, an external point of reference through which the self comes to know itself differently.

Brahma Kumari feminism, concerned as it is with a reassessment of female identity, works in partnership with this principle; at this level an 'otherworldly feminism' blends into forms of religious experience that are probably of very general importance in the Hindu world. From this standpoint the peculiarities of Brahma Kumari cosmology and historical theory diminish in importance. One must distinguish between the specific promise of such a tradition and its psychic rewards. The Brahma Kumaris promise a heaven to come, a paradise of (though it is not *just* this) perfect sexual equality. What the movement actually offers is a new way of experiencing the self, here and now, in which (among other things) gender differences are irrelevant. Such experiences are offered by other Hindu subtraditions too. For those who are fully committed to the movement, it also offers a manner of life, one of liminal siblinghood, in which an altered sense of self can be socially expressed in a communitarianism of extra-ordinary inwardness and intensity.

III. Sathya Sai Baba
and the Lesson of Trust

7. Sathya Sai Baba's Miracles

Magic

A more up-to-date young couple could scarcely be imagined. I met them for the first time on a Christmas afternoon in their impressively appointed house in one of the most expensive residential colonies in New Delhi. Then in their thirties, they were Punjabi Hindus whose families had been uprooted from Lahore at the time of the partition of the subcontinent between India and Pakistan. The chaos of those grim days seemed very distant from that pleasant sitting room. He was a very successful chartered accountant; she a housewife presiding over a neolocal household with three children. They spoke to me in fluent and expressive English. They had never been abroad, but their outlook was informed and cosmopolitan. They were in every way exemplary of modern Delhi's educated upper-middle class.

It all began, he told me, with his wife's sister's husband in Calcutta. This man was very rich and quite a libertine, an inveterate club-goer and heavy drinker. One evening as his bearer was about to bring his first whiskey, he picked up a copy of a book entitled *Sathyam, Shivam, Sundaram* (Kasturi, probably 1977), which his mother had left on a nearby table. The subject of this book was a deity-saint known as Sathya Sai Baba,[1] whose picture was on the cover. As he opened the book and began idly scanning its pages, his eye lighted on a sentence that read: 'You have not picked this book up by chance; it is by my will that you have done so.' This sentence, my informant told me, occurs nowhere in the actual printed book. His brother-in-law then began to read, and when his cronies called, he told them that he had decided to stop drinking for a while. In the end he became a devotee of Sathya Sai Baba and a transformed man. This story was the beginning of their own, my informant continued, for it was their astonishment at the alteration of the character of this incorrigible man that set in

---

[1] A more correct transliteration of his name would be *satya sāī bābā*. In the text to follow I shall use the nearly universal English version: Sathya Sai Baba.

motion a chain of events that led them, too, to become Sathya Sai Baba's devotees.

Sathya Sai Baba is modern India's most famous deity-saint. His somewhat heavy, cherubic face, framed by a cloud of curly afro-style hair, almost certainly has the highest degree of recognition (were such a thing ever to be measured) of all modern India's religious figures. In middle-class India, at least, the mere mention of his name usually suffices to elicit some comment, good or bad. As a type he is neither novel nor new. He is not the first living deity to set foot on the soil of India, nor will he be the last. Even in my limited circle of middle-class friends and neighbours in New Delhi, there were social networks that extended to several figures like Sathya Sai Baba, though not of his renown. Thousands of would-be Sathya Sai Babas probably pursue their divine careers in the relative obscurity of India's lesser cultural and social byways. But Sathya Sai Baba is the one who has risen to the top, the premier deity-saint of India's English-speaking and generally high-caste middle and upper-middle classes. Though his devotees are not all rich, as a group they tend to be both wealthier and more cosmopolitan than the generality of Radhasoami and Brahma Kumari devotees. Whatever else this wealth and status may mean, it has provided his cult with vast resources and unparalleled public visibility. The acclaim, however, is not universal. He has many detractors and is frequently accused of fraud and/or favoring only the rich and powerful. However, the size and influence of his indigenous (as opposed to international) following certainly justifies ranking him among the most important of modern India's religious personalities.

He is, at one level, a jet-age holy man. He is often to be found in automobiles and airplanes, traveling to meet his many followers throughout the subcontinent. And his followers, in their turn, are often people who better than any other represent the worldwide culture of middle-class modernity in its Indian form. Nor is the modernity of his cult only veneer. There is indeed something new, or newish, about Sathya Sai Baba's religious style. His personality resonates with the religious yearnings of the cosmopolitan and wealthy in a way that may not be unique, but is an impressive display of modernized saintliness. At a deeper level, however, there is something very ancient about Sathya Sai Baba's persona. He does the things a deity should: he receives the homage and devotion of his devotees, and he reciprocates with love and boons. And, above all, he performs miracles.

The remainder of that Christmas afternoon was given over to a very lengthy account of this couple's experiences as his devotees. For the most part this was an account of miracles. One of their children had been pronounced dead in the womb by doctors, but was restored to life by the deity-saint. When the wife developed a detached retina, Sathya Sai Baba saved her from blindness. One morning footprints of an infant were discovered before one of the many pictures of the deity-saint with which the interior of the house is filled. This was evidence of a nocturnal visitation by 'Baba.' (He is usually called *bābā* in conversation; also *svāmī*.) Red powder once oozed forth from one of these same pictures overnight. And another time, while they were praying, a garland that had been placed over one of the pictures leaped to the other side of the room. There was much, much more.

Avatār

Who is Sathya Sai Baba? As we shall see, this is a question with complex implications. From an outsider's standpoint he is a man born at a certain place and time with a personal biography. However, the matter cannot end here, since to his devotees Sathya Sai Baba is far more than an ordinary man. Also, as in the case of the Radhasoami gurus and Dada Lekhraj, the trick of recognizing him for what he 'really' is lies at the foundation of the religious experiences cultivated by his followers. Among other things, this means that the 'man himself' (as the outsider would say) is hard indeed to find. The strict facts of his personal biography and manner of life are buried beneath layer upon layer of hagiography (see esp. the works of Kasturi; also Gokak 1975). As far as I am aware, no objective account of Sathya Sai Baba's life has been written by anyone close to him. Indeed, such an account may be an inherent impossibility; it is unlikely that anyone who is allowed into his inner circles would *want* to write in such a vein. The word *defended* may be too strong, but the outside world is allowed only certain kinds of interactions with Baba, interactions that deviate very little from rather narrow devotional paradigms. He may be personally isolated even from his most trusted associates. One simply does not know.

Thus Sathya Sai Baba himself cannot be the actual subject of an account of his cult. For now, no supposedly 'real' Sathya Sai Baba can be any more real than an imagined character in fiction. All that is available are his public surfaces, his self as formally presented as an object for the devotional attitudes of his followers. But the humanly real Sathya Sai Baba is not of greatest interest in any case. Whoever he is, he is certainly more than the mere parlor magician many of his critics claim that he is. But even so, the most interesting Sathya Sai Baba, and in a sense the most real too, is the one who is worshipped by his devotees. This Sathya Sai Baba is what is known as an avatār, a 'descent' of God to earth. And of this Sathya Sai Baba one can indeed give an account, because his persona is fully available in the public domain of religious symbolism. At this level the extravagances of hagiography are not an impediment, but an important aid, to discovery.

His life story, as it emerges in the available materials,[2] consists of a core of basic facts surrounded by a great deal of elaboration. The facts are but the framework; the real tale is told by the elaborations. At the heart of this tale is the central theme of disclosure, which is also fundamental to the devotional attitudes assumed by his devotees today. As seen from the perspective of his devotees, Sathya Sai Baba's entire life has been one of signs and portents, uncanny occurrences that reveal at successively higher levels what is taken to be the truth about this only apparently human being.

Sathya Sai Baba was born in 1926 to a pious family of modest circumstances belonging to the Rāju caste[3] in the village of Puttaparthi in what is now the state of Andhra Pradesh. Named Satyanarayana, he was the last of four children. We are told that his birth was heralded by miracles. The strings of a *tambūrā* that was hanging in the house were plucked by a magical force just prior to his birth, and a cobra mysteriously appeared under the newborn infant's bedding (suggesting Vishnu's serpent-bed). It is said that during his early childhood he exhibited many signs of his very special character. He was unusually intelligent and an instinctive vegetarian. His character is described as sympathetic toward the poor and destitute, and much given to charitable acts. He was also, we learn, able to materialize food for himself.

[2] Virtually all existing accounts of Sathya Sai Baba's life are based on the hagiographic writings of Kasturi (1975b, 1975c, 1977). Kasturi is a retired history professor and college principal of Mysore University. He is a longtime devotee of Sathya Sai Baba, his secretary, and a central figure in the cult. The account that follows is based on Kasturi 1975b and 1977.

[3] Information on the Rājus can be found in Thurston and Rangachari (1909, 247–56).

Sathya Sai Baba's education began in a rustic village school and culminated at a high school at Uravakonda, some ninety kilometers from his native village. There is no evidence that he ever distinguished himself as a student. During his school years his main interests seem to have been in singing bhajans (devotional songs) and performing in traditional dramas. These dramas were based on episodes from Hindu mythology, and the young Satyanarayana was apparently a skilled actor. During this period there were many more uncanny occurrences. For example, he is said to have once prevented one of his teachers from rising from a chair by causing it to become tightly fixed to his backside. He also materialized sweets and other items for his friends.

The great watershed of his younger years, and the first great 'disclosure,' occurred in 1940 when he was thirteen years old. In March of that year, while at Uravakonda, he fell into a seizure of some kind, which at the time was thought to be caused by a scorpion sting. He recovered quite quickly, but then began behaving very strangely. Long periods of silence would give way to crying, laughing, fainting spells, and intense bouts of singing and scripture recitation. Doctors could do little. After his parents returned him to Puttaparthi, exorcists were employed, also to no avail. Finally on a morning in May he arose and began materializing items for members of his household and neighbors. His father was called, and in a flash of anger at being told to treat his son as a god, he threatened the boy with a stick. In response Satyanarayana said, 'I am Sai Baba. I belong to Apastamba Sutra, the spiritual school of Sage Apastamba and am of the Spiritual Lineage of Bharadwaja; I am Sai Baba; I have come to ward off all your troubles; keep your houses clean and pure' [Kasturi 1977, 47).[4] This was the first time Sathya Sai Baba explicitly declared his true (though partial) identity.

Although it might have meant little to Satyanarayana's (now Sai Baba's) fellow villagers, the name Sai Baba was a famous one at the time. Sai Baba was a much celebrated and rather mysterious holy man who years before had lived at the town of Shirdi in Maharashtra. There is no need here for an extended discussion of his most interesting

---

[4] Bharadvaja is one of the mythical Seven Sages (rishis), mind-born sons of Brahmā and ancestors of the Brahmanical gotras (lineages). See Mitchiner 1982. Some Rājus have adopted the Brahmanical gotra system (Thurston and Rangachari 1909, 249, 251), but the relevance of this to Sathya Sai Baba's claim is not clear. Apastamba is the putative author of an important body of dharmashāstra.

figure, but a few details are essential.[5] Sai Baba first appeared in
Shirdi as a teenaged boy in 1872. He was dressed as a Muslim
mendicant but professed to know nothing of his origin. Tradition
declared later that he was born of Brāhmaṇ parents but had been
raised by a Muslim fakīr. When he arrived at Shirdi, he took up
residence in an empty mosque (having been expelled from a local
Hindu temple), where he remained for the rest of his days. Over the
course of the ensuing years he attracted a very large following and
continued to be the focus of a widespread cult after his death in 1918.[6]
His saintly style was notably eclectic, a blend of Hindu and Muslim
elements. His trademark was a perpetually burning fire. He distributed
the ashes from this fire to his followers, who ate it or applied it to their
bodies. He was famous as a curer and miracle-worker, and the ash he
distributed was regarded as a material vehicle for his mysterious
powers. This is a theme we shall encounter again.

Having made the astonishing claim that he was a reincarnation of
this great Maharashtrian saint, Sathya Sai Baba returned to school,
but by now his educational career was in shambles. He began to
create an enormous sensation by materializing sacred ash (called
vibhūti) and other items and substances. There were many other
miracles as well. Finally, in October 1940, he announced to his
brother's wife (he was living in his brother's house in Uravakonda)
that he was no longer 'your Sathya' (ibid., 52). This was the decisive
break with earthly relatives that marks the career of any holy man. He
then returned to Puttaparthi and, living apart from his family, began
to accept devotees.

Over the years that followed Sathya Sai Baba's reputation grew
very rapidly. The main basis of his fame was the miracles. Materializations, astonishing cures, and much else of the same sort drew
increasingly large crowds to Puttaparthi. During the 1940s he also
began to travel to Madras and elsewhere in South India, and soon he
had a large regional following. In 1950 the construction of his āshram
at Puttaparthi was completed (it has grown since then), and by this
time this once obscure village had become a notable feature of the
sacred geography of South India. During the 1950s his fame spread to
the rest of the country (partly a result of tours to the sacred centers of

[5] For an excellent discussion of Shirdi Sai Baba and the entire Sai Baba tradition, see
White's 'The Sai Movement: Approaches to the Study of Indian Saints' (1972).

[6] There is at least one temple dedicated to Shirdi Sai Baba in New Delhi. Some of the
habitues of this temple expressed to me strong disapproval of the cult of Sathya Sai
Baba.

the North), and he became firmly established as a religious figure of
national (and to some degree international) reputation.[7]

The second great 'disclosure' occurred in June of 1963, and is quite
reminiscent of the first disclosure in 1940. On the morning of June
29th, while at his āshram, Sathya Sai Baba had another seizure. A
witness (his close associate, N Kasturi) describes it thus: 'The face
twitched and muscles drew the mouth to the left . . . . the tongue lolled.
The left eye appeared to have lost its sight' (1975b, 79). A physician
who was called to the scene diagnosed the illness as tubercular
meningitis. The ailing saint was in what appeared to be a coma for
part of the time, although there were periods in which he was at least
aware enough of his surroundings to refuse injections and to communicate with his grieving devotees by means of gestures and a few
indistinct words.

On the sixth day the pain abated somewhat, and on the eighth day
he appeared before a large crowd. Still visibly ill, he was propped into
position in his chair. He first turned to one of his assistants (N.
Kasturi) and asked him to announce to the crowd that the illness from
which he seemed to be suffering was not really his, but something he
had taken upon himself for the relief of a deserving devotee (a claim he
had also later made about his indisposition in 1940). He then sprinkled
water on himself, and by so doing, apparently cured himself
instantaneously and completely.

In the discourse that followed he reiterated, in full voice, that he
had taken on the illness to save a devotee. Then he went on to say that
he would disclose something that he had kept to himself for his
thirty-seven years of life. He was, he said, actually Shiva and Shakti
(Shiva's consort) in embodied form. At a deeper level of significance,
his apparent illness was actually that borne by Shakti because she had
once neglected the sage Bharadvaja, causing him to become ill. Just
as Shiva cured Bharadvaja by sprinkling water on him, Shiva had
now cured Shakti in Sathya Sai Baba's body. He further let it be
known that there would be a total of three Sai incarnations, all in the
lineage (gotra) of Bharadvaja. Shirdi Sai Baba was Shakti alone, and

---

[7] Although Sathya Sai Baba has travelled in East Africa, he has not, unlike some of
India's other modern deity-saints, put a great deal of emphasis on internationalization.
He treats foreign devotees with particular consideration, but his constituency is basically
Indian. For a non-Indian devotee's perceptions of Sathya Sai Baba, see Murphet 1975.
For an admiring but somewhat more distanced account, see Schulman 1971. The
animus of Brooke's book (1979) is too strong for one to have much confidence in its
accuracy.

Sathya Sai Baba is Shiva and Shakti together. Still to come is an incarnation of Shiva alone. He will take the form of Prem Sai, to be born in Karnataka State.

These pivotal assertions marked the formal completion of Sathya Sai Baba's publically available identity. One notable feature of this rather complex statement is the promise of a third incarnation. As D. A. Swallow points out, this assertion has important organizational implications: Sathya Sai Baba's promise that he will be reborn yet again obviates, at least in theory, potentially difficult succession rivalries that might arise within the cult (1982, 136–37). None of those in his immediate circle can have any basis (in the prevailing theory of Sathya Sai Baba's identity) for preparing the ground for claiming his sacred authority after his death.

But what is central is the claim to be an avatār of Shiva (and, of course, of Shakti too). Moreover, this claim is quite overt. Unlike the Radhasoami sant satgurus, Sathya Sai Baba's assertion of divine status is expressed in the first person; he states it boldly and repeatedly. He has come in the present age of wickedness and misery, he says, not merely to alleviate individual misfortunes (though he does do this for his devotees), but to set the whole world right, to usher in a 'Sai Age.' In the form of Shirdi Sai Baba his mission was to establish Hindu-Muslim unity; in his present incarnation he will reestablish Vedic and Shastric religion. As Prem Sai he will bring all of this work to completion. His present incarnation, he says, has four phases. For the first sixteen years he engaged in playful pranks (*bālalīlās*), and during the second sixteen years he displayed miracles (*mahimās*). The third sixteen-year period is reserved for teaching (updesh) and further miracles, and the remainder of his life will be devoted to the intensive teaching of spiritual discipline (*sādhanā*) to restricted groups. He will die at the age of ninety-six, but his body will stay young until then.

Because all the gods are ultimately one, Sathya Sai Baba is all the gods (and goddesses too) of the Hindu pantheon—and, indeed, in his view he is the deity of every religion. His devotees call him *Bhagavān*, which is to say, simply, 'God.' But his dominant identity is Shiva, and it is around the traditional image of Shiva that some of the most important symbolic accouterments of the cult are centered (on this see esp. Swallow 1982). Iconographically he is frequently portrayed in association with Shiva or the linga, which is Shiva's principal material representation for purposes of worship. In popular prints he is often represented standing inside a linga. In the cult's sacred year the most important occurrence is the festival of mahāshivrātri, 'the great night of Shiva.' On this occasion he materializes vast quantities of sacred ash from his hand inside an inverted pot. The ash then pours over a silver image of Shirdi Sai Baba (in parallel with the bathing of the deity [abhisheka] in a temple rite), after which it is distributed to devotees. On the same occasion he materializes lingas within his body, which he then ejects, with signs of pain and difficulty, from his mouth.

In many ways at the symbolic center of the cult, this sacred ash is a particularly unambiguous link with Shiva. Ash is basic to Shaivite ritual; markings of it are worn by Shiva's priests, and it is distributed to his worshippers from his altar. Ash is also associated with Kāma (Kāmdev), who was reduced to ashes (as we have seen in chapter 6) by Shiva's fire of anger. It embodies Shiva's ascetic powers, and is associated with the burning grounds, one of Shiva's favorite haunts. Sathya Sai Baba's use of ash also recalls the figure of Shirdi Sai Baba, who distributed ash to his followers from his perpetually burning fire.

Since the revelation of 1963 the cult has continued to grow. Although national in scope, it has only one true center—the person of Sathya Sai Baba himself. Its raison d'etre is the worship and service of this living deity. As already noted, the cult has a rather narrow—but socially and culturally very influential—constituency, which is basically drawn from urban India's English-educated elites. Since there are no formal ties of membership, it seems unlikely that we will ever know how many devotees there actually are. The cult has no well-defined boundaries in any case. Among my neighbors in New Delhi there were some who did not identify themselves as actual devotees, but who nonetheless considered Sathya Sai Baba to be in some sense a living deity. Of course there were also many who regarded him as a fraud and worse. But all of my neighbors at least knew of him; in middle-class India one would have to be asleep not to.

The Cult in the World

One of the most remarkable features of Sathya Sai Baba's cult is that he has managed to preserve the imagery and atmosphere of a purely personal constituency, despite the fact that many of his devotees see him rarely, and then often only from a distance. Though rooted in the South, his cult is far less regionally focused than the Radhasoami or

Brahma Kumari movements. He is a frequent traveller to various parts of India where he meets groups of devotees, and many followers travel to Puttaparthi to see him. But there are obvious physical limits on the degree to which his person can be accessible to followers. Nonetheless, despite its size and complexity, the cult expresses, and is energized by, Sathya Sai Baba's personal charisma. The cult-in-the-world is a kind of devotional empire, far-flung but totally dependent on the authority of its sovereign.

Baba, I was told, does not accept donations of money and does not own property. However, donations are accepted and property held by a legal entity known as the Central Shri Sathya Sai Trust. Donations to the trust can be made at any branch office of the Canara Bank (a large concern with branches all over the subcontinent). In each Indian state there is also a State Trust with its own Council of Management. The councils of management are composed of distinguished and prominent persons from a variety of backgrounds. Sathya Sai Baba himself, I was told, is the sole trustee of the various trusts.

Under the umbrella of the trusts is a vast organization, the cult's infrastructure, that engages in a number of quite diverse activities. These activities include the support and management of the cult's various devotional epicenters. Sathya Sai Baba's main āshram (known as Prashanti Nilayam) is at Puttaparthi, but he also has a colony at Whitehead (near Bangalore) and maintains residences at Bombay, Hyderabad (in Andhra Pradesh), and Madras. Through its Educational and Publication Foundation, the cult publishes a monthly magazine called *Sanathana Sarathi* in English, Hindi and Telugu. This same organizational arm also publishes and distributes numerous books dealing with Sathya Sai Baba or containing collections of his discourses.

Social service is another major emphasis of the cult. With junior and senior branches, the *sevā dal* (service corps) sponsors a variety of charitable and philanthropic activities: feeding the poor, assisting the authorities in relief work during disasters, visiting the sick, and so on. During the Delhi flooding of 1978 the local sevā dal was involved in distributing food to victims.

Education is another field in which Sathya Sai Baba's organizations are quite active. In 1979 four 'Sathya Sai Colleges' existed: three for girls (at Anantpur, Bhopal and Jaipur) and one for boys (at Bangalore). Plans were afoot for a college in each state of the Indian union. The educational arm of the cult also sponsors summer courses in 'Indian culture and spirituality' for college students. Major efforts are devoted to what is called the *bāl vikās* (child development) program. The purpose of this program is to supplement the secular education of children with 'spiritual' instruction. The classes are held once a week for an hour or so, usually in individual homes. There are said to be over eight hundred such classes taking place in India.

The bāl vikās classes exemplify well some of the most characteristic features of the general outlook of Sathya Sai Baba's cult. In consonance with a common doctrine of most forms of neo-Hinduism, Sathya Sai Baba interprets his message as religiously universal. Therefore, the bāl vikās program is deemed to be 'nonsectarian.' Nonetheless, the symbolism deployed in the classes is distinctly Hindu. Classes take place before an altarlike arrangement consisting of a picture or pictures of Sathya Sai Baba and an empty chair (actually occupied, in spirit, by the deity-saint himself). Classes begin with the chanting of the sacred syllable *om*, followed by a prayer (in Sanskrit) and the singing of devotional songs (bhajans). Then follows a lecture. The one I heard was on guruship: just as the deities Brahmā, Vishnu, and Shiva preside over creation, preservation, and destruction—the children were told—so a guru creates a new person, preserves the goodness in him, and destroys the bad. Then follows an interlude of meditation on Sathya Sai Baba's form. At the conclusion of the class each child receives a *tilak* of sacred ash on the forehead (a standard Hindu practice). What Muslims make of this kind of ecumenism I do not know; I was told that there were three or four Muslim children in the class of sixty-five that I attended. Even if some concessions are made to other religions in these classes, they are clearly locked into essentially Hindu devotional patterns.

The cult of Sathya Sai Baba does not make great demands on its adherents. This is not to say that a devotee might not make considerable demands on himself or herself, but the imposition of rigid rules is foreign to the spirit of Sathya Sai Baba's teachings. He favors a moderate and sāttvik (in essence, vegetarian) diet, and avoidance of alcohol and smoking. These are not radical injunctions in a Hindu context. Though celibate himself, Sathya Sai Baba does not advocate the celibate life for his devotees. He holds the householder's (*grihastha*'s) life in high esteem, and encourages celibacy only after the age of fifty (see Kasturi n.d.b, 445). One of my devotee-informants happened to have nearly destroyed his marriage by vowing celibacy without consulting his spouse (also a devotee), but this was done on his own, not because of any teaching of the cult.

In contrast to the Radhasoami and Brahma Kumari movements, the cult does not consider itself to be in tension with the religious usages of the surrounding community. The cult does not have pre-scribed rites that might conflict with other ceremonial requirements, nor does it see its tenets as at odds in any way with what is said to be the true essence of other religions. Given Sathya Sai Baba's divine identity, all worship of God—in whatever form—is actually worship of him in any case.

One can participate in the cult at practically any level. Placing a picture of Sathya Sai Baba in one's family shrine (or a statuette on the dashboard of one's car) is participation of a kind. More committed devotees are likely to attend sessions of devotional singing, which are held on a regular basis (usually monthly) in devotees' homes. Special sessions are also held in conjunction with major Hindu festivals such as mahāshivrātri, *gurupūrṇimā*, dashehrā, and *janmāshṭamī*. These events take place in the presence of the usual altarlike display of an empty chair (actually occupied) and numerous pictures of Sathya Sai Baba, Shirdi Sai Baba, and various deities. Attendees tend to be well dressed and obviously affluent, and I suspect that in some circles these events carry a certain social cachet. The main event is the singing of devotional songs, most of which are overtly addressed to Sathya Sai Baba himself. A book containing suitable bhajans (*Shrī satya* n.d.) is owned by many devotees. The singing is followed by a period of silent meditation, and then āratī is performed in the usual fashion before the altar. Devotees receive prasād as they leave.

At a higher level of commitment devotees not only participate in these observances but are actively involved in the educational and social service activities of the cult. Such individuals are also likely to be frequent visitors to Puttaparthi, and might even have purchased some form of permanent accommodations there. One of my informants, for example, joined two other devotees to pay Rs 12 000 for permanent rights in a place to stay during visits to the āshram. Hard-core devotees are often easily identifiable as such by the interior decor of their houses. The houses of strong devotees are usually stuffed with pictures of Sathya Sai Baba and other cultic bric-a-brac: books, recordings of Sai bhajans, busts, life-sized plaster replicas of his feet, and so on. Highly committed devotees use the phrase *sāī rām* as a salutation.

Sathya Sai Baba is, among other things, a teacher. He is a frequent giver of discourses, now compiled in several volumes. He usually speaks in Telugu, and before a Hindi-speaking audience an interpreter is required. One of his most characteristic rhetorical devices is the ad hoc (and often false) etymology. For example, he has stated that *Hindu* means 'one who is nonviolent' by the combination of *hinsā* (violence) and *dūr* (distant).

In the case of Sathya Sai Baba's teachings we are not, as in the case of the Radhasoami and Brahma Kumari movements, dealing with an elaborated and internally rationalized doctrinal system of which an extended account has to be given. Sathya Sai Baba's doctrines are basically an eclectic blend of elements drawn from a variety of well-known philosophical and devotional traditions. Virtually everything 'spiritual' is accorded its own value, including non-Hindu religions too. His ethics are basically common coin in the Hindu world, though certainly not to be dismissed on that account. Tolerance, gentleness, and kindness toward others are among his most frequently stated values. Whatever else he or she might feel, a Hindu auditor or reader of Sathya Sai Baba's discourses would probably not react to any of his teachings with surprise.

Nor does Sathya Sai Baba teach anything resembling the distinctively rationalized systems of disciplined introspection we have encountered in the Radhasoami and Brahma Kumari movements. That is, he does not have a meditational 'system' of his own. In fact, although he pays due respect to matters of salvation, the atmosphere of his cult is really not very soteriological at all. My informants dwelt little on questions of ultimate salvation; what mattered mainly to them was Sathya Sai Baba himself, and what he did or did not do to alleviate the misfortunes of life in this world.

Nonetheless, Sathya Sai Baba does strongly encourage his followers to engage in sādhanā (spiritual discipline). Identification with the body, he says, is a delusion; the reality of the person is the self or 'soul', the ātmā, encased within five material sheaths (*koshas*). By means of the repetition of the Lord's name, and meditation (dhyān) on his form, one can remove the effects of past karmas and directly experience the true reality of the self within. He urges daily meditation, preferably at 3:00 or 4:00 A.M. Recommendations on technique, not distinctive in any way, are scattered throughout his discourses and are also a prominent feature of the bāl vikās curriculum. Devotees should meditate on Sathya Sai Baba's form or on the flame of a lamp. If a lamp is used, the meditator should stare at the flame, mentally fix its image between his or her eyebrows, and then imagine its light filling up the body (see Sathya Sai Baba 1976, 75–78). The light is the Lord, and by experiencing oneself as the light, one realizes one's identity with God, who all along has been within. The final goal, therefore, is merger with God, who is, in fact, Baba. The result will be the eradication of harmful motives and tendencies, and feelings of deep inner peace (*prashānti*).

Under the rather cluttered eclecticism of Sathya Sai Baba's teachings are a few very consistent themes. One is a persistent note of cultural nationalism of a kind that sometimes verges on nativism. Although he welcomes foreigners as followers, he regards Western cultural influences as highly destructive in India. He believes that many Indians have sold themselves to the West and have become alienated from their own heritage. How, he asks, can Western values be applicable in any sense to Indian life? Though India has won its freedom, he says, 'The attitudes and the habits of the West still dominate the mind of the educated and the leaders' (Kasturi n.d.a, 147). Indians should not try to imitate others, but should adhere to 'the folkways that have been preserved by the folk-mind of this land' (Kasturi n.d.b, 43). He particularly deplores what he regards as the prevailing ignorance of the Hindu textual tradition, which is indeed true of many of his followers. Instead of being taught Sanskrit *stotras*, he says, Indian children are made to recite such nonsense as 'Baa, baa black sheep.' Correcting all of this is a major goal of his educational ventures. Sathya Sai Baba's harsh judgment of the Westernization of India, which is expressed repeatedly in his discourses, is not a minor theme. These are obviously matters that touch with particular directness on the life experiences of his English-educated, middle-class followers.

However, his discontent with the state of present-day India does not mean that he advocates radical reform of existing economic or social institutions. On these matters his views are in many ways profoundly conservative. For example, he is adamantly against strikes: for him the ideal social order is one based on noncompetitive complementation, a view deeply conditioned by the ideology of caste. 'The owner,' he says, 'is the heart of the organization; those who work in it in the various fields of activity necessary to carry out its objectives are the limbs. The heart has to keep the limbs active; the limbs have to sustain the heart' (Kasturi 1975a, 80). It is true that God showers his grace on all, and is indifferent to caste distinctions, but this does not mean that all human beings are the same. Innate capacities differ: 'The cry of equality now being used as a slogan is a vain and meaningless cry; for how can man, inheriting a multiplicity of impulses, skills, qualities, tendencies, attitudes, and even diseases from his ancestors and from his own history [Karmic history] be all of the same stamp?' (Kasturi 1970b, 29). Sathya Sai Baba urges his followers to treat others with decency and charity, but he does not advocate the upsetting of existing hierarchies.

He is no feminist, but by his own lights he has a deep concern for the welfare of women, as evidenced by the attention he has given to women's education. There are many women among his most ardent devotees in Delhi. He keeps a somewhat wary distance from his female followers, or so I am told. This is only prudent, given endemic suspicions about relations between male gurus and female followers. His views on the innate characteristics of women are of a piece with his views on caste, and are hardly enlightened, at least from a feminist point of view. Women are trusting, compassionate, humble, and shy. They are also weak (in some ways) and quick to petty anger. A virtuous woman is a treasure, but she has a circumscribed place in the order of things. Women should strive to realize *strī-dharma*, the inherent virtues of womanhood, which means that they should not be 'seen or talked about' and should stay 'away from the public gaze'; they should be 'silent invisible partners and inspirers, and teachers' (ibid., 65).

But anyone familiar with the cult of Sathya Sai Baba will know that this discussion of doctrines and teachings is, though not irrelevant, to a considerable degree beside the point. As far as I know, not one of my informants became involved in the cult because of Sathya Sai Baba's teachings as such, nor did many of them advert to doctrinal matters when describing their experiences as devotees. It is of course important that Sathya Sai Baba pronounces and teaches, and the content of what he says has its importance too. But for most devotees Baba's teachings are little more than a tambūrālike background drone. For them what is important about what he says is not its content, but the fact that *he* is the one saying it.

When devotee-informants talk about Sathya Sai Baba, what one hears is not theology, but account after account of their personal experiences as devotees. What emerges as one general theme in these accounts is the same kind of visual, tactile, and alimentary intimacy that is so central to devotional Hinduism in general, and that we have seen exemplified with particular clarity in the Radhasoami materials. His devotees long to see him, to hear him, to be near him, to have private audiences with him, to touch him (especially his feet), and to receive and consume, or use in other ways, substances and objects that have been touched by him or that originate from him. But above all, what one hears about are the miracles. In this respect, the account with which this chapter began is entirely typical. It is largely because of the miracles that devotees are drawn to him in the first place. The miracles, moreover, seem to play a vital role in sustaining the allegiance of his devotees. Miracles are the staple of any conversation about Sathya Sai Baba among his devotees, and are the principal topic of the literature concerning him as well. Any attempt to understand this cult, therefore, must try to come to terms with the miraculous.

Knowing Better

It would be easy not to take the cult of Sathya Sai Baba seriously. Because of its surfaces of modernity and the apparent estrangement of its many wealthy and English-educated adherents from 'grassroots Hinduism' (Bharati 1981, 87), it would be tempting to dismiss the cult as in some sense inauthentic, a less-than-best avenue to an understanding of anything truly Hindu. But in my view this would be a mistake. Not only is this cult deeply and authentically Hindu, as I hope to show, but the very cultural alienation of its main constituency sets in bold relief certain features of the Hindu tradition that we might not otherwise see as clearly.

In its emphasis on the miraculous the cult of Sathya Sai Baba seems to invert what common sense would lead us to expect. There is certainly nothing new about the miraculous in the Hindu world. Indeed, in this world the credibility of miraculous occurrences is never really the main issue; what matters most is what such events, in specific instances, actually *mean*. But Sathya Sai Baba's following is notably cosmopolitan, consisting of many people who at least outwardly are as strongly attuned as anyone to the more international cult of scientific rationality. These people, we are inclined to think, really 'ought to know better.' And yet the miraculous is absolutely central to what the Sai Baba phenomenon is about. This circumstance pushes to the fore questions that we might not otherwise ask. From what, exactly, do these miracles derive their convincingness, a convincingness so great that it seems to pull people into convictions ostensibly at odds with what their own subculture deems to be common sense and considered judgment? What is the source of the energy of Sathya Sai Baba's 'magic,' an energy that is apparently strong enough to have life-transforming effects on his devotees? Does it arise from cunning theatrics? Or is its true source something else?

8. The Reenchantment of the World

The Puzzle of
the Miraculous

The English word *miracle* is tendentious and heavily loaded, and for this reason it has a doubtful role in the language of cross-cultural interpretation. And yet without this word it would be difficult indeed to talk about the inner spirit of the cult of Sathya Sai Baba. What should we mean by *miracle*? Obviously to characterize miracles as occurrences that seem to contravene natural laws is not to clarify matters very much, because by so doing we smuggle in a premise and an evaluation that are likely to distort the interior realities of other cultures. The idea of natural law has a specifically Western historical and cultural context. If belief in the miraculous is, for the modern West, the disreputable opposite of scientific rationality, this judgment is sustained by an intellectual tradition that is by no means universal.

The traditional Hindu world sees nothing either startling or foolish about the idea that deities or other unseen beings can affect the world of normal experience in various ways. Nor is there anything remarkable in the idea that human beings can cultivate extraordinary powers— powers operating outside the realm of visible cause and effect, which can work good or evil in the world. In this tradition it is taken for granted that there are certain occurrences that are quite 'real,' and at a certain level intelligible to a rational mind, but that are nonetheless remarkable in a way that discloses the presence of normally invisible powers operating behind the facade of everyday experience. Most people do not have the power, let us say, to materialize objects. Some very few do.

That such things do from time to time occur is therefore not in itself surprising, and certainly not a blow at the foundations of rationality. But such occurrences are nevertheless extraordinary, and thus have special meaning. Just what this meaning might be in specific cases is a question to which we shall return, but for the present I only want to stress that perhaps the first step necessary in applying the term *miracle* to traditional Hindu materials is to understand that in this culture the miraculous lacks any element of truly radical surprise.

But the matter is more complex than this. Indian civilization has never been a monolith, and scientific rationalism is very much a part of the Indian scene. That its sources may have been historically extrinsic is beside the point; what matters is that there exists in India a living and extremely influential subculture in which this outlook is well understood and held in high esteem. I refer primarily to India's English-speaking elites, but the boundaries of this subculture are by no means strictly limited by English-medium education. For those influenced by this subculture, the miraculous has entered a new (or at least nontraditional) frame of reference.

This does not necessarily mean that we should expect pervasive scientific rationalism in *any* group in Indian society. As Boas pointed out many years ago, an application of the actual methods of science in attempts to understand the world is hardly normative for most people in Western cultures (1963, 199), and Indians, of whatever background, are probably no more prone than Euro-Americans to invoke strictly scientific canons of validity in trying to make sense of life's experiences. Science, in the strict sense, is probably nobody's 'common sense,' and indeed, as Geertz points out, science in its own way is as 'trans-commonsensical' as religion (1971, 103). But the scientific outlook certainly has a cultural impact outside its own narrow boundaries; if it does not create societies of scientists, it has nonetheless constituted a challenge to the 'religious ease' (ibid., 102) of tradition, or at least has done so for some people in many cultures.

Sathya Sai Baba's main constituency, consisting largely of those whom Bharati calls 'urban alienates' (1981, 87–88), is clearly drawn from the sector of Indian society for which this religious unease is most real. It is not that 'belief' in things like miracles is not possible within this elite subculture; the cult of Sathya Sai Baba itself provides ample evidence to the contrary. But in this sociocultural context the miraculous is burdened in a way that it is not in more traditional Hindu settings. Here the miraculous must justify itself in special ways. In this context the miraculous is not only extranormal, but also challenges what have become new conventions concerning what it is reasonable to believe. Put somewhat differently, this is a cultural setting in which miracles are, in a strong rather than a weak sense, 'miraculous,' requiring a leap across an incredulity that does not appear to be a factor in the traditional Hindu world.

The real surprise about the cult of Sathya Sai Baba is not so much that miracle working is part of the picture, but that miracles should be so central to the cult, given the cosmopolitan sophistication of Sathya Sai Baba's main constituency. If there is religious disequilibrium within the community from which his devotees are drawn, then it has apparently pushed them not into skepticism but its opposite. This religious modernism not only incorporates but centers upon what modern rationalism tends to understand as an archaic gullibility. That this startles us suggests that the relationship between 'modernity' and traditional religious outlooks may be more subtle than the simple antagonism it is commonly believed to be.

Types of Miracles

On one point let there be no mistake: miracles are crucial and central to the cult of Sathya Sai Baba. There is little doubt that some of the cult's apologists, particularly when representing the cult to Westerners, would like to see this aspect of his reputation downplayed. One is, therefore, often told that the miracles are really only a superficial aspect of his mission. However, this was not the view of most of my devotee-informants, who never seemed to tire of telling of miracles they had experienced, witnessed, or of which they had heard. Nor, evidently, is it the view of Sathya Sai Baba himself, who has characterized the miracles as 'evidence' (*nidarshan*) of his divinity (Kasturi 1975c, 139) and an important means of effecting the kinds of inner changes in his devotees necessary for their spiritual welfare. He sometimes calls his miracles his 'visiting cards,' signs of his *shakti* (power) by which he may be known for what he really is. The miracles are also fundamental to the perceptions of nondevotee onlookers to whom Sathya Sai Baba tends to be known primarily as a miracle worker, and who usually link the question of his credibility to the meaning and/or validity of his miracles.

The miracles in question are quite various. He is said to leave his body to aid his devotees in distant places. He cures incurable illnesses, and is even said to have raised the dead. Sometimes, as we have seen, he effects cures by taking a devotee's illness, or the karmic effects responsible for the illness, upon himself. He is also believed to have performed surgical operations on devotees at a distance. More commonly, cures are accomplished by means of substances or objects he gives his devotees. He also performs miracles of omniscience. He is aware of everything, and therefore he knows his devotees' problems even before they tell him. A major genre of miracle stories concerns instances in which Baba has told devotees what they wanted to say before they got a chance to say it. He has turned water into gasoline by dipping his hand in it. He has changed sand into religious books. One could go on and on. For Sathya Sai Baba, anything is possible. 'If you were to turn into a dancing girl before my eyes,' a devotee remarked to me, 'I would not be surprised.'

Sathya Sai Baba's most important miracle style, however, and the one that is his true forte and the main basis of his fame, is his apparent materialization of objects and substances from nothing. He is believed to be able to produce practically anything: images of deities, sweets, books, pictures of himself, amulets, jewelry (he once materialized a ring for the American ambassador), watches, and much else besides. But of all of his magical productions, the most significant by far is sacred ash (vibhūti), of which he is reported to materialize an average of over one pound per day (Kasturi 1977, 140). He usually does so with a wave of his right hand, and the result is given to devotees. They consume it, apply it to their bodies, or use it in other ways. The ash is believed to have an active power deriving from its source, and the use of sacred ash dramatically mobilizes all of the symbolism surrounding the figure of Shiva as defined in Puranic mythology—or at least it does so for those devotees who are familiar with these symbols.[1] Each materialization of ash is a vivid reiteration of Sathya Sai Baba's identity as Shiva/Shakti.

Sathya Sai Baba's physical presence is not necessary for miracles to occur. In fact, it is very likely that most 'Sai' miracles occur in his absence, since they are taking place, devotees believe, everywhere constantly. Informants report sometimes smelling him (the odor is described as sweet, like scented vibhūti or perfume) in their houses. This, of course, means that he is nearby, despite the fact that he might apparently be hundreds of kilometers away. Mysterious things are said to happen during congregational sessions of bhajan-singing: sacred ash may appear on his pictures or on the floor. He frequently appears in devotees' dreams, and because he is believed to appear in dreams only when he wills it, every dream of him is a kind of miraculous communication.

---

[1] Swallow's account (1982) provides a comprehensive and highly persuasive analysis of the significance of Sathya Sai Baba's production of ash (and other characteristic behaviors) vis-à-vis the mythology and symbolism of Shiva.

Moreover, there are several miraculous households in Delhi and New Delhi in which his magical influence is believed to be constantly manifested from afar. Footprints of sacred ash appear on floors, mysterious bites are taken out of edibles, garlands over his pictures change position, writing appears in closed notebooks, and his pictures exude sacred ash, red powder (*kumkum*), and amrit (nectar, a sweet-tasting liquid). In one such household, devotees deposit envelopes containing inquiries and petitions at the family altar. Sacred ash appears in some of these envelopes, indicating an affirmative response.

The miraculous household with which I was most familiar was that of a family of South Indian Brāhmans, who lived in a wealthy New Delhi residential colony. The household head was a business executive, and his wife a talented amateur musician. The first indication of domestic magic occurred four years prior to my contact with the family, when sacred ash mysteriously appeared on the hood of a newly purchased family car. Soon sacred ash began to emerge from the many pictures of Sathya Sai Baba in the family's prayer room and elsewhere in the house. The ash appears in the form of shallow cones on the outside of the glass covering the framed pictures, and the whole house is redolent with its smell. By the time I came on the scene the house had acquired considerable notoriety, and had become a regular gathering place for devotees. All of this occurred within what appears to be a common paradigm. There were other similar households in the Delhi area, and I heard of many more in other cities. These houses are, in effect, unofficial subcenters of the cult.

As far as I am aware, Sathya Sai Baba does not disclaim association with the miraculous events taking place in these households; moreover, the supposed miracles taking place in his absence do not in any way challenge or compromise his charismatic authority. In fact they have the opposite effect, because all of these mysterious phenomena simply add to the general atmosphere of the miraculous that lingers around the cult, and probably contribute to its remarkable ability to sustain its energy despite the physical remoteness of its presiding deity.

In this connection, however, Sathya Sai Baba is on record as adamantly condemning instances in which he is said to have possessed devotees (see Kasturi 1975b, 191–92). Sathya Sai Baba does not have human mediums, or at least not if he can put a stop to it. Whatever else this might mean, it clearly has the effect of minimizing the possibility of the decentralization of his personal sacred authority. If the miraculous households have become semiautonomous unofficial centers of the cult, so long as Sathya Sai Baba lives they will be completely dependent upon him for their legitimacy, and no potential rivals will be able to assume his role.

The Role of the Miraculous

The miraculous is often an important factor in recruitment to the cult. Most of my informants were highly voluble about their conversion experiences, which they tended to see as deeply important episodes in their life histories. A degree of alienation from traditional Hinduism was clear in the self-portrayal of many of these informants, who sometimes characterized themselves as having been worldly skeptics prior to their contact with Baba. Many, too, were people whose acquaintance with the symbolism and usages of popular Hinduism seemed relatively superficial. Some of them were also very troubled people at the time of their conversions, though whether they were more troubled than India's higher bourgeoisie generally is impossible for me to say. Frequently, however, details of truly serious difficulties emerged in the course of their accounts of themselves: illnesses, family problems, financial difficulties, and—something that should never be dismissed as trivial—the ennui of retirement from active professional life. A significant number of Sathya Sai Baba's devotees are impelled into the cult as a result of such difficulties.

But the critical precipitating factor in many of these cases was a direct experience of what was taken to be the miraculous. A powerful theme in these accounts is that of a passage from indifference or skepticism to faith through a personal confrontation with Sathya Sai Baba's power. Thus, an ex-beefeating former military officer reported that his attitude of amused disbelief changed completely when a picture of Sathya Sai Baba seemed to appear in one of his wife's earrings. For him this was the decisive break with what he regards as his benighted past, although his faith was further consolidated when Sathya Sai Baba materialized ash on his behalf and demonstrated an apparent ability to read his mind. Another informant, a U.S.-educated Punjabi businessman, recalls accompanying his father-in-law, basically as a lark, to see Sathya Sai Baba in Bangalore. Upon seeing an ash-materialization with his own eyes, he became a staunch devotee. A Punjabi chartered accountant (whom we have already met at the beginning of chapter 7), tells of the anguish that he and his wife felt upon being told by the attending physicians that their soon-to-be-born child would be born dead. As a last resort he prayed to a picture of Sathya Sai Baba while his wife's mother (a devotee) rubbed sacred ash on his wife's body. This was the first time in his life, he said, that he had ever 'really prayed.' The child was born alive, and this event finally cemented his belief in Sathya Sai Baba's powers. Subsequently he and his wife became mainstays of the Delhi community of Sai devotees.

In the literature of the cult there is a personal account of a conversion that seems to be paradigmatic of the type. One of India's most distinguished scientists, an erstwhile director of the All India Institute of Science, was jolted out of what was evidently a moderate case of scientific dogmatism when, before his very eyes, Sathya Sai Baba apparently transmuted a handful of sand into a copy of the *Bhagavad Gītā*. Having witnessed more occurrences of the same kind, he had to admit that he was having experiences that were beyond the capacity of his rational mind to explain. He agreed that Sathya Sai Baba is 'beyond science' (Bhagavantham 1976, 233).

This instance is paradigmatic because it seems to exhibit features that are important in many conversions to the cult. That the subject is a distinguished scientist is an exemplification of the worldly sophistication that seems characteristic of many of Sathya Sai Baba's key followers. And the attention given in his account to the tension between his scientific training and his belief in Sathya Sai Baba is a particularly clear articulation of what seems to be a widely shared perception among devotees—namely, that scientific rationality is fundamentally challenged and in some sense transcended by Sathya Sai Baba's magic.

Moreover, this case also illustrates well the 'threshold-crossing' character of many conversions to the cult. For many there appears to be a moment, though it may be a protracted one, of something tantamount to intellectual surrender. After this moment what is taken to be the evidence of *personal experience* is accepted in a way that eclipses what are, perhaps, less immediate and less felt rationalistic or scientific abstractions about what the world is like.

The question of predisposition is bypassed in this formulation. The scientist, and others like him, may be people who are predisposed in some way to be convinced of the validity of miracles, or have a thirst for the extraordinary. I have no evidence that bears on this question one way or another. But what is most important is the dynamic of the conversion process itself. Crucial here is the acknowledgement that occurs when a changed view of things is expressed in verbal or other forms of behavior (on this, see Festinger 1964). Having said that the miracles are in some sense genuine, or having acted as if they were so, the believer is then held fast in a net of behavioral and attitudinal consistency; he or she cannot easily turn back without making nonsense of what is now a coherent pattern of conviction and action visible to an audience consisting of himself or herself and others. At this point belief may become both stubborn and defensive in a way that is likely to drive the believer into the company of fellow believers, and is also likely to impress nonbelievers as an extreme credulity.

But this does not advance matters very much. While Sathya Sai Baba's miracles play a role in recruitment to his cult, this does not mean that we can fully understand them as a mere recruiting device. For one thing, this perspective ignores the fact that it is possible to 'believe' in the miracles without believing in Sathya Sai Baba. Many nondevotees are quite convinced that he can materialize ash and all the rest, but they do not see this as evidence of divinity. Some, indeed, consider his powers to be quite sinister. But, in addition, to see the miracles only as a blandishment to potential converts would be to fail to take into account the most crucial fact of all—that is, the miracles have not only to do with the inception of belief, but also with its consolidation and fulfillment. What is most important is not belief *in* the miracles but what devotees come to believe *about* the miracles. If devotees in some sense 'surrender,' they surrender to something that is apparently very meaningful to them. Let's see what this something is.

The very first thing that must be understood about Sathya Sai Baba is that he is, in every sense that matters, a deity to his devotees. As in the case of the Radhasoami sant satgurus, what his devotees want most of all is to establish personal devotional relationships with him. These are relationships of hierarchical intimacy, falling within standard Hindu patterns. Practically everything that Sathya Sai Baba's devotees say, do, and think about him can be seen as exemplifying these patterns.

Thus, devotees want to hear his discourses (*sambhāshan*). But as we have already seen, the actual content of his discourses is, while important, not the fundamental thing. What really distinguishes Sathya Sai Baba's discourses is not the philosophy or doctrine expressed therein (which is hardly novel), but the fact that they come from his mouth. They are his *vachanāmrit*, his speech-nectar, to be aurally imbibed by his devotees. Simply listening to him is in some way elevating, an improvement of the listener's nature. Devotees do not attend such lectures as one might go, let us say, to a lecture at a university, but as an act of worship.

Seeing and being seen, darshan, is also fundamental to what goes on in relations between Sathya Sai Baba and his devotees. His pictures are everywhere around his devotees; when he arrives in a city or town, his local devotees flock to catch even a distant glimpse of him. Amrit (nectar) is said to 'rain' from his eyes.[2] Devotees seek to fall under his gaze (drishṭi), and say they feel happiness and at peace when his glance lights on them. His devotees evidently feel a kind of power emanating from his eyes. Describing what it feels like to be looked at by Sathya Sai Baba, one young informant told of his experience of attempting to take Baba's photograph. Baba was slowly walking along a row of devotees in which my informant was seated. Just when my informant had him in the sight of his camera, the deity-saint looked at him and smiled, upon which my informant froze and could not release the shutter. Sathya Sai Baba's very glance in some way pierces his devotees, and evokes powerful inner feelings.

But even more important, and more avidly sought, is *sparshan*, touching. Devotees will seize any opportunity to touch Baba, or even to touch things that he has touched. I am told that one of the greatest honors that can be bestowed on a devotee is to walk behind him carrying the handkerchief with which he wipes his hand after materializing sacred ash. And as in the case of the Radhasoami sant satgurus, Sathya Sai Baba's feet figure prominently in devotees' longings for contact with him. They clamor to touch his feet, and some keep plaster casts of his feet in their homes as objects of worship. There is a particular photograph of the deity-saint, one seen in devotees' homes, that is an especially eloquent testimony to what his feet mean to his devotees. In this picture Baba stands erect with his hands behind his back, a nearly featureless (and lingalike) saffron column. At the top is his face, greatly accentuated by his halo of long, frizzy, black hair. Down at the bottom of the column, just peeping out from under the fringe of his garment, are four divine toes. 'See,' said a devotee, 'how he gives us a glimpse of his feet.' The picture is an invitation to hierarchical intimacy. It also portrays an act of grace; in offering his feet to be touched, the deity-saint is also offering his divine protection.

---

[2] In the literature of the cult, good examples of the language used by devotees to describe encounters with Sathya Sai Baba can be found in Rao (1975).

It is in this wider devotional setting that the miracles must be understood. On this point it is best to begin with the obvious—namely, that Sathya Sai Baba does not produce just impressive spectacles; he also produces things. And even when physical objects and substances are not involved, his miracles usually have a context. That context consists of relationships between him and particular devotees. What is most important about his miraculous productions is not really what he materializes (although the fact that much of it is sacred ash is obviously significant), but what he does with it—almost invariably he gives it to someone. This suggests that what matters most is not the thing in itself, but the way it connects him with others—in short, its significance as a vehicle for a relationship (see also White 1972, 874).

Seen in this light, the passage of materialized objects and substances from Sathya Sai Baba to his followers mobilizes very familiar patterns in Hindu devotional worship. In previous chapters we have already encountered the practice of receiving a deity's or august personage's prasād (leavings). We have noted that, among other things, such transactions exemplify hierarchical intimacy, and involve the transfer of desirable qualities of the donor (the deity) to the ingesting recipient who is thereby benefited. In the case of Sathya Sai Baba, the ash, the amrit, the sweets, the jewelry, and all the other parapheranalia of his magic are functional equivalents of this, received and taken by his devotees as a form of prasād. Produced *by* his power, they in some sense embody his inner virtue and power; when taken in what amounts to an act of worship, they transfer this power beneficially, as his 'grace,' to the recipients. Thus, the ash cures illnesses. The amulets and all the rest, far from being mere souvenirs, protect the ingestors and possessors from harm.

In fact, these items and substances seem to be conceived as media for their donor's actual presence. When Sathya Sai Baba presents his devotees with materialized objects, he often says that through them he will be close to the recipients. One informant recalled that when Baba presented him with a materialized ring, Baba stated that between the ring and himself was a 'golden thread' which would ensure that as long as the ring was worn Baba would always be there. This same motif of 'presence' seems to be involved in most of his miracles. When he transports himself to other locations, he does so to be near some devotee in a time of great need. And the real meaning of the startling phenomena in the miraculous households—the footprints, the materializations of ash and amrit from pictures, and so on—is that he is really there, even if he does not appear to be.

What all this suggests is that the power that is carried or manifested by the substances and objects he gives to others is not simply an impersonal force of some kind, but arises in the context of interactions and relations between Sathya Sai Baba and particular others. It is not power as such, but power-as-presence in the lives of specific persons.

Accountability

But I have not yet touched upon another crucial feature of Sathya Sai Baba's miracles, and indeed of most of his acts—their perceived indeterminancy. Though not as evident in the literature of the cult, one of the most striking themes in informants' accounts of their relationships with Baba is the apparent capriciousness of what he does. He is perceived as mercurial, and prone to sudden and inexplicable changes of demeanor and pace. Nobody ever really knows when or for whom he will produce ash or objects, or when or on whom he will bestow other kinds of favors. He often does so when least expected, 'out of the blue.' He surrounds himself with an atmosphere of surprise; he is playful and mischievous (*naṭkhaṭ*, a word used by a Hindi-speaking informant), and even a bit of a tease.

For example, in early 1979 many devotees believed that he would be coming to Delhi in March. One informant, a strong devotee, recalled to me later that he had personally asked him to come and that Baba had told him that he would. But he did not come (because Delhi in March is 'too hot,' we heard). When my informant related this tale to some people who are close to Baba, they laughed and said, 'You didn't really believe him, did you?' This remark and the incident that occasioned it are entirely consonant with the atmosphere of the cult. Another informant told of how, during a visit to the āshram at Puttaparthi, Baba had refused to allow him to touch his feet, but then later quite inexplicably called him for that most desirable of boons, a personal interview. This kind of thing, my informant said, is 'Baba's *līlā*' (play, sport), then adding, 'He does what he wants.' Such stories are extremely common.

Of course one might interpret such occurrences as simply the inevitable consequences of the hubbub and confusion surrounding a deity-saint with a national following—Baba forgetting to whom he had said what. But this would be to miss an important point—within the tradition in which Sathya Sai Baba operates, unaccountability is an extremely important characteristic of divinity.

In the Hindu world the gods are often playful. The world itself was created in divine play. When the gods play, they display a liminal dimension of their divinity. Sportive Krishna, John Hawley shows, is a boundary breaker and a confounder of convention whose love overflows the structures of social propriety (1983, 270–87). David Kinsley has pointed out that divine play expresses the 'otherness' of the deities. The gods are, by nature, free; they act, 'but their acts cannot be understood simply within the structure of theological or ethical systems. In their complete otherness their actions can only be called līlā . . . "sport," "play," or "dalliance" ' (Kinsley 1979, xi). But even as the play of the gods expresses divine otherness, it also expresses nearness and intimacy. The gods 'play with' their devotees, and their play can therefore define a certain kind of relationship. 'Like a love affair, to which it is repeatedly compared,' Kinsley writes, 'the devotee's relationship to God is constantly changing, full of surprises, hidden delights and ecstasies. It is unpredictable and spontaneous. It is an end in itself' (ibid., 202).

Kinsley's phrasing captures well a very important feature of Sathya Sai Baba's demeanor as perceived by many of his devotees. When one informant recalled feeling a nearly irresistable urge to 'pinch his cheek,' I believe him to have been expressing a widely shared sentiment arising from a powerful image of Baba as playful child. His miracles are, of course, evidences of extraordinary powers, but extraordinary powers are nothing new in the Hindu world. However, the fact that his devotees usually refer to his miracles as his 'līlās,' his sports, puts them in a different perspective. They are not mere 'wonders' (*chamatkārs*), nor are they the same as the magical 'accomplishments' (*siddhis*) of human adepts. To understand them as līlās puts them in a special category. Their essence is 'play,' and as such they are expressions of divine unaccountability. At this level the very haphazardness of Sathya Sai Baba's acts—magical or not— becomes a kind of evidence in support of his claim to divinity.

Moreover, the emphasis on the playfulness of his divine character also insists that his acts be understood within a special context—that of relations with particular others, his 'playmates.' These relationships are intimate, full of surprise and delight (though, as we shall see, sometimes pain as well), and, finally, ends in themselves.

It is in this general context that questions of skepticism seem most relevant. I have no quantitative data, but in the course of numerous conversations about Sathya Sai Baba with nondevotees two general perspectives on his miracles emerged. One was an attitude of pure (and in some cases dogmatic) skepticism—that is, the view that the materializations are really nothing more than sleight of hand or mechanical trickery of some other kind. This is, in fact, a common opinion. Indian audiences of wonder workers are quite attuned to the idea of fraud as a possibility, and many of the strongest devotees among my informants said that this is precisely what they thought Sathya Sai Baba's magic must be before they actually saw it.

The other point of view, which was expressed in varying ways and degrees by informants of quite diverse backgrounds, holds that the magic is 'real' enough, but that it does not mean what Sathya Sai Baba and his devotees claim that it means. Although some accuse him of sorcery, the most common opinion in this category seems to be that Sathya Sai Baba's powers are really the same as the siddhis, the magical accomplishments cultivated by numerous purely human yogic adepts. To express skepticism at this level is not necessarily a belittling or disapprobation of Baba or his powers (though it is some-times just that). Disbelief in his divinity is not inconsistent with genuine respect for Sathya Sai Baba as a religious leader or saintly figure.

This skepticism about the meaning of his magic defines with greater precision than anything else what it really is to be a genuine devotee of Sathya Sai Baba. It is not enough to believe that he has extraordinary powers. One must believe that his powers have extraordinary impli-cations. For his devotees Sathya Sai Baba's miracles are not 'just magic'; they are his līlās, his sports as God. For the siddhis of yogic adepts there are explanations, which, on their own premises, are as rational as anything dished up by modern science. But for his devotees, Sathya Sai Baba's miracles hold something deeply impenetrable. For them there is something essential about Sathya Sai Baba that, finally, cannot be 'explained away' in *any* terms. From this standpoint his magic is just another surface of a divinely inexplicable character.

But this position does not mean that Sathya Sai Baba's acts are completely outside the universe of accountability. Although informants portray an essentially unpredictable Baba, they also subject his acts to certain kinds of interpretation. For example, one informant recalled that Sathya Sai Baba once promised him a golden locket, but then failed to deliver. The informant now realizes that the only reason he wanted the locket was to 'show off,' and thus the apparently broken promise was actually a valuable lesson in humility. Indeed, Baba himself sometimes interprets his own acts. For instance, he can cure the apparently incurable, but he does not always do so. The reason is that it is occasionally best that the heavy karmic debts from past lives be repaid (though he can undo, or take upon himself, karmic effects if he wishes). Therefore, the unaccountability of his acts seems in essence to be prospective; one can never be quite sure of what he is going to do next (though he of course knows). But retrospectively his acts are at least susceptible to certain kinds of interpretation.

Sathya Sai Baba's apparent capriciousness is obviously compelled by the theodicy dilemma as it impinges on his relationships with devotees. Human ignorance and divine omniscience are the basic ingredients of the resulting formulation. Sathya Sai Baba knows everything; we do not. He never sleeps, his devotees say, and is always aware. 'He knows we are standing here now,' one informant remarked to me. He therefore knows, as devotees never tire of saying, everyone's 'past, present and future.' In other words, his awareness is precisely what history-bound human awareness can never be, given general Hindu premises about the nature of the self's predicament in history. His awareness is transhistorical, which is to say, divine.

His favors are certainly bestowed on some whom the world regards as virtuous, but not always; nor is it always clear that they are withheld from the less-than-virtuous. But it must be remembered that it is not within the power of human understanding to know who, in fact, is deserving, particularly in a world governed by karmic cause and effect extending beyond single earthly life spans. Not only do we not know what is hidden in the hearts of others, or for that matter even our own, but we can have no idea of the world-careers of the selves that we are and that surround us. Knowing nothing of these things, even a loving deity's favor must seem inexplicable to us. All that we can really conclude, in fact, is that even his apparent indifference is his love. 'Some complain,' he once said, 'that I did not give them this or that, but that is because their vision is limited to the immediate future or the present; whereas I know what is in store and so I have to safeguard them from greater grief' (Kasturi 1970a, 182).

Stated somewhat differently, against the background of misfortunes that occur, and must occur, in the lives of his devotees, it is logically necessary that Sathya Sai Baba's favor must be unaccountable to be believable. In this context the very opacity of his acts becomes evidence of his divine omniscience. Even more strikingly, what an outsider might see as absolute untrustworthiness becomes the basis for something resembling absolute trust.

Sathya Sai Baba's acts thus represent a curious amalgam of determination and indetermination. It is a question of points of view. From a limited human perspective he seems inexplicable. But embedded in the discourse of his cult seems to be an assumption that there exists some frame of reference within which his acts are but the visible exterior of an activity that is inwardly deeply meaningful. This does not mean that his acts can ever be in any human sense finally accountable. Although he may allude to his purposes in explaining to a devotee why, say, the illness of a child was not cured, the idea that 'if one only knew what *he* knows then everything he does would seem inevitable' is not quite at the forefront of devotee's minds. I have never heard such an idea deployed in talk about him (though it would not surprise me). But what is implicit in such talk is the idea that although his acts may be impenetrable, they are not meaningless.

Hence, a paradox and an apparent contradiction in terms: we are dealing, it would seem, with determined indetermination. But somewhere in the conceptual chasm between the accountable and the unaccountable there is another possibility that is perhaps (as the writings of Geertz suggest; see esp. 1966) uniquely the domain of religious thought and experience. It is sometimes possible for things to be meaningful without being fully accountable. I think Sathya Sai Baba's magical play is an example of this. When an informant says that the purpose of some instance of apparent indifference is to demolish pride, the point is not only that where Sathya Sai Baba finds pride he demolishes it (though this is a major theme in his relations with devotees), but that there is something about his acts, however obscure they may seem to us, that permits such explications—right or wrong—reasonably to be made. What we do not know, he knows; and thus even if his play encompasses its own ends, this does not mean that it is pointless.

Trust and Identity

It would be misleading, however, to present Sathya Sai Baba's divine persona as if it were merely an occasion for abstract karmic calculations. That perspective would leave out what is most present in informants' accounts of their relationships with him—very powerful emotions. What must be stressed is the strong emphasis on love-in-intimacy that is so characteristic of devotees' feelings about him, even when such relations are to all outside appearances far from intimate;

indeed, in the ideological framework of the cult intimate relations can and do exist even when there has been no physical encounter with Baba at all. One of the most remarkable features of this cult is its atmosphere of intense personalism maintained in the face of the large numbers and relative anonymity of devotees. Sathya Sai Baba does not so much have relationships with devotees 'in general' as he has specific relationships with particular devotees for whom these relationships are charged with deep personal meaning.[3]

What is this meaning? In part it involves questions of identity. Certainly the theme of identity is very strong in Sathya Sai Baba's teachings. He often speaks of the delusions most people have about who they really are. He once said that in every person there are three persons: the one you think you are, the one others think you are, and the one you really are, which is ātmā, soul; and soul is really the same (according to the usual formula) as God (Rao 1975, 81). The devotee should seek, of course, to realize inwardly this essential truth of self.

Moreover, for many devotees the religious problem of identity is given additional content and urgency by their peculiar position in Indian society. Many of these individuals are to some degree culturally rootless, distanced from their tradition by background and education. For some in this situation the problem of identity is likely to be more than a mere soteriological abstraction, but a puzzle that presents itself every day. It is therefore possible that the nativistic tendencies in Sathya Sai Baba's teachings provide a link between more traditional concepts of the predicament of the self in the world and perplexities inherent in the lives of many members of modern India's most favored groups.

But by contrast with the Brahma Kumari and Radhasoami movements—movements in which questions of identity are also crucial—what is striking about the cult of Sathya Sai Baba is that so little emphasis is given to identity-conferring internal experiences. While he does encourage his devotees to engage in meditation, I think it likely that for most devotees a sense of spiritual self depends less on hard-won contemplative insight than it does on complete trust in *his* powers, powers that are constantly validated by miracles.

Who is the devotee? The point is, the devotee cannot really know.

---

[3] I certainly do not mean to suggest that the worship of Sathya Sai Baba is without collective, communitarian dimensions. However loosely, his devotees do constitute a community of believers, and the ties that link them can, at least in principle, transcend social boundaries of other kinds. On this point see White (1972, 875).

He or she knows neither the worst about himself or herself, nor, in a kind of inversion of Puritanism, the best. But Sathya Sai Baba does know, because he knows the world as the Supreme Being does. He knows the real devotee, 'past, present and future,' that bundle of motives and inclinations embarked on a transtemporal world career. Or, rather, when he enters a relationship with a devotee, the relationship in some measure defines a self, as all social interactions do. But because of Baba's unique character, and particularly his omniscience, the self so defined cannot be the evident one. The self known to, watched over, loved by, and ultimately (ideally) blended with Baba is more inclusive, less partial, and in some sense more real than the one of which the devotee—and all human others—are normally aware.

By standing for this relationship, and indeed by serving as its material embodiments, Baba's miraculous productions—and all of the things his devotees take from him, whether miraculously produced or not—possess a potential self-transformative 'power.' Curative properties and the rest apart, this is the ultimate 'value' of such things. But as always, the efficacy of this power (and probably of the curative power as well) depends on who Baba is really understood to be. The devotee must enter into interactions of heightened significance with him—interactions occurring on what is felt to be a plane different from that of interactions with normal human others. The accounts of informants certainly suggest that their association with Sathya Sai Baba has this character; he is someone whom his devotees recognize, 'appearances to the contrary notwithstanding,' as the Absolute. The basis of this recognition is the miracles. The playful, seemingly chaotic displays of power—power that is not 'acquired' (as siddhis are) but is intrinsic to his nature—make of Sathya Sai Baba what his devotees depend upon him to be.

I am certainly not suggesting that the result for devotees is anything as simple as mere self-esteem buttressed by apparent divine approbation. 'Pride,' as we have noted, can be demolished by encounters with Baba. What is truly remarkable about relationships between the deity-saint and his devotees is that even his seeming indifference or neglect can be seen as somehow positive in implication. Informants speak of what is apparently a very common experience of new devotees: strong affirmative reactions from Baba at first, followed by coolness and neglect. But this does not matter, because his indifference is only apparent, never a matter of neglect. Even his anger, informants say, is really his love (*prem*). That is, beyond mere pride or self-esteem (regarded universally in the Hindu world as spiritually fatal), devotees, through their relations with Baba, can come to feel about themselves something else. This something is an enlarged sense of self that, for those who pass the test of his ostensible neglect or indifference, is seemingly more valuable than self-esteem.

But who then is this person who is in some way 'completed' through a relationship with Baba? It is not easy to say; indeed, I am far from sure that devotees themselves have very coherent ideas about this, and in any case the ultimate rewards of devotion to Sathya Sai Baba are certainly idiosyncratic, depending on highly specific features of individual life experiences.

For some devotees the emphasis is no doubt on salvation in the classical sense; for them the fulfillment of their relationship with Baba is what they take to be self-realization in union with God. For many, I suspect, there is also a heightening of a sense of cultural identity as Hindus or Indians, which is by no means inconsistent with a more strictly religious realization of self. There are other themes visible, too, at least in outer contour. A devotee of Sathya Sai Baba is certainly a safer person, being under God's direct protection, but of course this does not mean that such a person is unaffected by the often painful vicissitudes of life. He or she is also in some sense a more valued person, but of course the worth in question is not necessarily visible on the surfaces of things. It is fully realized only in the knowledge of an all-knowing other. This is a knowledge the devotee cannot actually share, but he or she can communicate with it through a sense of that all-knowing other's intimate, personal, and total presence in his or her life. Above all, such a person is a more loved person, since Baba's love, being all-knowing, is all-forgiving even if it appears to be unforgiving. More than anything else, Baba's devotees are the beloved of God.

What is finally most at issue is trust. Aside from his many 'teachings,' what Sathya Sai Baba mainly teaches his devotees is a certain quality of optimism that Erik Erikson has called 'basic trust,' 'the assumption that "somebody is there," without which we cannot live' (Erikson 1962, 118).[4] A critical factor in identity formation, such trust arises at first in the individual's earliest interactions with a maternal figure—the first social 'other'—and is consolidated by later phases of parental care. As Erikson notes, it is often given collective expression

[4] I would like to thank Catherine Bateson for suggesting the applicability of Erikson's insights to these materials.

in religious images of surrender. Its ultimate fulfillment is the individual's feeling that he or she is *someone* with a place in an ultimately beneficent cosmos. The school of this trust, and the essential condition of its existence, is a sense of being loved; in the case of Sathya Sai Baba's devotees it is supported by their absolute confidence in his love, the physical and moral confusions of the world notwithstanding. For his true devotees he is 'always there.' In what is perhaps his greatest 'surprise' of all, it is at this point that Baba's playful, childlike persona grades into an image of Sathya Sai Baba as divine parent.

In any case, it is clear that many of his devotees are more serene persons as a result of their relationships with Baba. This is what many informants say of themselves, and I can think of no reason to doubt them. It would be consistent with Sathya Sai Baba's own emphasis on 'courage,' and perhaps also with his promise that the sincere devotee will have his darshan at the moment of death. When informants speak, as they often do, of the 'peace of mind' they get from Sathya Sai Baba, they are referring to a genuine inner sense of security that the deity-saint's presence, in whatever medium, confers. Love and trust are its vital ingredients. Sathya Sai Baba's chaotic playfulness is, of course, ultimately indistinguishable from the chaos of human existence itself. To learn to trust him, therefore, is to learn to trust life.

These points might at least in some measure help to explain what could seem at first glance to be a mere credulous innocence in people who ought to know better. Sathya Sai Baba's magic is obviously in tension with scientific rationality, but for his devotees it engages with it only obliquely. The so-called miracles seem to derive their real energy from their role as media for deity-devotee relationships. This being so, it is finally these relationships for which the miracles are 'evidence,' and therefore it is on the basis of a devotee's feeling about such relationships that his or her final assessment of the 'validity' of the miracles is likely to be formulated. Devotees 'recognize' Sathya Sai Baba through the miracles, but in a circular chain of implication of a sort that is probably peculiar to religion, they 'recognize' the miracles because of their faith in Sathya Sai Baba.

In other words, the deity-saint's acts, of which the miracles are considered by devotees to be quintessential examples, have as much to do with a devotee's feelings and hopes about himself or herself as about Sathya Sai Baba and the things he can or cannot do. In this context one's feelings about oneself and about Baba are fused. This is Sathya Sai Baba's true magic. Whatever the devotee's inner understanding of himself or herself might in the end turn out to be (and here we must be agnostic), to the degree that this understanding is valued by the devotee, the miracles must be accepted as genuine signs of divinity. Therefore, as good as Sathya Sai Baba's theatrics might be, and by all accounts they are very good indeed, the true source of the verisimilitude of his self-presentation lies only partly in physical appearances. At least as important is his devotees' assent to their own hopefulness about themselves.

The Miraculous and the World

No mere conjuring show for the credulous, Sathya Sai Baba's magic cements his links with Shirdi Sai Baba and (more importantly) with Shiva, provides a medium for particularly vivid deity-devotee trans-actions, and supplies a stage for a theater of identities. In this sense it blends with its Hindu background, not just as magic, but as a phenomenon that on many levels exemplifies principles lying deep in what is probably the symbolic infrastructure of all forms of Hinduism. These are principles that we have also seen manifested, though differently and in different degrees, in the Radhasoami and Brahma Kumari movements.

But congruence at this level does not mean identity or even similarity, and in many ways the cult of Sathya Sai Baba seems almost antagonistically different from the Radhasoami and Brahma Kumari movements. A major difference is the matter of miracles. It is not just that the Radhasoami and Brahma Kumari movements pay little heed to the miraculous; in fact they are both in some degree actively hostile to the whole idea. A few miracles are reported of the Radhasoami sant satgurus, but against this Babuji Maharaj (the last of the Soami Bagh gurus) insists that faith founded on the miraculous is superficial and that miracles are only performed by 'lower incar-nations' (Phelps 1947, 117). He does not, it should be noted, deny that such powers exists.

A prominent Brahma Kumari writer has harshly criticized 'godmen' who magically produce vibhūti and other things (he is obviously referring to Sathya Sai Baba). Again, like Babuji Maharaj, he does not claim that such powers (he calls them siddhis) are unreal, but he regards them as deeply flawed. A watch produced by such power, he says, will not last as long as one produced in a factory, and the remarkable cures do not protect against future illness. Nothing, in short, that results from such powers is either permanent or truly valuable. Such powers, he says, are spiritually hazardous temptations for the practitioner, and a dangerous diversion from the true path for his followers (Chandar 1977, 220–26).

Involved in these stern judgments is far more than a matter of religious taste. The question of the meaning of the miraculous seems to be related, in these materials at least, to the more general question of what stance is to be taken toward the world.

We must remind ourselves that within the Radhasoami and Brahma Kumari traditions alike, the view taken toward the world of normal experience is hardly a sanguine one. For the Brahma Kumaris, heaven may be earthly, but it is not of *this* world. While they await their paradisiacal inheritance, deitary and other rules of association keep the world at a distance; also, whatever its salvationary implications, celibacy has had the effect of producing deep rifts between movement members and their own families, and also between the movement as a whole and the surrounding society. The Brahma Kumaris' goal is separation from the world; one is to become a sākshī, a mere witness to the body and the world. One is to see the world going about its business, bad business in the end, while inwardly remaining completely disengaged.

The Radhasoami movement has never been as overtly hostile toward the world as the Brahma Kumari movement, nor in fact has it ever been as radically rejected by the world. There is something about it of a religion of busy men of affairs, men who are often very good at what they do, as exemplified in the careers of most of the sant satgurus. Moreover, the Dayalbagh community has reached what appears to be a comfortable accommodation with a practical ethic of work-as-worship.[5] But at the level of doctrine, particularly in the Soami Bagh tradition, the world is strongly devalued. It is portrayed as a prison and a trap, an 'alien country,' within which nothing of genuine value can ever be found.

Most important, however, is not the ostensive value or lack of it accorded to worldly things, but the related question of where the proper arena for redemptively significant experience can be found. A critical feature of the Brahma Kumari and Radhasoami traditions

[5] As Weber showed in his classic analysis of ascetic Protestantism (1958), an ethic of work in the world is not necessarily a form of worldliness. However, exactly how the Dayal Bagh community reconciles the emphasis given to their various enterprises with Radhasoami beliefs has not been studied.

is that the experiential realization of the devotee's spiritual achievement is intensely inward, or at least it is in theory. If there are
evidentiary miracles at all, miracles of 'recognition,' they are essentially 'miracles within,' occurring against an internal landscape.

For the Brahma Kumaris there is the minor outer miracle of the
glowing faces and lights, but this is supposed to be highly contextualized
by the yogic practitioner's inward feelings of detachment from the
body and communion with the Supreme Soul, and is held to result
from the awakening of a purely inner faculty of awareness.

Probably because of the metaphoric elaborations of the sant (and
tantric) tradition from which it derives, the Radhasoami vision of the
internal landscape, especially as seen in the poetic imagery of the
self's ascent through internal-upper regions, is far richer than anything
the Brahma Kumari tradition has produced. And although many
devotees probably do not actually experience these celestial marvels,
the Radhasoami tradition also makes available the rich experiential
possibilities of intimate flow-exchanges with the sant satgurus. If the
devotee does not actually see heavens beyond heaven, he or she can at
least feel love for the guru and his leavings, which really comes to the
same thing. This too is inwardly focused, for the love must come from
within the devotee. If there is any miracle, it is not that the guru's
spittle somehow changes to nectar; it is that the devotee comes to see it
and taste it for the nectar it always was. The same is true of the souls
the Brahma Kumaris come to see in others.

Echoes of these themes also reverberate in the cult of Sathya Sai
Baba, but between the outlook fostered by this cult and the world
views of the Radhasoami and Brahma Kumari movements there is at
least this bedrock difference: for Sathya Sai Baba's devotees it *really
matters* that ash can be produced from nowhere and that water can be
magically changed into gasoline. That is, for Sathya Sai Baba's
devotees the miracles are not necessarily 'within,' but 'out there.'
What is required is simple assent. What is asked is not so much that
the devotee, with hard-won insight, see things as different from what
appearances insistently suggest, but that the devotee give way to
appearances altogether, and subside into the artless faith that at least
some things seen are precisely what they seem to be—that is, that
Sathya Sai Baba's miracles are, in fact, miraculous. It is true that the
ash is more than 'mere' ash, but—for many—what mainly makes it so
is that it was (apparently) produced from nowhere.

In both the Radhasoami and Brahma Kumari traditions the theme of enlightened vision is strong; having experienced a higher reality, the devotee can never look out on the same world again. And in both cases this new world, or rather the world now seen in its undisguised reality, is one that in theory can only be experienced negatively. The ideal Radhasoami devotee, as portrayed in Radhasoami devotional poetry, lives in a world in which even wife, children, and kinsmen (strong positive values for the unawakened) are 'snakes,' and in which all normal pleasures are the snares of Kāl. This is a devastated world, from which all that matters has been abstracted—except, of course, for guru. The Brahma Kumari practitioner of rāja yoga learns to distinguish soul from material nature, and having done so sees material nature itself with a clarity unavailable to the unenlightened. From this perspective the world of the kaliyug is utterly benighted, and utterly separate, too, from the souls we essentially are.

Transformed vision is also an explicit theme in Sathya Sai Baba's teachings. Because the world appears when we open our eyes, he says, the world (*srishti*) is created by our seeing it (*drishti*). Therefore, he continues, the kind of world you live in is a product of your point of view. If you cultivate a divinity-oriented viewpoint, you will see everything 'suffused with divinity.' Others will be 'mirrors,' because by seeing God in them, you will see him in yourself (Kasturi n.d.c, 110). These ideas are obviously very similar to concepts central to the Radhasoami and Brahma Kumari traditions.

But what kind of world do Sathya Sai Baba's devotees look out upon? To some degree it is rather like the world that surrounds Radhasoami and Brahma Kumari devotees. It is a determined world. Just as everything that happens does so because it is written into the script of history for the Brahma Kumaris, and just as everything that happens does so because of karmic effects and the Lord's mauj for the Radhasoami devotee, so for Sathya Sai Baba's followers everything that occurs does so by his ordainment. They speak of this constantly, even in connection with what may seem to be the most trivial events; nothing happens that he does not will. Moreover, the world of Sathya Sai Baba's devotees, like that portrayed by the Radhasoami and Brahma Kumari traditions, is one in which one can never know what is going to happen next. If all is determined, from the standpoint of the individual, nothing is fixed. From our vantage all that happens is an expression of God's fathomless play.

But one of the most striking features of the world as seen by Sathya Sai Baba's devotees is that this is a world in which his magic has somehow flooded outward. Their world is something like an enchanted garden. This is a point on which it is difficult to be ethnographically precise, but it is real enough. It emerges mainly in the tone in which informants report their experiences as members of the cult: a sense of heightened expectation, a feeling that the world has become a place of wonders to be constantly scrutinized for ever-newer marvels. These are people for whom the miraculous has somehow become part of the very furniture of normal existence.

It is largely a matter of little things. An informant reported an altercation with someone while staying at Baba's āshram; immediately upon leaving the room his eye lighted on a sign with some slogan about the evils of anger. Another informant reports longing for a guava, having seen a few unimpressive specimens for sale while on a motor trip. When her car halted, a man suddenly appeared by its side with two plump and juicy ones, which he sold her for eight annas. This, of course, was Baba himself. Another informant tells of how she was frightened by the dark clouds surrounding an aircraft in which she was descending for a landing at Nagpur. But then, just as the thought of Baba flashed through her mind, the plane passed through a momentary shaft of sunlight.

No one of these small accounts means anything by itself, but they are all typical of a genre that conveys something quite characteristic of the atmosphere of Sathya Sai Baba's cult. It is as if the most unremarkable surfaces of normal life are marked with potential magical meaning of a sort that is unnoticed by others. On one occasion I sat with a devotee as he tried to show me how the chaos of lines on his palm was actually the Roman characters S and R (for 'sāī rām'). This is a diminutive but typical example of what seems to be generally true of the way Sathya Sai Baba's most committed devotees look at the world. They inhabit a world in which signs and evidences of his love and grace are pervasive. *Any* trouble vanquished or illness cured is by his grace. And troubles *not* vanquished are likewise signs of his love, because he always watches over his devotees with omniscient and all-powerful concern.

From the standpoint of Radhasoami and Brahma Kumari teachings this is all deeply naive. It is not that they deny that life has its pleasant, even magical, surprises; nor, in the case of the Radhasoami tradition, is it denial of the Lord's occasional intervention to help a devotee. It is, rather, the more fundamental denial that pleasant surprises in this world, magical or not, can have any real meaning.

Though they have little genuine affinity with the inner spirit of ascetic Protestantism, these are nevertheless religious movements that have, in the Weberian sense, stripped the world of magic, and have done so with impressive thoroughness. By contrast, the Sathya Sai Baba cult may be something of a Weberian reversal, an example of the re-enchantment of the world. Here are urban sophisticates, who come from a class and background in which much of popular Hinduism is dismissed as mere 'superstition,' finding their religious selves at the feet of someone who is—to outward appearances at least—a magician, and coming to live in a world in which the miraculous is a pervasive, significant fact.

One must not make more of a puzzle of this than it deserves to be. Most of India's wealthy urban sophisticates are not followers of Sathya Sai Baba, and therefore we cannot conclude that there is some general feature of life in this milieu to which Sathya Sai Baba is an obvious or necessary response. But most of those who follow him are of this background, and this suggests that there must be something in Sathya Sai Baba's sacred persona that resonates at some level with experiences peculiar to India's bicultural elites.

The material we have seen suggests several possibilities. We have already noted the potential overlap between ambivalences of cultural identity and the religious problem of self. Moreover, as Swallow has pointed out (1982, 153), many of Sathya Sai Baba's followers live in a world that is, by traditional standards, disconcertingly disoriented. In the world of middle-class India existential trust may be at a real premium; for its denizens, allegiance to Baba might serve to revive a sense of the efficacy of a tradition that otherwise seems to be rendered increasingly irrelevant by modern conditions of life. For those among his devotees whose religious lives were relatively unenergized before they entered his cult—and they are many—devotion to Sathya Sai Baba may also represent a way of reclaiming the religious culture of childhood that makes less than onerous demands on spiritual sensibilities that are not, for whatever reason, very complicated. In the absence of more fully internalized traditional cultural resources, devotion to Sathya Sai Baba (or figures like him) must be particularly attractive at moments of personal crisis.

Sathya Sai Baba's cult makes a strong appeal to feelings of simple cultural nationalism in some devotees. In some it also appeals to a sense of social altruism that has an honored place in India's modern culture of nationhood. The emphasis on social service provides an opportunity for devotees to do good in the world, but Sathya Sai Baba's profound conservatism on fundamentals like caste and gender ensures that doing good is unlikely to challenge his devotees' more basic sense of propriety and order. And then, too, the simple chic that has come to be associated with Sai-related activities probably exerts a pull in its own right.

Sathya Sai Baba's genius is that in the midst of this tangle of motives, some of which have little to do with religious yearnings as such, he is able to use ancient religious symbolisms of extraordinary psychological efficacy in a way that appears to be deeply satisfying to his followers. Through his use of traditional imagery he has succeeded, as Swallow puts it, 'in persuading his followers to think of their many individual and complex problems in terms of traditional dilemmas and conflicts' (1982, 155).

Beyond all this, however, another element in Sathya Sai Baba's appeal is the fact that he does not demand that his devotees become enemies of the world. It is not that he encourages unregenerate worldliness. Although he does not require his followers to cast away their worldly wealth, he certainly does not sanction unbridled materialist strivings. But he himself is thoroughly in the world, a social deity (despite his identification with Shiva) par excellence. Through his magic he has made the world into an arena for his sanctity, and of course he has also encouraged the belief that the world can be made a better place by means of education and charitable service. Perhaps inadvertently he has found a rather surprising point of contact between religious traditionalism and a certain kind of modernity. By this I mean that his emphasis on miraculous transformations has created an anything-is-possible atmosphere that does not challenge what in many of his devotees are lifetime habits of intellectual and affective extroversion. There is a kind of hopefulness here that things can turn out well in the world that seems fundamentally consonant with the outlook of the affluent, the comfortable, the smart, and the up-to-date. A world that can be enchanted is a world that one need not, and should not, hate or leave.

IV. Conclusion

9. Images

Plurality

Just how pluralistic is Hindu religious culture? The confusions to
which this deceptively innocent question leads are notorious, and
sometimes far from innocuous, since political identities can be at
stake. The question of the plurality of our present three religious
movements is not so perilous, but it bristles with difficulties nonetheless.

Are these movements Hindu at all? Two of them say not; the
exception is Sathya Sai Baba's cult. The Soami Bagh tradition regards
the Radhasoami faith as a wholly new and unique religious dispensation; it is not a form of Hinduism, or anything else. The Brahma
Kumari tradition holds that present-day Hinduism is a degenerated
version of the 'original religion' of the gods and goddesses of the first
half of the historical cycle (*ādi sanātan devi-devatā dharm*); Indians
became 'Hindus' when they fell from grace. The sect regards its own
activities in the sangamyug not as a 'form' of Hinduism, but as its
transhistorical source. Sathya Sai Baba, by contrast, strongly identifies
with the Hindu tradition and urges his followers to recover this
tradition in their own lives as a way of reconstituting a religious
culture of Indian nationhood. On the other hand, and perhaps
inconsistently, he has also attempted to dissolve the 'Hinduness' of
his message by stressing an ecumenism symbolized by the presence of
the cross and the crescent on the cult's logo. Is this cult Hindu? Of
course it is, but in a sense it defines the Hindu world as the whole
world.

But just as we must doubt Sathya Sai Baba's implicit premise that
the worship of Jesus is really the worship of him, so too we must
dissent, with all due respect, from Radhasoami and Brahma Kumari
judgments about their relationships with the Hindu tradition. Most
of the basic ingredients of the Radhasoami faith are drawn from
devotional and tantric Hinduism, and if the faith is new, it nevertheless
cannot be fully understood outside a Hindu context. The same is true

of the Brahma Kumaris. Virtually every element of their vision of the world has been drawn from the Hindu tradition, as I have tried to show. Thus, there is a prima facie case for unity at some level, between these three religious movements.

However, to move beyond generalities in an attempt to see what, if anything, these movements actually have in common raises difficult questions. One thing is certain: if there is common ground between them, it is not a matter of 'beliefs,' or at least not in any simple sense. No reader of this book could fail to see that the belief systems of these three movements are different. Nor, to move to a somewhat higher level of abstraction, can it be a matter of what is sometimes called 'world-view.' These traditions construct quite different visions of the way things are; they portray different worlds in which quite different kinds of specific beliefs and behaviors make sense. To the Brahma Kumaris the obsession of Sathya Sai Baba's devotees with the miraculous is fatuous, and from the Radhasoami standpoint the Brahma Kumaris' desire for an earthly paradise is really tantamount to a desire to rush into the jaws of Kāl. What are perceived as major schisms in Christendom are but minor quibbles by comparison with the doctrinal chasms that separate these groups.

And yet all three groups seem to share something that in some way provides a common framework for concepts and beliefs that are very different in detail. The word *presupposition* comes to mind, but to employ it in this context would be somewhat misleading. It would be to inject a bit too much of the strategy of syllogistic reasoning into systems to which the spirit of formal logic is really quite foreign. Lekhraj's question was never 'How can we deduce what the world is really like?' but 'Who are you?' His system was an essentially intuitive construct, arising from visionary experiences. Its plausibility rested finally on how well it gave direction and focus to his followers' own sense of being—as one of the formulas of the movement puts it—'long lost and now found again children.' This indifference to disembodied intellection is likewise characteristic of the Radhasoami movement and the cult of Sathya Sai Baba.

What these traditions have in common is both less abstract and deeper than logical presuppositions. The common elements between them are best characterized as certain loosely floating images. By *images* I mean certain concepts, carried by sets or clusters of symbols, that represent partial world-constructions. They are particular angles of vision on the world, world-glimpses if you will, that shape the possibilities of a religiously constructed world while never determining what it will look like in detail. They are not so much logical premises as they are elements in the plausibility infrastructure of Hindu religious culture; beliefs are not deduced from them, but beliefs must accommodate them in order to be believable. I call them 'loosely floating' because there is apparently no rigid molecular arrangement in which they must appear as constituent atoms. Different combinations and permutations are possible, and the same images may be differently emphasized in different contexts. In fact, such differences of emphasis are largely what distinguish the three movements under discussion.

History and Forgetfulness

One such image is that of cyclical history; all three traditions are committed at some level to the Hindu yuga theory of how world-time passes. But beyond this minimal concept, our three traditions do not share anything that could be called a common 'theory of history.' The whole matter of history is treated quite differently in each of them.

In the cult of Sathya Sai Baba there is relatively little talk of history at all. Baba does allude to the standard yuga image from time to time, and—in common with all Hindu thinking—situates the contemporary world in the crepuscular kaliyug. Also, in the symbolism of the cult he is implicitly assimilated to the image of Kalkin; he is here on earth to reestablish dharma and to usher in a 'Sai Age.' But historical interpretation is not where the cult's energies are really focused.

In the Radhasoami tradition matters are very different; here history is not only integral to the faith's conception of its own nature and meaning, but is also the principal battleground for schismatic disputes. In the midst of this, the yuga theory becomes partially submerged. At one level the tradition encompasses yugic history within a wider cosmogony of its own, a first creation 'prior' to history's restarts. This cosmogony gives temporal expression to the idea of the self's vast alienation from its original source and 'true home,' and in the process provides a rationale for what is deemed to be the higher enlightenment of sants. Only sants know of the true final goal, a final goal that is in some sense also the beginning of time. In turn, the yuga theory itself is turned to Radhasoami uses; the moral and physical squalor of the kaliyug is subjected to a partial transvaluation, and our present age emerges as one of great and (in the case of Soami Bagh) unique spiritual opportunity.

Of these groups, it is the Brahma Kumari movement that has most invested itself in historical theorizing. The result is a vision of history that is quite unusual in the Hindu world, but nonetheless thoroughly Hindu in inspiration. To know exactly why Lekhraj came to the conclusions he did would require entering his mind. But, short of that, we can at least surmise that one of his tasks was somehow to find a way of conceiving liberation through sannyās (world renunciation) as a reasonable option for women. Seemingly, this fusion of intrinsically antagonistic concepts—those of world renunciation and legitimate womanhood—required a kind of spiritual white heat, and this was supplied by the image of the world at the very brink of doom. This, in turn, required a drastic acceleration of the traditional historical cycle, with results that we have traced. The vision of high-speed Hindu history may yet prove unstable. Whether the theory of reiterative five-thousand-year cycles can, in the long run, withstand the assault of scientific disconfirmation remains to be seen. The fate of biblical chronology in the educated West does not inspire confidence.

What's the meaning of these rather different concepts of how the history of the cosmos passes? To compare them with the cosmogonic theories of modern astrophysics would be missing the main point. The Radhasoami account of the creation does read a bit like a Hindu version of Steven Weinberg's *The First Three Minutes*, and there is also something vaguely thermodynamic about the image of the declining universe common to all three groups. But these schemes are not actually about the world as such, but about the human situation *in* the world. They are about why our experiences are what they are, what kind of disposition toward the world makes sense under the circumstances, and what basis exists for ultimate human hope. They are, in sum, less descriptions than evaluations of the world.

The convincingness of these schemes is, in part, a matter of how they are supported by experience, but their relationship with experience is far from simple. It is likely, for example, that the Radhasoami vision of how things are is not based on experiences of the world as an 'alien country,' but rather that the world is experienced this way from the perspective of the Radhasoami vision, a vision that gives content and direction to otherwise inchoate anxiety and discontent. Likewise, it is not because of contemporary calamities that the Brahma Kumaris have a sense of impending doom, but such occurrences certainly vindicate this sense of things when comprehended within the Brahma Kumari frame of reference. Characteristic of these schemes is that the world of experience and the world as projected by belief are brought into a mutual accommodation that is—at least from the inside—virtually seamless.

Although our three movements treat the matter of history in quite different ways, there is one point on which all three converge. This common theme is the image of the forgetful self in history, the self that has lost itself in time. Because of this distinctively negative view of the situation of the self in history, escaping history is seen as a goal in each of these traditions. In the Radhasoami case the devotee strives to thwart Kāl, who is time and death, by ascending to a region in which time does not exist. The Brahma Kumaris seek a temporal paradise, but to get there they must first make a detour through the experience of themselves as atemporal souls cultivated in rāja yoga. Sathya Sai Baba is many things, but chiefly a being for whom 'past, present and future' are one. If few of his devotees have transtemporal experiences, they can at least enter into a relationship with transtemporal awareness through interactions with him.

Fundamental to these ideas is the concept of the amnesia of the transmigrating self. The self in history forgets; the only memory carried from birth to birth is in the form of unconscious tendencies (*sanskārs*). Indeed, it may be an implicit logical necessity that a transmigrating self *has* to forget if it is to exist in history at all. Not only would full memory of past lives make nonsense of the theodicy of karma, but a totally recollective self would be unable to establish social relationships with others. By their very nature social roles are only partial disclosures of the selves behind them (cf. Goffman 1959), and this is even more true when the selves in question have transmigratory world-careers. Such a self, if fully disclosed to itself or to others, would be a chaos of innumerable personae, incapable of ordered social relationships.[1] Therefore, an historical person must be self-forgetful. And this seems to mean, conversely, that in order to recover memory, such a self will in some measure have to withdraw

[1] With his usual insight, Babuji Maharaj (in Phelps 1947, 86–87) had the following to say on the subject of memory: 'The cutting of recollections of past lives in the present life is necessary to the present life, else the latter could not take the course which it takes without that recollection.' Recollection of past lives, that is, would interfere with the course of one's present life, and 'in order that karma should be exhausted it was necessary that your life should have been lived as you actually lived it.' Moreover, one's conduct in the present life would be influenced by sentiments inherited from past lives: 'Suppose for instance that your mother of this life was your son of your past life, would it be possible to yield her the reverence due to a mother if you remembered your past life?' Thus, confusion of roles.

from normal society and enter into new kinds of interactions with a very special 'other,' which is a point that I shall enlarge upon later in this chapter.

Eliade (1963) has shown that the theme of memory and forgetfulness is not only deep in the Indian materials, but is transculturally distributed. Forgetfulness is sleep, bondage, and death; memory is wakefulness, liberation, and eternal life. Forgetfulness is ignorance of who you really are, and remembrance is recovery of one's true (that is, primordial) self, lost behind the appearances of a changing world. Such ideas are associated with an indifference to the things the West has learned to consider most important about history. The act of memory that matters most of all is one that bypasses history in transhistorical recollection. These themes are found in all three traditions, and are represented with particular clarity in the Radhasoami materials where we encounter the image of the lost self, forgetful of its origin, 'eaten' by time and death, trying, in effect, to ascend to its beginning.

Ingesting

Another powerful image in these materials is that of worshippers seeking identification and union with objects of worship by means of intimate transactions. This image should not surprise us, since transactions of this kind seem to be a nearly invariant feature of Hindu liturgical usage. The basic pattern is one in which devotees establish hierarchical intimacy with a deity by taking the deity's leavings as prasād.

These behaviors are not fully intelligible unless seen against the background of ideas of personhood very different from those prevailing in the modern West. Marriott (1976) has argued persuasively that in the general ambiance of traditional Hindu thought the social actor is conceived as an internally composite transactor of what he calls 'substance-codes'—trait-conferring 'codes for conduct' directly embodied as flowing, exchangeable substances. Conceived this way, social actors are not 'individuals,' but 'dividuals,' divisible persons who are dependent for their nature as beings on their exchanges with others. Beings so constituted (that is, conceiving themselves as so constituted) must calculate inputs, internal resistances, and outputs in a way that probably has its closest counterpart elsewhere in the management of oil refineries or the design of electronic circuitry. The point of the game is at least to preserve one's own nature, and to improve it if possible. Actors, therefore, try to maximize their inputs from others whose substance-codes are subtler, lighter, more powerful, and thus improving; they also seek to maximize the netherward release of coarser, heavier, debasing wastes. In so doing, they participate in a wider social and cosmic world that is itself a true flux: flowing, eddying, ceaselessly changing. This is a world in which no boundary is impermeable, and in which every actor's nature is heterogeneous and always subject to potential change.

In a world conceived this way, identity is obviously an issue. Kakar suggests that the Hindu 'preoccupation' with questions of identity may reflect a 'fundamental anxiety aroused by an image of the body in unflagging transformation' (1982, 235). From this standpoint, prasād-taking and its many analogues are part of the strategy of dividual beings attempting to achieve identity improvement and, ultimately, identity stability. In this world, as everywhere, actors can manipulate their identities by 'identifying with' others, but here this principle is culturally expressed in a transactional-substantialist idiom.

While these points apply to the Hindu world generally, I know of no body of ethnographic data illustrating them better than the Radhasoami materials, especially as seen in the Soami Bagh tradition. The historical person, as embodied self, is portrayed with clarity and directness as a fluid entity, a 'current' engaged in constant flowlike interactions with its surroundings. So constituted, the devotee seeks to find a source of subtle, value-laden current that will radically improve his or her own nature. The sant satguru (and/or his relics) represents something approximating a spiggot of fine and improving subtle substance. Instead of 'eating delusion' (as we normally do), devotees change their natures for the better by eating, drinking, and in other ways assimilating this higher nature, imaged as higher awareness (chaitanya), into their own. Here redemptive awareness is not a property of disembodied psyche, but seems to be a quasi-physical current that can be mingled into a devotee's own inner nature. But there is also an apparent reciprocity to this process. Devotees take, but they also give, and in giving they give themselves to the Supreme Being. In so doing, they are 'purified' by the Supreme Being, their attachments and karmic residues stripped away by his superior powers of discrimination and transformative alimentation. Therefore, when devotees assimilate a true guru's currents, it is as if they are being given back to themselves, but in a transformed condition.

This transformative ability, indeed, seems to be the true essence of divine 'power.'

The entire encounter tends in the direction of spiritual-substantial merger between worshipper and worshipped. The devotee is portrayed as ultimately sharing directly in the Supreme Being's nature, which is full self-awareness. In a conflation that may be unique to Indic materials, a change of identity is a change in one's capacity to be aware of one's identity. This heightened self-awareness is entirely free from the obfuscations (conceived as coarse physiomoral accretions) imposed by existence in the belly of time.

Kakar argues that the intense veneration of holy men in the Hindu world can be related to the retention in the adult male personality structure of Heinz Kohut's 'idealized parental imago,' which is expressed in the paradigm, 'You are perfect, but I am part of you' (Kakar 1978, 128–39). Whether or not one agrees with Kakar's overall analysis of the Hindu psyche, it is clear that transactions between devotees and divine beings are enactments of precisely this conviction. Devotees are purified by assimilating, and being assimilated by, objects of worship; they are perfected by blending with the perfect.

In the cult of Sathya Sai Baba we do not encounter anything approximating the doctrinally and poetically elaborated imagery of physiological engagement that we find in the Radhasoami tradition, but the same principles are clearly in evidence. Sathya Sai Baba is a giver of things and substances that act as media for hierarchical intimacy between him and his devotees. By means of his words (his discourse-nectar), his magical productions, contact with his feet, and his food-leavings (which can be taken from his altar whether or not he is physically present), his divine nature comes into contact with, and is assimilated by, his devotees. And just as the Radhasoami sant satgurus do, he can take the karmic detritus of his devotees onto himself. The point of devotion to Sathya Sai Baba is to evoke his presence in one's life, to achieve intimacy with him (though the relationship may seem to be very distant), and finally to achieve merger with him. When he says that he is 'within' his devotees, as God is within them, this is more than a metaphysical cliché, for Baba does indeed become an internal presence in the lives, bodies and being of his true devotees.

The theme of ingestion is also present among the Brahma Kumaris, but with the critical difference that it tends to be expressed in less overtly physiological ways. Prasād-taking occurs, but it is not much emphasized in this group. Here we also find relatively little concern with the geography of the body. This seems to reflect the radical soul-nature dualism that is so basic to this movement's beliefs. Radhasoami teachings hold that all of creation has its origin in currents emanating from the Supreme Being; thus, he himself is present, in the form of subtle currents, in all beings and all things. For the Brahma Kumaris, however, the Supreme Soul (Shiv Bābā)—and the souls of persons—were and are utterly distinct from bodies and material nature. How, the Brahma Kumaris ask, could a perfect being be immanent in a material world in which evil exists? There was never a time when material nature was a part of the Supreme Soul, since material nature is, in fact, sourceless. Its cycles of five thousand years have no beginning and did not arise from him. And just as material nature was never part of the Supreme Soul, so we, as souls, have never been part of it.

This conception of the world puts deity-devotee transactions in a frame of reference interestingly different from that of the Radhasoami tradition. In Radhasoami teachings the image of physiological engagement is just that; self is realized as body interacts with body. But among the Brahma Kumaris, radical dualism ensures that souls can never be reached through bodies or things of the body. Therefore, although Lekhraj did indeed dispense prasād to his followers, and although bhog is offered and prasād taken from the Supreme Soul nowadays too, these practices are not central to the life of the sect.

Rather, at one level what is central are transactions in the medium of gyān, or subtle knowledge. The Brahma Kumaris regard knowledge as a faculty of the soul, and its assimilation as a potential refinement of the soul, helping to render it self-aware. The Supreme Soul is a source of redeeming knowledge, delivered through Lekhraj and his visionary surrogates. It is not so much foot nectar as knowledge nectar (gyān amrit) that the Brahma Kumaris drink. At a higher level, devotees engage in an even more intimate interaction with the Supreme Soul in the context of rāja yoga. Here they interact directly with the Supreme Soul, soul to soul, through media that are soullike and ethereal. Brilliance and power are the two principal characteristics of soul, and it is by means of these that devotees commune and achieve union with the Supreme Soul, as depicted in many Brahma Kumari pictures that show a white line of light or power connecting the heads of practitioners with the egg-shaped emblem of Shiv Bābā above.

The presence of these concepts in the background is consistent with the relative deemphasis of visible expressions of deference and hierarchy in Brahma Kumari life. The relationship between the Supreme Soul and his devotees is, of course, a hierarchical one. He is, after all, 'supreme,' and he stays at the apex of the universe never to descend, as we do, into material nature to 'forget.' Moreover, the incorporation of his knowledge nectar into his devotees' self-awareness suggests hierarchical intimacy, an assimilation of the higher nature of a higher being. But in human terms radical hierarchy depends on body geography, on the placing of heads on feet, or the ingesting of another's saliva, and so on. Even though the Supreme Soul may enter human bodies (as he entered Lekhraj's body), the Brahma Kumaris cannot, finally, interact with the Supreme Soul as bodies; he has no body, and neither, as souls, do they. The positioning of points of ingress against others' points of egress, so productive of radical hierarchy in other Hindu systems, lacks a meaningful context here.

Likewise, the relations that matter most between devotees themselves, even between devotees of differing degrees of spiritual attainment, must be noncorporeal in the end. The Brahma Kumaris stress constantly that human others simply should not be seen as bodies, and especially not as sexed bodies, but only as souls. As souls they traffic with each other in power, light, and subtle knowledge. There is, of course, a hierarchy in the movement, which after all is the Pāṇḍava 'army.' Souls, moreover, do indeed have differing degrees of value, which will be expressed directly in the hierarchy of the satyug to come. But for the present this is irrelevant to relationships between devotees as bodies, and therefore we find a distinct flattening of the usual highly corporeal expressions of deference. It should also be noted that a muting of expressions of hierarchy is consistent with the atmosphere of liminality so important to the Brahma Kumari conception of the sangamyug (cf. Turner 1969).

Seeing

According to a well-known Puranic myth, Pārvatī once covered Shiva's three eyes with her hands in play. The world then went dark. This episode points to the existence of another basic image in Hindu religious culture, which has to do with eyes, seeing, and the powers of seeing. Despite the obvious importance of ocular matters in the Hindu world, this subject has not been much discussed (excepting Eck 1981). In the existing literature most of the attention has been reserved for the so-called evil eye, the glance of envy that steals the virtues of objects or persons against whom it is directed (for more details see Maloney 1976). The materials we have seen, however, suggest that ocular aggression is only one element in a wider pattern. In conformity with Simmel's dictum that the interaction of glances is 'the most direct and purest reciprocity that exists anywhere' (1981, 98), the axial principle in this pattern seems to be that visual contact affords an extremely intimate form of communion between persons or beings. The evidence we have seen also suggests that visual interaction between worshippers and higher beings has transactionlike aspects of great soteriological importance.

The evil eye has its exact inverse in what the Radhasoami tradition, with characteristic explicitness, calls the 'glance of mercy.' One of the most powerful impulses in this tradition is to see, and be seen by, a sant satguru. The theme of reciprocal gazing is expressed vividly in the poetic literature of the movement, and is also strikingly evident in the actual interactions taking place between gurus and their devotees. Implicit in these behaviors is the notion that seeing is extrusive, involving an externalization of inner powers that can affect, and be affected by, that which is seen. Just as the evil eye in some sense touches its object harmfully, the benevolent gaze of a guru touches his devotee beneficially.

Moreover, in the imagery of Radhasoami poetry the benevolent effect of the guru's gaze seems to result in a modification of the devotee's own power of seeing. Gazes mingle, and as they do, the devotee's inner powers of awareness are awakened; 'external darshan' makes possible 'internal darshan' in which the devotee's sight-current is turned around, from outward to inward and upward. Then, as the devotee mixes gazes with the guru's inner form, he or she acquires higher powers of seeing in degrees. Whole worlds, invisible to the unawakened, disclose themselves to his or her inner sight. And as the devotee ascends, the guru is seen with growing insight, resulting in a complete epiphany at the end of the journey. Having had such experiences, the devotee sees this world differently too; for the fully awakened, the world of normal experience can only be a spiritual desert.

The theme of awakened vision is also very powerful in the Brahma Kumari tradition, though here it is not expressed in the poetic imagery of Radhasoami sacred literature. This tradition, in fact, was based from the beginning on special powers of sight. Things seen in visions inspired Lekhraj's prophecies. His was the first power of sight to be awakened; then, by spiritual mimicry, came the awakening of that of his followers. Seeing has been central to this tradition ever since.

At one level the importance of sight to the Brahma Kumaris is evident in the continuing emphasis (though less than before) on visions as a medium for the communication of 'knowledge.' Visions have been tamed and routinized today in the Thursday morning seances in which sisters of the movement rise to the subtle world to communicate with Lekhraj in his subtle form. Sound does not exist in this realm, and so communication occurs through movement—that is, through vision—alone.

But the final goal of Brahma Kumari life is the awakening and cultivation of what they call 'soul consciousness' in yogic practice. The procedures employed in the teaching and practice of rāja yoga are directly parallel to the poetically portrayed visual interactions between the Radhasoami sant satguru and his devotees. Here too gazes mingle, and here too there is thought to be an awakening of the seeker's powers of inner vision. Many devotees experience this as an 'actual' seeing of light. If all goes well, the teacher's frame of reference is visually communicated to the student, who then sees himself or herself, and others too, in a totally new way—as souls, not as bodies. And with this comes, in theory, a total shift of outlook; the whole world now looks different, as a drama in which the self, now seen for what it really is, merely acts out its preordained, but disengaged, part.

Similar ideas are strongly present in the cult of Sathya Sai Baba. His devotees seek to see him, and hope that his benevolent gaze, which evokes strong inner feelings, will light upon them. Moreover, his devotees, like their Radhasoami and Brahma Kumari counterparts, come to 'see things differently.' When they look at Sathya Sai Baba, they see not a man with magical powers, but God himself. Ideally, when they look at others, they see not the mere physical beings that the unenlightened see, but instead they perceive in others what Sathya Sai Baba calls 'mirrors.' By this he means that they see themselves in others by seeing the divinity that is present in every being. The world is seen differently too—not as the devastated wilderness of the Radhasoami tradition, nor as the sink of vice that surrounds the Brahma Kumaris, but as a place of potential enchantment and a suitable environment for positive values. These values may not be ultimate values, but they are values that count for something.

Sathya Sai Baba himself clearly believes that the world is vision-created. The world is not just the source of the things we see, but also a product of our powers of seeing. This concept, which seems to be deeply embedded in many forms of Hindu thought, is illustrated in what strikes me as a diagnostically remarkable interchange (from Hislop 1978, 79) between Baba and a Western devotee.

> *Sai:* For us the world exists only if we are there to see it. If we are blind, we do not see it. If we are in a faint it does not exist for us. For us the world is as we see it. It takes shape according to our viewpoint. If your viewpoint is that all is God, then everything we see is God [this is something he says repeatedly]. Suppose we take a picture with a camera. Do the trees enter the lens and impress themselves on the film, or does the camera reach out and grasp the trees?
>
> *H:* The trees impress themselves on the camera.
>
> *Sai:* Wrong! I take a picture of a person who does not want his picture taken. Will the refusal prevent the picture? Or, put it in the other way. The person wants his picture taken. Will that result in the picture? The heart is like a film that can capture the image of Swami. If the film is latent and clear, it can capture Swami even if he does not want . . . .

Baba probably did not know how odd these several assertions must have sounded to his interlocutor. More or less offhandedly, he was expressing an understanding of ocular process very different from Western common sense, and in the process saying something of great importance about the situation of beings in the world. The point he was making is far more subtle than the notion that the world looks different through differently colored glasses. It involves the idea that visual awareness is extrusive, transformative, and creative; seeing is somehow implicated in the construction of things seen. What is extruded from a seeing subject is not just a current of vision, but in some sense a world; thus when Shiva's all-seeing eyes are covered, the cosmos winks out. To the degree that we see only partially, and this is a necessary feature of temporal existence, we live as partial selves in partial worlds. The problem of identity, is, in this sense, a problem of vision. To be different, we must see differently. What is needed is participation in a higher power of vision, which will enable us to see the world and ourselves in illuminated completeness, 'past, present and future.' Then the world will *be* completed, and ourselves with it. For this to happen, however, we must come to see our selves and the world as they are seen by the Lord.

Recognizing

Throughout this account I have been concerned with a notoriously slippery concept, and it is now time to attempt some clarification. The concept is often represented by the term *realization*. Devotees, I have suggested, attempt to realize extraordinary identities in interactions with guru-deities. The question is, just how seriously, and in what sense, do we take this realization? Do we, or should we, mean that devotees actually 'make real' new identities? Or is it self-deception, a kind of elaborate enactment of optimistic fantasies? In what sense can persons actually be souls, or emanations of the Supreme Being?

I believe that these matters are a good deal less metaphysical than they might seem at first. Obviously the question of the existence of, let us say, souls as actual 'things' is entirely beyond the purview of an account such as this. However, in the world of thought and feeling in which our three movements operate, it is not clear that this is the right question anyway. Here the problem of the existence of entities like souls really comes down to questions of identity.

Do souls exist? It depends. One might just as well ask the question of any identity. The answer would surely have to be 'yes and no.' If social psychology has taught us anything, it is that identities are social constructions, features of interactions between actors and others. At one level identities, whether perceived from the inside out or the outside in, must be fictions. Such constructed identities do not characterize or even name the actual bundles of psychophysiological processes that constitute living individuals. But, on the other hand, within the web of social life, which is the true environment of constructed identities, identities are precisely as real as actors take them to be.

An obvious corollary of this view is that there is no such thing as an autonomous identity. Identities require cooperation; they arise within social relationships, of which the dyad is the irreducible atom. Therefore, for us to speak of such things as souls requires us to speak of relationships. The question, then, is this: are there relationships in which such identities are deployed? The answer is yes, because such relationships are, in large measure, what our three religious movements are about.

But identities also have an inward, subjective dimension, which is critical in these materials. At issue is what is usually called 'self.' Quite obviously, self and identity are closely related, but they are not quite the same. Identity is a public thing, fully at home in the open marketplace of social life. Self is the subjective, reflexive side of identity—that is, identity absorbed into one's basic sense of who one is. As has often been noted, by George Herbert Mead in particular, the peculiar paradox of self is that it is at once both subject and object to itself. It is, however, no less social for its inwardness. Although we may be 'alone with ourselves,' a self is no more autonomous in the end than more purely outward social identities. To be a self at all, one must enter into relations with others. Through such relations a sense of self arises.

Classic work in this field suggests that the key to selfhood is the implication of powers of imagination and empathy in social interaction. Cooley, for example, long ago proposed that feelings of selfhood can arise from how an actor imagines himself or herself to appear and be judged in the minds of others. Such a self he called a 'looking-glass self,' with social others serving as mirrors (1902, 151–52). That most subtle of social theorists, George Herbert Mead, saw the problem of selfhood in similar terms. How, Mead asked, can the individual 'become an object to himself?' (1934, 138). The answer lies in social interactions: 'The individual experiences himself as such, not directly, but only indirectly, from the particular standpoints of other individual members of the same social group, or from the generalized standpoint of the social group as a whole to which he belongs' (ibid.). That is, the self cannot create itself; it arises only when an ego makes an object of itself by learning to enter into the reactions of social others to itself.

What I have characterized as the religious problem of identity (as in Lekhraj's question, 'Who are you?') can be seen as a problem of the social psychology of selfhood in a very special frame of reference.[2] The question is, how can a person assume an identity as self that is quite different from those employed in his or her normal interactions with social others? Let there be no mistake on one point: this is precisely a matter of self, not merely of enacted identity. In the case of the Brahma Kumaris, for example, it is not enough for a person to *think* that he or she is a soul, to *be called* a soul, or even to behave *as if* this were true. What is required, rather, is that the devotee actually

---

[2] Berger (1969, 37–38) has suggested that deities, functioning as social others, can stabilize the identification of individuals with conventional social roles. In my view this is certainly true. What is at issue in these pages, however, is identity-transformation. I suspect that the dynamic of inner recognition explored here also plays a role in the deity-worshipper encounters alluded to by Berger.

experience himself or herself in this new and extraordinary identity. This requires that the devotee become an 'object,' a new *kind* of object, to himself or herself. If Mead is right, the devotee will have to borrow, and in some sense enter, some relevant other's point of view. Moreover, this other will have to be an extraordinary person, whose awareness of the devotee—or so the devotee must believe—is expanded and enlarged, and who can thereby confer on the devotee an identity that entirely supersedes all the other identities that he or she has absorbed in the course of normal social life.

The problem of how a devotee can realize his or her identity as a soul, or emanation of the Supreme Being, therefore resolves into the question of whether the devotee can actually experience such an extraordinary 'other' as reality. Whether such others 'really exist' is quite beside the point; what matters is whether and in what sense they exist in the imaginations of devotees. Put somewhat differently, what is required is that the existence of an extraordinary, transcendental other-awareness be made a fact of the devotee's inner life. The childlike submission and dependency of the devotee, so frequently a feature of devotional interactions, is probably often an important factor in this, helping to diminish older feelings of selfhood, and creating a psychic environment hospitable to the sense of the presence of an all-powerful other (see Kakar 1982, 145). To the degree that such a being finally becomes a feature of the devotee's inner landscape, experienced as real, the devotee can participate in an alternative awareness through which can arise a new or deepened sense of self. That this occurs by indirection matters little, for indirection is apparently the key to the social psychology of all forms of selfhood. And if the fact of this special being's existence acquires the energy to push aside other inner facts, this new sense of self can become 'realer' than any other. Thus, the devotee 'realizes' his or her 'true' identity.[3]

In the materials we have surveyed, these principles are expressed with the most striking clarity in the teachings of the Radhasoami faith (in its Soami Bagh form). The sant satguru is a highly 'significant other.' In transactions with him—that is, in giving and taking from him, in seeing him and being seen, in hearing (i.e., 'drinking the

---

[3] Of course this can be a two-way street. When a living guru or deity-saint is involved in such encounters, it is likely that his or her own sense of self is engaged (Kakar 1982, 149–50). He too has an inner landscape, and when it is populated by worshipping devotees, this surely provokes and supports feelings of deity like power. Or so one might surmise. These are matters about which the materials presented here reveal nothing.

nectar of') his discourses, and all the rest—the devotee is conceived to be improving his or her own nature by assimilating and blending with the guru's superior nature. That is, the devotee becomes like the sant satguru, and in so doing shares his or her guru's higher nature, which nature is manifested as higher self-awareness. This is Cooley's leap of imagination into the perceptions and awareness of others, but conceived in a physical or quasi-physical way; ego and other come into intimate contact and mingle. As idealized in the imaginative constructions of Radhasoami teachings, this interactive process culminates when ego merges (somewhat short of complete absorption) with the other and in so doing sees the world, and himself or herself, as this transcendental other sees them—which is to say, he or she now sees all with perfected, encompassing, atemporal clarity. In this way, dividual beings become individuals, completed and stable selves.

Indispensable to this process, however, is a critical shift in the devotee's own inward perception of the transactions in which he or she is engaged. It is not enough simply to 'act out'; only genuine convictions will suffice. I believe this is what Babuji Maharaj is really saying when he stresses the importance of the devotee's inner feelings about the meaning of taking a sant satguru's prasād. Prasād is redemptively inefficacious unless its consumption provokes and supports an actual altered awareness of things. It is insufficient for the devotee merely to believe that he or she is imbibing a higher nature. Rather, the devotee must actually experience that interaction as identity transformative. The interaction itself, therefore, should be a 'perceiving of things' in a new and extraordinary way. And so it is. Prasād looks like filth, but 'really' (that is, to an awakened awareness) it is identity-transforming divine substance. It transforms identity, however, only when the devotee *actually feels love for it*, its appearances to the contrary notwithstanding. Simply stated, to feel such love is indeed to become a different kind of self, because in so doing one enters a new relationship with appearances.

In other words, the redemptive efficacy of a devotee's relationship with a sant satguru depends on the devotee's own real conviction that there is in *fact* a higher, more powerful 'other' whose definition of the situation—whose 'awareness'—encompasses and supersedes his or her own. This conviction is probably powerfully buttressed by the devotee's perception of himself or herself in surrender, each gesture of homage being both a diminution of the devotee's normal self and a further confirmation of the reality of the superiority and redemptive power of his or her guru. The spectacle of other devotees offering similar homage gives additional reinforcement to this idea. In this sense the sant satguru becomes a shared other, defining a satsang as a devotional community. But what is absolutely crucial is that the guru's 'redemptive power' be given real focus in the devotee's own inner life. Although the devotional situation is socially constructed, and although the symbolisms involved are public and shared, in the final analysis it is the devotee alone who can regard as nectar what the world sees as filth.

At the heart of the devotee's experience is an implicit logic of 'recognition.' If guru is God, then one should love his leavings, and if one loves his leavings, he must be God. The very act of taking his leavings thus becomes a kind of motor-psychic form of knowing, a distinguishing of higher reality from gross appearances. In this sense, when a devotee takes the leavings of the Lord with love, he or she *really does* assimilate a higher power of awareness. If one takes his spittle, then he must be the Lord; if he is the Lord, then his spittle purifies; and indeed one is purified, for one can see—appearances to the contrary notwithstanding—that he is the Lord, because how else would one be taking his spittle with love? Thus the salvific power of prasād. To take it with the proper attitude is psychically to project, and then to participate in, the being and awareness of the ultimate identity-conferring other; in Kakar's words, it is an expression of 'the need to bestow *mana* on our superiors and leaders in order to partake of the *mana* ourselves' (1978, 137).

This interpretation makes new sense of the common assertion by Hindus that the image of a deity is, finally, only an 'aid.' Tantric theory holds that objects perceived are actually in the possession of the perceiving mind (Woodroffe 1978, 87–88). In the materials we have discussed, particularly those dealing with vision, we have found echoes of this view. Within the framework of such a concept, it is quite possible for a beneficial 'other' to be generated by the self as a modification of itself. From a non-Indic standpoint, we might say that in treating an apparently human guru as a superior being to be 'taken from,' the devotee is simply realizing possibilities for self-transformation that are, as deposits of social experience, already internalized as part of his or her personality structure. The devotee externalizes, for and from himself or herself, an interactional frame of reference that encompasses all normal frames of reference, and on that account is 'realer than' (Geertz 1966) all normal frames of reference too. The deity-guru then becomes an (apparently) external point of focus for an internalized version of Mead's 'generalized other.' Here is Cooley's mirror in a form that is powerful in its self-transformative possibilities. But in the final analysis it is a social-psychic extension—projected onto another—of the devotee's internal processes of self-recognition, an extension of self serving as mirror for the self. Nor need the crucial other even be animate, as it is in the case of the Radhasoami gurus. An inanimate image will (and does in many forms of Hindu tradition) suffice; what is crucial is not what it is, but how it is seen. The ignorant will see only stone or metal; the awakened will see divinity, and the truly awakened will see themselves anew.

Among the Brahma Kumaris these principles are in evidence, but somewhat differently expressed. As we have noted, body imagery is less stressed than in the Radhasoami tradition, the main emphasis being on the more ethereal realm of pure vision. The Brahma Kumaris also rely much less on devotional humility as a means of weakening a devotee's accustomed sense of self, employing instead the imagery of 'dying' to older social roles. Here one seeks an awakening of spiritual vision, which is accomplished by allowing a superior frame of reference, a superior *way* of seeing, to overwhelm and overpower one's own; this is done by means of interaction with spiritually powerful others in whose mode of awareness one learns to share. Here the devotional 'other,' whether it be a fellow yogic practitioner or the Supreme Soul, is genuinely very mirrorlike. To be realized as soul is to be able to see the souls that others are; thus, to see the soul in another is to begin to see oneself as soul. But of course the devotee must *really see*, as many devotees 'really' do. It is never enough merely to think that one is a soul; it is only when 'recognition' of the other becomes an inner fact, 'appearances to the contrary notwithstanding,' that one's own transformation becomes an inner fact as well. As we have seen in chapter 6, one of the most remarkable features of the Brahma Kumari movement is the way these ancient principles have been linked, in an unexpected conjunction, with issues of gender identity.

Within the world as constructed by the cult of Sathya Sai Baba we find the same themes, but with still different emphases. As in the Radhasoami case, an important aspect of the devotee's transformation is the attenuation of the older self through humility and surrender. Here too we find an intense physicality in guru-devotee interactions, or at least as such interactions are idealized. By taking Sathya Sai Baba's prasād and other productions and emanations—including, apparently, his visual emanations—devotees mingle his higher nature with theirs and are improved thereby. In their inner feelings about such transactions, devotees apparently find validation for their sense of his extraordinary identity, and thus by reflex, a basis for a transformed sense of who and what they are. If for many the trick of 'recognition' requires the crutch of magical performances (at least at first), it is not different in principle from what we see in our other two cases.

But in comparison with the other groups, what is most striking about the cult of Sathya Sai Baba is the way it uses the world itself as a screen for the projection of an extraordinary, divine persona. This is very different from a mere question of resignation to events as ordained by God, and far more positive in tone. The crux of the matter is the devotee's cultivation of trust in what appears to be untrustworthy, a psychic act that seems parallel to the Radhasoami devotee's love of his or her guru's leavings, which look to all the world like filth. The world is a treacherous place, full of misfortunes, pain, and afflictions that seem to strike randomly. In its apparent capriciousness, however, the world expresses Baba's nature. If our experiences in the world are beyond our immediate understanding, this does not mean that they are meaningless. To an awakened awareness all experiences of the world, painful or not, are expressions of God's love. Like the snake that turns out, on closer inspection, to be a rope (an axial Indic metaphor), the world's hazards dissolve into Baba's benevolence to his awakened devotees. For them, in a sense, the world itself is the redemptive mirror.

The point is to know who you really are. But in South Asian religions the knowledge in question is not simply a miscalculation of some kind, quickly repaired by hearing a discourse or reading a book. The mistake, rather, is a fundamental misunderstanding in the very grain of day-to-day experience arising from the most basic habits of mind and emotion. It is not just a question of learning that the self is, after all, not what one thought it was before. It is, rather, a matter of actually learning to experience oneself in a new way.

A significant feature of interaction with deities and deitylike personages is that it is, among other things, a way in which a very special sense of self and the world, which has little basis in the experience of everyday life, can be assimilated to a devotee's inner life. The devotee's identity, his or her 'true' identity, is invested with reality by indirection; the devotee discovers a new sense of who he or she is (that is, discovers an identity that was supposedly the real one all along) by surrendering to—indeed becoming 'submerged' within—the awareness of an other for whom he or she believes this identity to be real. Far from being an impediment, the fact that the other might seem to outsiders to be fictitious can actually be an aid. A major part of the devotee's challenge is to struggle with, and overcome, mere appearance.

At its heart this process of self-discovery is more affective than intellectual. In all three of our traditions what is required of the devotee is not so much understanding as feelings, especially feelings of love and trust. Trust is the key, since it is trust indeed when one not only surrenders one's life ('body, mind and wealth') but also one's very sense of self to another. Beyond a certain point, moreover, there is nothing particularly esoteric or exotic in any of this. The religious attitudes cultivated by our three traditions cannot be fully understood apart from visions deeply rooted in the Hindu tradition. But to the degree that they involve the construction or reconstruction of self through interaction, they express a theme that ramifies outward into the social experience of men and women everywhere.

Glossary

amrit	Nectar.
ansh	Part, emanation.
ārati	Hindu ceremony in which a lamp or other object is moved in a circular fashion before a deity or august personage. In the Radhasoami tradition, reciprocal gazing between devotee and guru while *ārati* hymns are sung.
āshram	In the Hindu tradition, one of the four traditional stages of life. Also a retreat for the cultivation of the spiritual life.
ātmā	The essential self, the soul.
avatār	Earthly descent of a deity.
Bābūjī Mahārāj (Rāi Sāheb Mādhav Prasād Sinha)	Friend and school chum of Maharāj Sāheb; fifth *sant satguru* in the Soami Bagh tradition, presiding from 1913 to 1949.
basant panchmī	'Spring Fifth,' a vernal celebration taking place on the fifth day of the waxing half of the lunar month of *māgh* (January–February).
Bhagavad Gītā	The 'Song of God,' a text forming part of the *Mahābhārata* and consisting of a dialogue between Arjuna and his charioteer, Krishna.
Bhagavān	God.
bhaiyā dūj	'Brother second,' a Hindu festival celebrating the brother-sister tie and occurring on the second day of the waxing half of the lunar month of *kārtik* (October–November).
bhajan	Devotional song. In the Radhasoami tradition, the practice of listening to sounds emanating from higher regions.

227

bhakta	A devotee.
bhakti	Religious devotion.
Brahm	God, the supreme spirit. In Radhasoami teachings the lord of *brahmāṇḍ*, identified with Kāl.
Brahmā	Hindu deity who creates the world.
brahmacharya	Celibacy. Also the first of the four traditional stages of life (*āshrams*).
Brāhmaṇ	Topmost of the four *varṇas*, consisting of priests and teachers.
brahmāṇḍ	The universe. In Radhasoami cosmology, the middle layer among the three main levels of creation.
Buājī Sāhebā	Sister of Maharaj Saheb and fourth *sant satguru* in the Soami Bagh tradition; nominally presided from 1907 to 1913.
Chāchājī Sāheb (Lālā Pratāp Singh Seṭh)	Younger brother and biographer of Soamiji Maharaj.
chaitanya (also *chetan*)	Conscious, alert; consciousness, spirit. In the Radhasoami tradition, often glossed in English as 'spirituality.'
chakor	Bird said to drink moonlight.
Charan Singh	Current guru of the Radhasoami congregation headquartered at Beas.
chaurāsī	Eighty-four. In the Hindu tradition, the cycle of 8,400,000 forms through which the unliberated self transmigrates. Soami Bagh teachings reduce this number to eighty-four.
Dādā Lekhrāj	Sindhi businessman who founded the Brahma Kumari movement.
darshan	Sight, vision. The seeing of a deity or august personage.
dashehrā	Hindu festival celebrating Rāma's victory over Rāvaṇa as recounted in the *Rāmāyaṇa*; celebrated on the tenth day of the waning half of the lunar month of *kvār* (September–October).

dayāl desh	'Region of the Merciful,' in Radhasoami cosmology the topmost of the three main levels of creation. Also called *sat desh*.
dhār	Current, flow.
dharma	Duty, righteousness, inherent moral nature; religion.
dhyān	Attention, meditation. In Radhasoami teachings, the contemplation of the Supreme Being in the form of the *sant satguru*.
divālī	Hindu 'festival of lights,' dedicated to the goddess Lakshmī, and celebrated on the full moon day of the lunar month of *kārtik* (October–November).
drishṭi	Sight, glance, seeing.
Durgā	The 'Inaccessible One,' the goddess in a weapon-bearing form.
dvāparyug	Third of the four recurrent ages (*yuga*s) of Hindu historical cosmology.
gopī	Cowherder woman. The *gopī*s of Braj were youthful Krishna's amorous partners.
guru	Teacher, spiritual master
gurumukh	One who faces the guru. In the Soami Bagh tradition, a *sant satguru*'s principal disciple who will be his successor.
guru pūrṇimā	Full moon day of the lunar month of *āshāṛh* (June–July) dedicated to the worship of guru.
gyān	Knowledge.
hansa	Wild goose, swan; a liberated self. In the Radhasoami tradition, a person of high spiritual attainments or one who dwells in high celestial regions.
holī	Hindu saturnalia beginning on the full moon night of the lunar month of *phālgun* (February–March).
Huzūr Mahārāj (Rāi Sāligrām Sāheb Bahādur)	Second *sant satguru* in the Soami Bagh (and Agra) tradition; presided 1878–98.
janmāshṭamī	Krishna's birthday, celebrated on the eighth day of the waning half of the lunar month of *bhādrapad* (August–September).

jīva	Life; the embodied, transmigrating self.
jīvan mukti	Liberation in life—i.e., liberation while still existing in the body.
Kabīr	Mystic poet of the late fifteenth and early sixteenth centuries. In the Radhasoami tradition, regarded as an early *sant*.
Kāl	Time, death. In the Radhasoami tradition, a being who is lord of time and death, and the dominant force in lower regions of the cosmos.
Kālī	The 'Black One,' a fearsome form of the goddess associated with death and destruction.
kaliyug	Fourth, last, and most degraded of the four recurrent ages (*yuga*s) of Hindu historical cosmology; the present epoch.
Kalkin	Tenth *avatār* of Vishnu who restores virtue at the *kaliyug*'s end.
Kāma (or *Kāmdev*)	Hindu god of love or lust.
kanyā	A virgin.
karma	Action, with inevitable 'fruits' (*phal*) to be reaped by the actor.
Kāyastha	North Indian caste of scribes.
Khatrī	Punjab caste of merchants, moneylenders, land-owners, and government officials.
Krishṇa	*Avatār* of Vishnu and one of the most important deities in the Hindu pantheon; sported with *gopī*s of Braj, hero of the *Mahābhārata*, and Arjuna's teacher in the *Bhagavad Gītā*.
Kshatriya	Second in rank of the four *varṇa*s; rulers and warriors.
kumār	Unmarried male, a boy, a prince.
kumārī	Unmarried female, a virgin, a girl, a princess.
Lakshmī	Wife of Vishnu and the Hindu goddess of wealth and good fortune.
Lekhrāj	See *Dādā Lekhrāj*.
līlā	Sport, play.

linga	A sign; a phallus, the phallic representation of Shiva.
Mādhav Prasād Sinha	See *Bābūjī Mahārāj*.
Mahābhārata	Sanskrit epic dating from roughly 300 B.C. to A.D. 300 that recounts the story of the war between the Kauravas and the Pāndavas; includes the *Bhagavad Gītā*.
Mahārāj Sāheb (Brahma Shankar Mishra)	Third *sant satguru* in the Soami Bagh tradition; presided from 1898–1907.
mahāshivrātri	'Great night of Shiva, a festival dedicated to Shiva occurring on the fourteenth of the waning half of the lunar month of *phālgun* (February–March).
man	Mind, heart; the faculty that processes sense data.
mantra	Sacred utterance.
mauj	Whim, delight, pleasure, wave. In the Radhasoami tradition, the Supreme Being's desireless will-as-pleasure.
māyā	Illusion, delusion, magic, trick; divine (and feminine) creative power. In the Radhasoami tradition, also matter.
mukti	Liberation, salvation.
muralī	Flute, Krishna's flute. Among the Brahma Kumaris, one of Dada Lekhraj's sermons.
nām	Name
Nānak (Guru Nānak)	A religious teacher and innovator of the late fifteenth and early sixteenth centuries; the founder of Sikhism.
Nārāyaṇ	An epithet of Vishnu.
navrātra (navrātri)	'Nine nights,' a festival dedicated to the goddess and celebrated in the lunar months of *chaitra* (March–April) and *kvār* (September–October).
nij	Own, true, proper.
om	Sacred syllable; the supreme *mantra*.
Om Rādhe	Woman who was Dada Lekhraj's principal disciple and assistant.

Pāṇḍava	The *Pāṇḍava*s are the five sons of king Pāṇḍu and the heros of the *Mahābhārata*.
paramārth	The supreme goal, salvation; spiritual matters and pursuits.
paramārthī	One who seeks *paramārth*; having to do with *paramārth*.
paramātmā	Supreme Soul.
paramdhām	'Supreme Abode.' The location of the Supreme Soul according to Brahma Kumari teachings.
Pārvatī	Daughter of Himālaya and wife o: Shiva.
piṇḍ	Body; balls of cooked rice or flour offered to the dead. In the Radhasoami tradition, the lowest of the three main levels of creation.
prasād	Blessing, grace. Food leavings of a deity or august personage; objects or substances sanctified by contact with, or use by, a deity or august personage.
Prembānī Rādhāsvāmī	Collections of Huzūr Mahārāj's verse.
Prempatra Rādhāsvāmī	Collections of articles written by Huzūr Mahārāj for a journal of the same name.
pūjā	Worship, homage.
pujārī	Temple priest, a worshipper; one who worships.
pūjya	Worthy of worship.
Rādhāsoāmī	See *rādhāsvāmī*.
rādhāsvāmī	According to the teachings of the Agra wing of the Radhasoami movement, the true name of the Supreme Being. An appellation of Soamiji Maharaj. A salutation among *satsangī*s.
rādhāsvāmī dhām	'Abode of *rādhāsvāmī*.' The highest sublevel of *dayāl desh*, and the devotee's ultimate goal.
rāja yoga	System of *yoga* attributed to Patanjali; a system of *yoga* taught by the Brahma Kumaris.
rakshābandhan	Hindu festival in which sisters tie amulets to the wrists of their brothers; celebrated on the full moon day of the lunar month of *shrāvaṇ* (July–August).

Rāma	*Avatār* of Vishnu, hero of the epic *Rāmāyaṇa*, and important Hindu deity.
sādh	In Radhasoami teachings, an adept at spiritual practice who has risen to high celestial regions.
sādhu	Religious mendicant.
sākshī	Witness.
samādh	Resting place for the ashes of a holy person.
sangamyug	'Confluence age,' so named by the Brahma Kumaris because it is the age of transition from the present *kaliyug* to the *satyug* to come.
sannyās	World renunciation. The fourth and final stage of life in the Hindu tradition.
sannyāsī	A world-renouncer.
sant	Often glossed in English as 'saint.' A holy man. In Radhasoami teachings, one who has progressed spiritually to the highest levels of creation.
sant mat	'Creed of the *sants*.' The wider North Indian poet-saintly tradition to which the Radhasoami movement belongs. In Soami Bagh teachings, the Radhasoami faith itself.
sant satguru	True spiritual master who incarnates the Supreme Being.
saran	Protection, shelter.
Sār Bachan	Verse and prose discourses of Soamiji Maharaj. The most venerated texts in the Radhasoami tradition.
satsang	Company of the good; keeping the company of a *sant satguru*; keeping the 'inward' company of the true form of the *sant satguru*; congregational devotional services; a community of co-followers of a *sant satguru*.
satsangī	Disciple of a *sant satguru* and thus a member of a *satsang*.
sāttvik	Imbued with goodness; pure.
satyug	First and most blessed of the four recurrent ages (*yugas*) of Hindu historical cosmology.

sevā	Service; devotional service.
shabd	A word; sound. In the Radhasoami tradition, the universal sound current emanating from the Supreme Being.
shakti	Power, energy; energy personified as the goddess.
Shiva	The 'Auspicious.' One of the most important deities of the Hindu pantheon. Associated with the periodic destruction of the world, but also with creative power.
Shiv Bābā	Brahma Kumari appellation for Shiva, whom they regard as the Supreme Soul.
Shūdra	Lowest of the four *varṇas*. Those who serve the top three *varṇas*.
siddhi	Accomplishment; manifestation of success in yogic practice; paranormal power achieved by means of yogic practices or magical rites.
Sītā	Wife of Rama and heroine of the *Rāmāyaṇa*.
Soāmī Bāgh (*svāmī bāg*)	'Garden of the Master.' A religious colony at Agra, the location of Soamiji Maharaj's *samādh* and the headquarters of a branch of the Radhasoami movement.
Soāmījī Mahārāj (*svāmījī mahārāj*; *Shiv Dayāl Singh*)	Nineteenth-century divine who founded the Radhasoami movement (b. 1818, d. 1878).
sumiran (also *simran*)	Repetition, remembrance. In Radhasoami teachings, the repetition of the sacred name or names.
surat	In Radhasoami teachings, the essential self.
surat-shabd-yoga	The Radhasoami system of disciplined introspection.
svarūp	True form.
svatah sant	Autonomous *sant* who neither has nor needs a guru.
tambūrā	Four-stringed drone instrument.
tīsrā til	The 'third eye,' located between and behind the outer eyes. In Radhasoami teachings, this is the seat of the *surat* and the aperture of access to higher regions.

tretāyug	Second of the four recurrent ages (*yuga*s) of Hindu historical cosmology.
Tulsī Sāheb	A distinguished *sant* from Hathras, author of the *Ghaṭ Rāmāyaṇ*, who was an important spiritual influence on Soamiji Maharaj's family. According to the Punjab wing of the Radhasoami movement, he was Soamiji Maharaj's guru.
Vaishya	Third in rank of the four *varṇas*, traditionally traders and farmers.
varṇa	Four broad categories of Hindu society: Brāhmaṇs, Kshatriyas, Vaishyas, and Shūdras.
vibhūti	Sacred ash.
Vishṇu	One of the chief deities of the Hindu pantheon, conceived as the preserver of the universe.
yoga	Any of various systems of mental or physical discipline by which the practitioner may enhance physical well-being, acquire paranormal powers, or achieve or realize release from worldly bonds and/or union with the divine or with the underlying reality of the universe.
yogī	A practitioner of *yoga*.
yuga (Hindi *yug*)	An epoch or age in the Hindu system of historical cosmology, of which there are four: *satyug*, *tretāyug*, *dvāparyug*, and *kaliyug*.

References

Aitken, E. H.
   1907.   *Gazetteer of the province of Sind.* Karachi: Government of India.
Babb, Lawrence A.
   1981.   'Glancing: Visual interaction in Hinduism.' *Journal of Anthropological Research* 37: 387–401.

   ———.
   1982.   'Amnesia and remembrance in a Hindu theory of history.' *Asian Folklore Studies* 41: 49–66.

   ———.
   1983a.   'The physiology of redemption.' *History of Religions* 22: 298–312.

   ———.
   1983b.   'Sathya Sai Baba's magic.' *Anthropological Quarterly* 56: 116–24.

   ———.
   1984.   'Indigenous feminism in a modern Hindu sect.' *Signs* 9: 399–416.
Babuji Maharaj (Madhav Prasad Sinha).
   1972.   *Bachan bābūjī mahārāj,* pt. 1. Soami Bagh (Agra): Radhasoami Satsang.

   ———.
   1974.   *Discourses of Babuji Maharaj,* vol. 5. Trans. S. D. Maheshwari. Soami Bagh (Agra): S. D. Maheshwari.
Barthwal, Pitambar D.
   1978.   *Traditions of Indian mysticism based on nirguna school of Hindi poetry.* New Delhi: Heritage Publishers.
Basham, A. L.
   1977.   Forward. In *Hindu epics, myths and legends in popular illustrations* by V. Vitsaxis, ix–x. Delhi: Oxford University Press.
Berger, Peter L.
   1969.   *The sacred canopy: Elements of a sociological theory of religion.* New York: Doubleday, Anchor Books.
Bhagavantam, S.
   1976.   'Lord of miracles.' In *Sai Baba and his message: A challenge to behavioural sciences,* ed. S. P. Ruhela and D. Robinson, 228–35. Delhi: Vikas.

Bharati, Agehananda.
1981.   *Hindu views and ways and the Hindu-Muslim interface: An anthropological assessment.* New Delhi: Munshiram Manoharlal.
Boas, Franz.
1963.   *The mind of primitive man.* Rev. ed. New York: The Free Press.
Brooke, Tal.
1979.   *Sai Baba: Lord of the air.* New Delhi: Vikas.
Carstairs, G. Morris.
1961.   *The twice-born: A study of a community of high-caste Hindus.* Bloomington: Indiana University Press.
Chachaji Saheb (Lala Pratap Singh Seth).
1978.   *Biography of Soamiji Maharaj.* 2d ed. Trans. S. D. Maheshwari. Soami Bagh (Agra): S. D. Maheshwari.
Chandar, Jagdish ('Jagdish').
n.d.   *Ek adbhut jīvan-kahānī.* Mt. Abu: Prajapita Brahma Kumari Ishvariya Vishva-Vidyalaya.

———.
1977.   *The way and the goal of raja yoga.* 2d ed. Mt. Abu: Prajapita Brahma Kumari Ishvariya Vishva-Vidyalaya.
Church, Cornelia Dimmott.
1971.   *The yuga story: A myth of the four ages of the world as found in the Puranas.* Ph.D. diss. Syracuse University. Ann Arbor, Mich: University Microfilms.
Cohn, Norman.
1962.   'Medieval millenarism: Its bearing on the comparative study of millenarian movements.' In *Millenial dreams in action: Essays in comparative study,* ed. S. L. Thrupp, 31–43. Comparative Studies in Society and History, Supplement 2. The Hague: Mouton.
Cooley, Charles Horton.
1902.   *Human nature and the social order.* New York: Scribner's Sons.
Danielou, Alain.
1964.   *Hindu polytheism.* New York: Pantheon Books.
Eck, Diana.
1981.   *Darśan: Seeing the divine image in India.* Chambersburg, Pa.: Anima Books.
Eliade, Mircea.
1963.   'Mythologies of memory and forgetting.' *History of Religions* 2: 329–44.

———.
1971.   *The myth of the eternal return.* Trans. W. R. Trask. Princeton, N. J.: Princeton University Press.
Erikson, Erik H.
1962.   *Young man Luther: A study in psychoanalysis and history.* New York: Norton.

Farquhar, J. N.
    1977.   *Modern religious movements in India.* Reprint of 1914 ed. Delhi: Munshiram Manoharlal.

Festinger, Leon, H. W. Riecken and S. Schachter.
    1964.   *When prophecy fails.* New York: Harper and Row, Torchbook.

Fuchs, Stephen.
    1965.   *Rebellious prophets: A study of messianic movements in Indian religions.* Bombay: Asia Publishing House.

Geertz, Clifford.
    1966.   'Religion as a cultural system.' In *Anthropological approaches to the study of religion,* ed. M. Banton, 1–46. London: Tavistock.

————.
    1971.   *Islam observed: Religious development in Morocco and Indonesia.* Chicago: University of Chicago Press, Phoenix Books.

Gennep, Arnold van.
    1961.   *The rites of passage.* Trans. M. B. Vizedom and G. L. Caffee. Chicago: University of Chicago Press, Phoenix Books.

Goffman, Erving.
    1959.   *The presentation of self in everyday life.* Garden City, N.Y.: Doubleday, Anchor Books.

Gokak, Vinayak Krishna.
    1975.   *Bhagavan Sri Sathya Sai Baba (An interpretation).* New Delhi: Abhinav.

Gold, Daniel.
    1982.   'The lord as guru in north Indian religion: Hindu sant tradition and universals of religious perception.' Ph.D. diss. University of Chicago.

Hawley, John Stratton.
    1983.   *Krishna: The butter thief.* Princeton, N.J.: Princeton University Press.

Hawley, John Stratton, and Donna Marie Wulff, eds.
    1982.   *The divine consort: Radha and the goddesses of India.* Berkeley Religious Studies Series. Berkeley, Calif.: Graduate Theological Union.

Hayley, Audrey.
    1980.   'A commensal relationship with God: The nature of the offering in Assamese Vaishnavism.' In *Sacrifice,* ed. M. F. C. Bourdillon and M. Fortes. New York: Academic Press.

Hislop, J. S.
    1978.   *Conversation with Bhagavan Sri Sathya Sai Baba.* Bangalore: Sri Sathya Sai Education and Publication Foundation.

Hobsbawm, E. J.
    1959.   *Primitive rebels: Studies in archaic forms of social movement in the 19th and 20th centuries.* Manchester, England: Manchester University Press.

Huzur Maharaj (Rai Saligram Bahadur).

1952.   *Pilgrim's path, being a collection of extracts from some letters written by Param Guru Huzur Maharaj to outstation satsangis.* Dayal Bagh (Agra): Radhasoami Satsang Sabha.

———.

1972.   *Prembānī rādhāsvāmī,* vol. 1. 7th ed. Soami Bagh (Agra): Radhasoami Satsang.

———.

1973.   *Prempatra rādhāsvāmī,* pt. 1. 6th ed. Soami Bagh (Agra): Radhasoami Satsang.

Inden, Ronald B.

1976.   *Marriage and rank in Bengali culture: A history of caste and clan in middle period Bengal.* Berkeley and Los Angeles: University of California Press.

Inden, Ronald B., and Ralph W. Nicholas.

1977.   *Kinship in Bengali culture.* Chicago: University of Chicago Press.

Juergensmeyer, Mark.

1978.   'Radhasoami as a trans-national movement.' In *Understanding the new religions,* ed. Jacob Needleman and George Baker. New York: The Seabury Press.

———.

1982.   *Religion as social vision: The movement against untouchability in 20th-century Punjab.* Berkeley and Los Angeles: University of California Press.

———.

n.d.   *Radhasoami reality: The logic of a modern faith.* Forthcoming.

Kakar, Sudhir.

1978.   *The inner world: A psycho-analytic study of childhood and society in India.* Delhi: Oxford University Press.

———.

1982.   *Shamans, mystics and doctors: A psychological inquiry into India and its healing traditions.* New York: Alfred A. Knopf.

Kasturi, N.

n.d. a.   *Sathya Sai speaks,* vol. 5. Compiled from notes taken by N. Kasturi. Prasanti Nilayam: Sanathana Sarathi Office.

———.

n.d. b.   *Sathya Sai speaks,* vol. 7. Compiled from notes taken by N. Kasturi. Bombay: Sri Sathya Sai Education Foundation.

———.

n.d. c.   *Sathya Sai speaks,* vol. 9. Compiled by N. Kasturi. Tustin, Calif.: Sri Sathya Sai Baba Book Center of America.

———.

1970a.   *Sathya Sai speaks,* vol. 1. 4th ed. Discourses of Bhagavan Sri Sathya Sai Baba. Compiled from notes taken by N. Kasturi. Tustin, Calif.: Sri Sathya Sai Baba Book Center of America.

———.
1970b.   *Sathya Sai speaks*, vol. 3, 2d ed. Discourses of Sri Sathya Sai Baba. Compiled from notes taken by N. Kasturi. Tustin, Calif.: Sri Sathya Sai Baba Book Center of America.

———.
1975a.   *Sathya Sai speaks*, vol. 8. Compiled by N. Kasturi. Tustin, Calif.: Bhagavan Sri Sathya Sai Baba Book Center of America.

———.
·1975b.   *Sathyam, Shivam, Sundaram*, pt. 2. 3d ed. New Delhi: Bhagavan Sri Sathya Sai Seva Samithi.

———.
1975c.   *Sathyam, Sivam, Sundaram*, pt. 3. New Delhi: Bhagavan Sri Sathya Sai Seva Samithi.

———.
1977.   *Sathyam, Sivam, Sundaram*, pt. 1. American ed., 4th ed. Whitefield, India: Sri Sathya Sai Educational and Publication Foundation.
Kinsley, David R.
1979.   *The divine player: A study of Kṛṣṇa līlā*. Delhi: Motilal Banarsidass.
Kirpal Singh.
1971.   *A great saint. Baba Jaimal Singh: His life and teachings*. 3d ed. Delhi: Savan Ashram.
Maharaj Saheb (Brahma Shankar Mishra).
1973.   *Discourses on Radhasoami faith*. Soami Bagh (Agra): Radhasoami Satsang.

———.
1978.   *Discourses of Maharaj Saheb*. Trans. S. D. Maheshwari. Soami Bagh (Agra): S. D. Maheshwari.
Maheshwari, Sant Das.
1954.   *Radhasoami faith: History and tenets*. Soami Bagh (Agra): S. D. Maheshwari.

———.
1963.   *Truth unvarnished*, pt. 1. Soami Bagh (Agra): S. D. Maheshwari.

———.
1967.   *Glossary of Radhasoami faith (From Hindi into English)*. Soami Bagh (Agra): S. D. Maheshwari.

———.
1970.   *Truth unvarnished*, pt. 2. Soami Bagh (Agra): S. D. Maheshwari.

———.
1971a.   *Biography of Babuji Maharaj*. Soami Bagh (Agra): S. D. Maheshwari.

———.
1971b.   *Biography of Huzur Maharaj*. Soami Bagh (Agra): S. D. Maheshwari.
Maloney, C.
1976.   'Don't say "pretty baby" lest you zap it with your eye—The evil

eye in South Asia.' In *The evil eye*, ed. C. Maloney, 102–48. New York: Columbia University Press.

Marglin, Frederique A.
n.d.   *Wives of the God-King: The rituals of the Devadasis of Puri.* Delhi: Oxford University Press. In press.

Marriott, McKim.
1976.   'Hindu transactions: Diversity without dualism.' In *Transaction and meaning: Directions in the anthropology of exchange and symbolic behavior*, ed. B. Kapferer, 109–42. Philadelphia: Ishi Publishers.

————.
1978.   'Intimacy and rank in food.' Paper presented to the Tenth International Conference of Anthropological and Ethnological Sciences, New Delhi.

Mathur, Agam Prasad.
1974.   *Radhasoami faith: A historical study.* Delhi: Vikas.

Mead, George H.
1934.   *Mind, self and society.* Chicago: University of Chicago Press.

Mitchiner, John E.
1982.   *Traditions of the seven Rsis.* Delhi: Motilal Banarsidass.

Moffatt, Michael.
1979.   *An untouchable community in south India: Structure and consensus.* Princeton, N.J.: Princeton University Press.

Murphet, Howard.
1975.   *Sai Baba: Man of miracles.* Madras: Macmillan Company of India.

O'Flaherty, Wendy D.
1973.   *Asceticism and eroticism in the mythology of Śiva.* London: Oxford University Press.

————.
1975.   *Hindu myths: A sourcebook translated from the Sanskrit.* New York: Penguin.

————.
1976.   *The origins of evil in Hindu mythology.* Berkeley and Los Angeles: University of California Press.

————.
1980.   *Women, androgynes, and other mythical beasts.* Chicago: University of Chicago Press.

One week course for attainment of complete purity, peace and prosperity. n.d. 5th ed. Mt. Abu: Prajapita Brahma Kumari Ishvariya Vishva-Vidyalaya.

Parry, Jonathan.
1980.   'Ghosts, greed and sin: The occupational identity of the Benaras funeral priests.' *Man* 15: 88–111.

Phelps, Myron H.
1947.   *Notes of discourses on Radhasoami faith delivered by Babuji Maharaj in 1913–14.* (Phelps' notes). Soami Bagh (Agra): Radhasoami Satsang.

Pitā shrī.   n.d. Mt. Abu: Prajapita Brahma Kumari Ishvariya Vishva-
             Vidyalaya.
Puri, Lekh Raj.
    1972.   *Radha Swami teachings.* Beas: Radha Soami Satsang.
Purity and brahmacharya as solution of our problems. 1976. Delhi: Prajapita Brahma
             Kumari Ishvariya Vishva-Vidyalaya.
Radha Soami Satsang (Beas).
    1974.   *The Sar Bachan.* 6th ed. Trans. Sardar Seva Singh. Beas: Radha
             Soami Satsang.
Radhasoami Satsang (Soami Bagh).
    1970.   *Shabd kosh-santmat bēnī.* Soami Bagh (Agra): Radhasoami Satsang.
Radhasoami Satsang Sabha (Dayal Bagh).
    1961.   *Souvenir in commemoration of the first centenary of the Radhasoami
             Satsang (1861–1961).* Dayal Bagh (Agra): Radhasoami Satsang
             Sabha.
Rao, Dr. Panduranga.
    1975.   *Das-bārah din bābā ke sāth.* New Delhi: Bhagavan Sri Satya Sai
             Seva Samiti.
Roy, Manisha.
    1975.   *Bengali women.* Chicago: University of Chicago Press.
Sathya Sai Baba.
    1976.   *Sadhana: The inward path—Quotations from the divine discourse of
             Bhagavan Sri Sathya Sai Baba.* Whitefield, India: Sri Sathya Sai
             Educational and Publication Foundation.
S. B. Poetry. Sār Bachan, Poetry. Soamiji Maharaj 1976.
S. B. Prose. Sār Bachan, Prose. Soamiji Maharaj 1973.
Schulman, Arnold.
    1971.   *Baba.* New York: Viking Press.
Sharma, Ursula.
    1980.   *Women, work, and property in north-west India.* London and New
             York: Tavistock.
Shrī satya sāī bhajanāvalī. n.d. New Delhi: Gulab Printers.
Simmel, Georg.
    1981.   'On visual interaction.' In *Social psychology through symbolic inter-
             action.* 2d ed. ed. G. P. Stone and H. A. Faberman, 94–99. New
             York: John Wiley and Sons.
Smith, Wilfred Cantwell.
    1977.   *Islam in modern history.* Princeton, N.J.: Princeton University Press.
Soamiji Maharaj (Shiv Dayal Singh).
    1973.   *Sār bachan rādhāsvārnī, nasar yānī bārtik.* 14th ed. Soami Bagh
             (Agra): Radhasoami Satsang.
    ———.
    1976.   *Sār bachan rādhāsvāmī, nazm yānī chhand band.* 14th ed. 2 vols. Soami
             Bagh (Agra): Radhasoami Satsang.

Streitfeld, Harold.
  1982.   *A psychologist reports on the International Brahma Kumaris Movement.* San Francisco: The Kundalini Clinic.
Swallow, D. A.
  1982.   'Ashes and powers: Myth, rite and miracle in an Indian godman's cult.' *Modern Asian Studies* 16: 123–58.
Talmon, Yonina.
  1965.   'Pursuit of the millennium: The relation between religious and social change.' In *Reader in comparative religion: An anthropological approach*, ed. W. A. Lessa and E. Z. Vogt, 522–37. New York: Harper and Row.
Thakur, U. T.
  1959.   *Sindhi culture.* Bombay: University of Bombay.
Thurston, Edgar (assisted by K. Rangachari).
  1909.   *Castes and tribes of southern India*, vol. 6. Madras: Government Press.
Turner, Victor.
  1969.   *The ritual process.* Chicago: Aldine Publishing Company.
Wadley, Susan.
  1975.   *Shakti: Power in the conceptual structure of Karimpur religion.* Chicago: University of Chicago, Department of Anthropology.
Weber, Max.
  1958.   *The Protestant ethic and the spirit of capitalism.* Trans. Talcott Parsons. New York: Scribner's.
White, Charles, S. J.
  1972.   'The Sai Baba movement: Approaches to the study of Indian saints.' *Journal of Asian Studies* 31: 863–78.
Woodroffe, J.
  1978.   *The serpent power.* Madras: Ganesh and Company.
Zimmer, Heinrich.
  1962.   *Myths and symbols in Indian art and civilization.* New York: Harper and Row.

Index

Abhyās, 18, 32

Accountability for miracles, 186–90

Agra, 15

Agra branch of the Radhasoami movement, 7, 17; conflict with the Punjab branch, 22–23, 26, 32, 43, 46–47; cosmos interpreted by, 37–43; on the founder of the Radhasoami faith, 20–21; on succession, 21–22, 81–84

Alcohol, abstinence from, 56, 95, 169

Alienation from the world: in the Brahma Kumari movement, 103, 137–38; in the Radhasoami movement, 36, 43

Ambrosia, 66. See also Amrit

American Institute of Indian Studies, x

Amnesia, 12; in the Hindu tradition, 152, 209–10; historical, 128; and identity, 36, 149; of the world-career of souls, 115, 128

Amrit, 184, 185

Anand Swarup, 27. See also Sahibji Maharaj

Anglo-Indian bureaucracy, 22

Anus, and physiocosmology, 42

Apocalyptic tradition in Hinduism, 107–8. See also Doom

Āratī: defined, 52, 76; described, 76–77; and the redemption of family members, 55; and visual encounters between gurus and devotees, 76–77, 78

Asal baithak, 40

Ascendance of the self, 48–54, 210

Ash: materialized by Sathya Sai Baba, 179, 185; and "miraculous households," 150; in the Sai Baba tradition, 164; symbolic significance of, 167

Āshram of Sathya Sai Baba, 164, 168, 170, 186

Ātmā: defined, 110, 171; and the true self, 191. See also Identity; Self; Souls

Authority, submission to, 58. See also Humility

Avatār: defined, 3, 162; and Sathya Sai Baba, 162–67

Babuji Maharaj (Madhav Prasad Sinha), 16, 17, 29–30, 51; career of, 29, 84; and conflicts on spiritual succession, 19; death of, 29; guruship of, 29–30, 84; illness of, 66; lack of an official successor for, 16, 18, 30; on the leavings of a guru, 71–72; marriage ceremonies conducted by, 57; and the meaning of prasād, 221; on memory, 209–11; relics of, 16, 18, 19; religious discourses by, 29, 71; ritual gestures by the devotees of, 62

Bal vikas program for child development, 169, 171

Barthwal, Pitambar D., 6, 17n2

Basant panchmī, 21; and the founder of the Radhasoami movement, 21

Bateson, Catherine, 193n4

Beas, Punjab, Radhasoami movement in, 16, 17, 18, 23, 46, 47. See also Punjab branch of the Radhasoami movement

Berger, Peter L., 219n2

Bhagavad Gītā, 100, 137; and miracles by Sathya Sai Baba, 182

Bhagavān, Sathya Sai Baba as, 166

Bhajan: defined, 50; practice of, 52

Bhajan ghar, 17

Bhandārs, 41

Bhogs, 57, 58. See also Food offerings

Birth, 40

Kumari movement, 134; of Dada
Lekhraj, 99–100

Wadley, Susan, 70
Weinberg, Steven, 208
Well water, 62, 89
Western feminism, 142, 145, 153
Westernization of India, 172
White, Charles, 8, 185
Women: absentee husbands of, 97; attitudes of Sathya Sai Baba toward,
173; in centers of the Brahma Kumari movement, 131; chastity vowed
by, 102; dissatisfaction of, 97–98; gurus selected by, 101; and human reproduction, 115–17, 140, 142, inheritance by, 150; marriage into
nonsatsangī families, 19; *pardā* of, 26–
27; position in the family, 97, 102; renunciation by, 146; and salvation,
141; subordinate position in marriage, 141, 142, 149; spiritual leadership by, 106; spiritual virtues of,
149–50; true self of, 55; unmarried,
148; and visual interaction between
gurus and devotees, 27
Women's liberation, 11, 142

Women's movement: Brahma Kumari
movement as, 94
Work, 58
World: comparative viewpoints on, 196–
98; and the miraculous, 195–201;
predicted destruction of, 93, 94, 99,
109, 117, 123
Worldly life: attitudes of the Radhasoami
devotees toward, 54–58; flow of, 50

Yoga, xiii; and the ascent of the self, 48–
49; in the Brahma Kumari move-
ment, 94, 95, 103–4, 116, 119–20,
129–30; and human reproduction,
115, 116; *rāja yoga* aspect of, 119–21,
122–23, 129–30, 149, 154. *See also*
Surat-shabd-yoga
Yogeshvar gyānīs, 44
Yugas, xiii, 38; defined, 43; and Hindu historical cycles, 113; historical theory
based on, 43–44; and history interpreted by the Brahma Kumari movement, 113–17; and history interpreted by the Radhasoami
movement, 43–44

Zimmer, Heinrich, 108, 125, 127